POINT BLANK AND BEYOND

Point Blank and Beyond

L. Lacey-Johnson

To Alan, with best wishes.

Lionel Lacey Johnson

Airlife
England

Copyright © L. Lacey-Johnson, 1991

British Library Cataloguing in Publication Data
Lacey-Johnson, Lionel
    Point blank and beyond.
    1.   World War 2. European campaigns. Air operations by bomber aeroplanes.
    I.   Title
    940.544
    ISBN 1-85310-142-7

First published 1991 by Airlife Publishing Ltd.

Printed in England by Livesey Ltd, Shrewsbury.

Airlife Publishing Ltd.

101 Longden Road, Shrewsbury, England.

Contents

Acknowledgements

The research and gathering of information for this book have not only broadened my knowledge of this period of the Second World War, but has provided an opportunity to meet a great number of very kind and helpful people. I wish to thank first those people who belong to the organisations which I approached for help. Air Cdre H. A. Probert and G. Day, Ministry of Defence, Air Historical Branch; Miss Anne Crawford and the staff, Public Records Office at Kew; Herr Meyer, Bundesarchiv/Militararchiv at Freiburg; Mrs Jacqueline Withers, Commonwealth War Graves Commission; Douglas Radcliffe, Secretary of Bomber Command Association; Fred Sheppard, Royal Air Force Museum; Mrs Sheila Walton, Air Photo Library, Keele University; Mr Willis, Imperial War Museum; Fred Beck, Office of Air Force History, Washington DC; Jack Morley, one time Secretary of No 101 Squadron Association; and Jim Carpenter, Chairman of the Air Gunners' Association. All have helped by pointing me towards other sources of information and to contact some of the following individuals: Lord Zuckerman, the architect of the Transportation Plan; the late AM Sir Harold Martin and Lady Martin; Grp Capt Leonard Cheshire, who, with 'Mick' Martin, did so much to perfect the low-level marking techniques; AM Sir Alfred Ball, one time CO of No 542 PR Squadron; Grp Capt 'Benny' Goodman; Grp Capt Hamish Mahaddie; Sqn Ldr Jack Emmerson, and Wg Cdr John Tipton who both helped me to understand 'Oboe'; 1st Sgt Peter Loncke, Belgian Air Force who helped with the Bourg Leopold narrative; Louis Clement, one time Mayor of Voué where my brother is buried; Jack Worsfold; John Ackroyd and George Burton for their personal accounts; and Alan Castle and Ron Emeny for their help with the Mailly saga.

To all of these people I say 'Thank you' again. Finally, although she does not wish me to do so, I wish to thank my wife, Corinne, who has had to put up with the 'office', and who has waited so patiently for me to complete all those jobs about the house and garden which have been neglected for the past two years.

L. Lacey-Johnson

Foreword

by Marshal of the Royal Air Force
Sir Michael Beetham
GCB, CBE, DFC, AFC, FRAeS

Much controversy has surrounded the Stragic Bombing Offensive in the Second World War and the so-called area bombing of German cities.

What the critics fail to acknowledge is that, if there was to be any direct offensive action taken against Germany, there was until 1944 simply no alternative. Bomber Command, forced by the German defences to operate by night, just did not have the navigation aids to find specific military targets. Furthermore, the British public, having endured the bombing of London and other major cities, wanted some retribution on the German people. This Bomber Command was able to give with powerful effect. By 1944 radar bombing and navigation aids were available and the Command had developed the capability to bomb smaller targets with considerable accuracy.

With hindsight, perhaps Air Marshal Harris was wrong to persist with the bombing of cities at this stage but he believed at the time, not without considerable evidence, that by continuing his campaign German morale would break. However, when he was overruled and ordered to switch his heavy bombers to the support of Overlord, he did so with devastating effect, paralysing the continental rail network and paving the way for the successful invasion of Europe and final victory.

This role of the Bomber Force has not received the same detailed scrutiny as the main campaign nor received the credit it deserves. The situation is redressed in this book, in which the author has made a comprehensive study of the work of the strategic bombers in this phase of the war and pays them a generous tribute. The bomber crews have long felt aggrieved at the criticism they have received over area bombing when they were in fact carrying out Government policy and when they had suffered losses on the scale of trench warfare in the First World War. Coming as it does from an army officer, the recognition they receive in this book is all the more gratifying.

I hope you enjoy reading it as much as I have done.

Prologue

Many eminent historians and authors have examined already most of the facts and arguments relating to the parts played by the Bomber Commands of the RAF and the United States Eighth Army Air Force in bringing down Hitler's regime. There has been much retrospective criticism of the commanders of both these great forces over their belief that the bombing of Germany's industries and cities could end the war without a land battle. Being wise after the event, some alternative uses of these immensely powerful strategic forces have been suggested. However, in spite of the comprehensive nature of their excellent account of the Strategic Air Offensive Against Germany, Sir Charles Webster and Dr Noble Frankland did acknowledge that there were still some gaps to be explored, arising from the relationship of that offensive to other campaigns (such as the Battle of the Atlantic and the Allied Invasion of Normandy).

In deciding to examine the latter I must confess to having been motivated, at least initially, by the fact that one of my brothers was killed in action during a raid by RAF Bomber Command on the German tank training depot at Mailly Le Camp in May 1944. In researching the circumstances of his death I became involved in organising a memorial service and reunion in the French village of Voué, where my brother is buried, together with the rest of the crew of a No 101 Squadron Lancaster.

During that event (which took place in 1987) I met many aircrew and French civilians who not only regard the Mailly Le Camp raid as having been part of the essential preparations for 'Overlord', but also feel strongly that both Bomber Commands of the RAF and USAAF Eighth Air Force have never received proper recognition for the parts they played in the successful establishment of the Normandy beach-head. It seems that the attacks which were made on the railways and German military installations in northwest France and Belgium have become overshadowed by the devastating raids on Germany's industrial centres and cities which, because of their controversial nature, have received so much previous attention.

There appeared, therefore, to be some need not only to examine more closely the parts played by the heavy bombers during the preparatory and beach-head phases of the Allied assault on Normandy, but also to redress the balance of credit due to the crews of those bombers who, contrary to general belief, faced an enemy fighter force which, at the beginning of this period, was at or near its peak of efficiency.

From a soldier's point of view, battles are won or lost by the speed with which each side is able to react to the other's moves and by their abilities to provide reinforcements and supplies, whenever and wherever they are needed. It could be argued that superior wealth and resources alone made it inevitable that the Allies would win the war — eventually; but although some battles did go in their favour through possessing these advantages, some were lost as a result of over-reliance upon them.

My early research consisted of a study of the attacks made by RAF Bomber Command on the railways and German military installations in northwest France and the Low Countries during the spring of 1944. However, the controversy which surrounded the so called "Transportation Plan" led me to make a much wider examination of the dispositions and capabilities of all the Allied and German land and air forces, which were affected, in one way or the other, by the decision to place the strategic bombers in Europe, under the direction of General Eisenhower. Therefore, this book is concerned primarily with the part played by heavy bombers in carrying out Allied plans to so disrupt the German Army's communication and supply systems, that its ability to react to the Normandy landings was severely limited, even before the great land battle began. To be fair to those concerned, and in order to create a balance, it has been necessary (on occasions) to draw attention to the parts played by the Allied Expeditionary Air Force and the French Resistance.

I have broken the book down into three main parts: Background; The Attacks; and Results. In the fourth and final part (titled Conclusions) I have quoted statements made by Allied and German commanders shortly after the war ended. Some of these statements were made without the benefit of facts which are now available and contained in this book, and it seems to me that some of the views expressed were rather less balanced than they might have been. My hope is to place my readers in a position from whence they can make their own, and perhaps more valid, conclusions.

Finally, it is my view that factual and less glamorous accounts actually reflect to a greater extent the problems which faced the aircrews; and the courage of the men who often flew into battle, knowing that their odds of survival were as poor (if not worse) as their fathers' had been in the trenches of the First World War.

Part One

CHAPTER ONE
INTRODUCTION

In November 1942 growing United States involvement in the European war led to President Roosevelt suggesting a tripartite conference, involving the USA, Great Britain and Russia. The aim of the conference was to come to some agreement as to the future conduct of the war. For various reasons Stalin declined to attend, and only the President and Winston Churchill, together with their senior planning staffs, finally met in Casablanca in January 1943.

At this meeting the whole field of the war was surveyed by the Chiefs of Staff of both nations, and, quite naturally, some differences of opinion emerged. Not all the disagreements were international (some were of an interservice nature), but a serious divergence of views did occur over the sequence of future operations. It was thus a triumph for the British Chiefs of Staff who finally tabled a plan[1] which led to an agreed statement on the future conduct of the war. Part of the statement included a reference to 'The heaviest possible Air Offensive against the German War Effort' and on 4 February 1943 a directive was issued to the British and American Commands which gave them their tasks as follows:

> *Your primary object will be the progressive destruction and dislocation of the German military, industrial and economic systems, and the undermining of the morale of the German people to a point where their capacity for armed resistance is fatally weakened. Within that general concept your primary objectives will, for the present, be in the following priority:*
>
> *a.   German submarine yards*
>
> *b.   The German aircraft industry*
>
> *c.   Transportation*
>
> *d.   Oil Plants*
>
> *e.   Other targets of the enemy war industry*

At the beginning of this Combined Bomber Offensive, General Eaker, Commander of the USAAF Eighth Air Force in Britain (who had finally persuaded Churchill at Casablanca that his mostly untried B-17 Fortress bombers should be used in daylight only), made many brave but costly attacks on Bremen, Kiel, Hannover and Berlin. Air Marshal Harris, the Commander-in-Chief of RAF Bomber

Command, with the help of the latest blind bombing and navigation aids, concentrated more successfully, but again at some cost, on the great industrial area of the Ruhr.

American losses on the daylight raids without fighter cover brought Eaker to the conclusion that, if his plan was to succeed, he would have to defeat the German fighter forces first. Accordingly, he pressed for changes in the original Casablanca directive, thus making the first priority attacks on the German aircraft industry. Because the U-Boat war in the Atlantic was easing, the Chiefs of Staff accepted the need for the change and on 10 June 1943 they issued the 'Point Blank' directive. It was to form the basis of the new Combined Bomber Offensive (CBO) and, with timely alterations and additions, it survived the war (in spite of much acrimonious discussion and in-fighting between Allied planners and Commanders).

The Point Blank directive repeated the wording of the original instruction, reference was made again to the objective of 'undermining the morale of the German people'. That loose wording gave Air Marshal Harris plenty of scope to pursue the aims of his original directive. Whilst agreeing, on paper, with the policy of linking up American daylight bombing with night attacks by his own command, Harris was suspicious of any plan that might lead to an attempt to incorporate his Command into a joint Allied heavy bomber force.

His plans for the systematic destruction of German towns had been made following the War Cabinet's directive of February 1942 (well before Point Blank was drawn up) and he was loath to be diverted from his belief that Germany could be brought to her knees without a land battle in Western Europe. General Eaker, while having some sympathy with Harris's ideas, was somewhat disappointed at the lack of support he was receiving in the task of destroying the Luftwaffe. This was noted in Webster and Frankland's *History of the Strategic Air Offensive*:

> *For most of 1943 there was no Combined Bomber Offensive but on the contrary there was a bombing competition.*

It is outside the scope of this book to describe and analyse USAAF and Bomber Command raids of 1943, suffice to say that both the Americans and British achieved some success, but suffered heavy casualties. RAF aircrew morale was probably at its lowest ebb at the end of that year when they were in the middle of the battle of Berlin.

In general terms, the first priority of Point Blank (the destruction of the Luftwaffe's fighter arm) was not achieved in 1943. In spite of the delivery of 200,000 tons of bombs on Germany (twice the 1942 figure), German fighter production and capabilities had in fact increased and, although Hamburg had been crippled by a fire storm in July, the weather and lack of good radar responses from Berlin had saved that city from a similar fate. Even American attempts to halt the flow of armaments by cutting off the supply of ball bearings from Schweinfurt had brought disaster for the unescorted bombers. In one week in October 1943 the USAAF Eighth Air Force lost 148 aircraft; sixty of these were lost on 14 October, when the percentage of aircraft missing to those that were despatched rose to a staggering twenty per cent.

In spite of gloomy predictions by Harris that the German ball bearing industry had been dispersed[2], further attacks were made in February 1944 on Schweinfurt, Steyr and Cannstadt, this time with some support from RAF Bomber Command and the USAAF 15th Air Force; but Allied intelligence failed to appreciate the serious effects which these attacks were having and they ended in April. By September 1944 the German ball bearing industry had almost recovered fully.

It would be quite wrong, however, to suggest that the strategic bombing offensive had been a complete failure[3], it not only presented the Germans with serious industrial problems but also it lead to the drawing off of anti-aircraft guns and radar and much needed manpower from other theatres of war, so helping the Italian campaign and appeasing Stalin, who was constantly pressing Churchill to establish a third front. Also, the need to give priority to fighter aircraft meant that the Luftwaffe was left without any real effective bomber or ground force with which to attack the Allied armies during the build-up and execution of 'Overlord'.

I shall deal later with the introduction and the bombing of the V-1 and V-2 rocket sites in France. For the moment I shall deal with the period about which the reader should have a more detailed understanding.

Planning the invasion of Western Europe from the sea began early in 1943 when Britain's Gen Sir E W Morgan was appointed Chief of Staff to the Supreme Allied Commander (COSSAC) — Eisenhower was yet to be appointed. Morgan's initial plan was considered and approved in principle at a meeting of the Joint Chiefs of Staff in Quebec in August 1943. A feature of the plan was COSSAC's insistence that certain pre-conditions had to be fulfilled, if the invasion was to have a reasonable chance of succeeding. One such condition was the bombing of rail centres, airfields and coastal defence batteries within 150 miles of Caen in Normandy.

In November 1943 ACM Sir Trafford Leigh-Mallory was appointed Air Commander-in-Chief of the Allied Air Expeditionary Air Force, which consisted of the US 9th (Tactical) Air Force, and the RAF 2nd Tactical Air Force. He was asked to draw up a detailed Air Plan for 'Overlord', and in doing so it soon became clear that, in order to meet the army's requirements, he would need the support of RAF and USAAF heavy bombers, which were under the control of the Combined Chiefs of Staff.

At the turn of the year Leigh-Mallory's planners began to hold regular conferences to plan the airborne effort for 'Overlord'. Harris could see that Leigh-Mallory was receiving a great deal of support for his plans to use Bomber Command and the USAAF Eighth Air Force in the initial phases of the invasion, and in direct support of the Allied armies later. Always conscious of heavy aircrew losses, Harris was loath to commit them to a battle for which he considered they had not been trained. On 13 January 1944 he wrote the now well-known paper *The Employment of the Night Bomber Force in Connection with the Invasion of the Continent from the UK*.

Copies of the paper were sent to the Chief of the Air Staff; ACM Sir Charles Portal; to Leigh-Mallory; and Montgomery, the latter having been chosen to command the initial phases of 'Overlord'. It gave a clear picture of Harris's views on the capabilities of his command, and on the technical problems involved in planning and executing raids by heavy bombers. Above all, he stated that any easing of the strategic bombing of Germany, in favour of a tactical role in support of the invasion, would allow Germany to rebuild her armament potential, and indirectly jeopardise the Allied landings in the West. He concluded the paper with the opinion that, given the circumstances, the best use of Bomber Command would be for it to intensify the attacks on Germany's industries.

Harris was supported to a point by the American General Carl Spaatz, who had been appointed to command the US Strategic Air Forces in Europe. Nevertheless, Leigh-Mallory continued to press his case, and in particular wanted the heavy bombers to execute a plan which was being finalised by the Allied Air Forces Bombing Committee[4]. The plan, which was for the disruption of the railway systems in France and Belgium, was the brainchild of Prof Solly Zuckerman[5], assisted by Capt Sherrington and Mr Brant of the Railways Executive Committee; Brant had extensive pre-war knowledge of the French railway system. Zuckerman had been Scientific Advisor to Air Marshal Tedder in the Mediterranean and had produced a similar plan for the Mediterranean Air Force which was widely approved.

On 16 January 1944 Gen Dwight D Eisenhower was appointed Supreme Commander Allied Forces in Europe, and was charged with the liberation of Western Europe. ACM Sir Arthur Tedder was appointed Eisenhower's deputy.

Spaatz and Harris immediately opposed what was to become known as the 'Transportation Plan'; Harris for the reasons which he had already made known in his paper of 13 January, and Spaatz because he believed that oil was the key factor and therefore every effort should be made to disrupt its production and distribution in Germany.

In February there was much argument, during which Zuckerman

fought off repeated criticisms of his plan; but by March Eisenhower and Tedder were both supporting the Transportation Plan. However, Eisenhower was concerned about the possibility of heavy casualties amongst French and Belgian civilians, and the effect that these might have on their cooperation with the land forces — a point which Harris lost no time in emphasising. In early March it was agreed that Bomber Command should carry out trial attacks on six of the seventy-six rail targets selected by Zuckerman and Brant. The aim of the trials was to find out how accurately small targets could be hit at night, using new target marking techniques and blind bombing aids. Spaatz, meanwhile, was authorised to test his heavy bombers against oil targets deep into Germany and the Balkans.

The results of Bomber Command's trial were so successful that the Transportation Plan was reviewed on 25 March, at a special meeting called by the Chief of the Air Staff, Sir Charles Portal. Portal summed up the meeting by stating that he could see no suitable alternative to the plan.

On 14 April, following the receipt of Portal's summary of the 25 March meeting, the Combined Chiefs of Staff agreed to place the heavy bombers of Bomber Command and the USAAF Eighth Air Force under the control of Gen Eisenhower. On 15 April ACM Tedder issued a directive for attacks on seventy-nine rail targets in France and Belgium. The directive paved the way for the use of heavy bombers not only in the execution of the Transportation Plan, but also against German military depots in occupied France and in direct support of the Allied armies, once battle had been joined in Normandy.

On 18 April Eisenhower issued his first directive to both Commands. The instruction to Bomber Command reiterated the need to give maximum assistance in the aims for reducing the strength of the German Air Force and destroying and disrupting enemy rail communications. Harris had made his case and, characteristically, realising the 'inescapable commitment to Overlord'[6], set about his new task with devastating effect. In the months that followed, Bomber Command mounted some 8,000 sorties and dropped 41,000 tons of bombs on the thirty-seven rail targets allocated to them under the Transportation Plan. By the time of the Normandy landings well over half of the targets had been so badly damaged that no further attacks were considered necessary.

At the same time, USAAF attacks on oil targets (long-feared by Albert Speer) were no less successful; and although the USAAF Eighth Air Force was diverted often to attack V-1 and V-2 sites in the Pas de Calais area, there is no doubt that the attacks on German oil supplies, carried out in May, June and July, were responsible for a significant drop in the amount of fuel available to the Luftwaffe and the German Army in the latter half of 1944.

Notes

1 The War Diaries of Gen Sir Alan Brooke credit Field Marshal Dill with having played a large part in persuading the Americans to accept the plan, which was drafted by AM Sir John Slessor, and presented by the Chief of the Air Staff, Sir Charles Portal.

2 For a full and balanced account of the situation at the time see Speer *Inside the Third Reich* p286.

3 Ibid p284.

4 Intelligence departments, particularly AI3(c), had in fact been making intelligence appreciations on that subject since March 1943 (PRO AIR/40/1157).

5 Later Lord Zuckerman, OM, KCB.

6 A phrase he used in the paper of 13 January.

CHAPTER TWO
ALLIED INTELLIGENCE

'Manui Dat Cognitio Vires' is the motto of the Intelligence Corps and translated it reads 'Knowledge gives strength to the arm' symbolizing the need for good intelligence. Lack of good intelligence can lead to defences being taken off guard and attacks failing because the enemy has either moved or is holding the objective with forces far greater than those anticipated.

To many people the word intelligence conjures up visions of spies and covert activities of one sort or another, and although information from such sources has always helped to build up the intelligence picture, it rarely provides a complete one.

By including this subject in the book I hope to give my readers some idea of the demands made upon the Allied Intelligence Organization during the preparatory phase of 'Overlord'; and, in particular, I wish to examine the part played by the 'Intelligencers' during the planning and execution of operations flown by the heavy bombers at this time.

The first requirement was for background intelligence on potential targets: Which of the rail centres would be most used by the Germans in their reinforcement of the Normandy area? Where were most of the locomotives and wagons housed and repaired? Where were the permanent way depots located? And, later on, where were the supply and launching areas for the V-1 and V-2 missiles. These questions formed a fraction of the details required by the planners so that attacks and resources were not wasted on unimportant targets.

Having decided on the targets, the operational staffs would have needed to know the extent of the enemy defences, the proximity of friendly civilians, and the navigational factors in order to plan the attack. As the campaign developed, post-strike analyses were required so that decisions could be made about the requirement or otherwise for further attacks, and Luftwaffe reactions would have been closely monitored also so that routes to and from the targets would not take the bombers over the most heavily defended areas.

After the fall of France in 1940 there were large, if temporary, gaps in British sources of information. Air photo-reconnaissance was able (within the limitations of it's embryonic organisation) to provide some idea of the movements of the invasion barges which were gathering in the Channel ports. However, photo-reconnaissance could seldom answer the question '*Who* is it?'; on the other hand radio intercepts, field observations, interrogations of Prisoners of

War, and captured documents provided some of the answers from which it was possible to determine the type of enemy, its capabilities and probable intentions. Collecting information was, and still is, only part of the process of producing intelligence which emerges only after careful collation and interpretation of the facts which were obtained from many sources.

Counter-intelligence, concealment and deception all formed an integral part of intelligence for planning. In 1943 German Intelligence Staffs were faced with questions very similar to those which confronted the British in 1940: Where and when would the enemy land? Allied Intelligence Staffs, while appreciating that it would be impossible to conceal the preparations for 'Overlord', set about trying to convince the Germans that the invasion would take place somewhere other than Normandy. A bogus Order of Battle was concocted, involving 1st United States Army Group (FUSAG), which included a mythical 4th British Army, supposedly located both in eastern England and Scotland. A number of supporting ruses were employed, such as the placing of dummy landing craft and ammunition dumps near East Anglian ports, the careful leaking of intelligence probes, and (as we shall see later) the bombing of coastal defences well outside the real invasion area. The use of 'spoof' raids and the transmission of false radio messages on the eve of the Allied invasion all helped to mislead the Germans into believing that the attack was about to take place in the Calais area.

The Air Intelligence Branch of the Air Ministry provided Bomber Command with the information required to give its aircrews the best chances of survival against the Luftwaffe's defences, and to ensure that valuable resources were not wasted by attacking targets that could be dealt with by less expensive means. Together with other service intelligence organisations, Bomber Command's only way of collecting information was through direct contact with the enemy (Combat Intelligence). Intelligence regarding such matters as the development of new enemy aircraft, or the vulnerable points of a particular target, reached the Command via one or other of the Air Intelligence branches, which in turn had been privy to reports from one of the numerous special collection agencies.

This book will not deal with the responsibilities and work of all such intelligence organisations; it will deal only with those organisations which were more directly involved in producing intelligence in support of the plans and operations which are discussed in Part 2.

Coordination and administration of the British Intelligence Services was vested in a sub-committee of the Joint Chiefs of Staff Committee and was known as the Joint Intelligence Committee (JIC). The committee comprised the heads of the three Service intelligence branches; and senior representatives from other Government departments, such as the Foreign Office (whose representative acted as chairman), the Ministry of Economic Warfare (MEW), the Government Code and Cypher School (GC and CS), the Central Interpretation Unit (CIU), the Interservices Topographical Department (ISTD), the Secret Intelligence Service (SIS), and the Special Operations Executive (SOE). The Joint Intelligence Staff formed that part of the JIC which was responsible for the production of Intelligence Appreciations and Intelligence Summaries (INTSUMS), leaving the main committee free to control gathering activities and allocate priorities.

The preparation of target maps and illustrated dossiers for use by planners and Allied aircrews was the responsibility of a branch of Air Intelligence known as AI3(c). The annotated photograph in Part 2 of this book is typical of the work of AI3(c), which by the end of the war comprised some 370 men and women, who between them produced about 560,000 items of target material a week. The branch was based at High Wycombe, close to the Headquarters of RAF Bomber Command and the USAAF Eighth Air Force. It is important to note that although AI3(c) produced target intelligence, it did not select the targets, that was done by Intelligence and Planning Staffs at Commands, who worked to general directives issued by Whitehall. In the case of Bomber Command targets were often selected according to operational considerations, rather than in the strict order of priority laid down in the overall directives. The USAAF Eighth Air Force worked more closely to their 'Point Blank' directive, and later, when German fighter production became a priority, via a special committee consisting of members from AI2, AI3 and the RAF and USAAF Commands. The 'Jockey' Committee, as it was known, met weekly from June 1943 to the autumn of 1944, when it was incorporated into the Combined Strategic Targets Committee (CSTC).[1]

Commands were assisted in selecting targets and planning raids by some excellent intelligence reports, emanating from photographs taken from the air by aircraft of PRUs, and by special signals intelligence derived from breaking the German Enigma codes. 'Ultra' was the special caveat used in conjunction with the security classification 'Top Secret' to denote information obtained from that most valuable source. (Those people who are interested in this fascinating subject are recommended to read some of the many books which have emerged since the security restrictions were relaxed in 1974.)

The following extract from one of the many thousand 'Ultra' signals which were produced at Bletchley Park by the GC and CS is relevant to the subject being discussed:

Folio 119. 26 April 1944. Representation by Comd in Chief SW to OKW.
Continually increasing systematic destruction of railway supply

routes and supply installations by Allied aircraft and Guerillas necessitates urgent reinforcement of technical forces (principally electronic units) with a view to the most rapid restoration of damaged installations in order to supply the front line units. There is a lack of experienced personnel, especially for power stations, transformers, and driving and high tension cables.

The Signals Intelligence Station at Kingsdown (the RAF Y Organisation) also produced much valuable intelligence. By listening to radio transmissions from Luftwaffe pilots and their ground controllers, it was possible to deduce much information about enemy aircraft movements and combat tactics. Much of the information received via the two signals intelligence (SIGINT) organisations enabled Allied Intelligence Staffs to make accurate assessments of the effects of the attacks on railway systems in France and Belgium, and monitor the reactions of both the Luftwaffe and French civilians. The graphic and most dramatic evidence of damage to the targets was obtained by photographic reconnaissance.

The Central Interpretation Unit (CIU), later renamed the Allied Central Interpretation Unit (ACIU), was responsible for interpreting air photographs taken over northwest Europe. Many of the Photographic Interpreters (PIs) were recruited from industries or public services (such as electric power or railways) and therefore were well placed to give expert opinions on the flow, capacity and effects of the bombing of factories and utilities in Germany and Nazi-occupied Europe. The unit was based, for the most part, at Danesfield House, Medmenham. (Its survivors meet annually under the name of The Medmenham Club. One of the members was Constance Babington-Smith, author of the book *Evidence in Camera*, and who, as a young WAAF officer, was able to confirm the existence of the V-1 flying bomb at Peenemünde as early as June 1943.)

Topographical intelligence, which included the study of railway systems, was produced by the Interservice Topographical Department (ISTD). The organisation, which was set up in 1941, caused some initial difficulty for the JIC by becoming over-zealous and poaching on the preserves of both the CIU and Air Intelligence. However, once these problems were sorted out, the ISTD produced much sought-after intelligence, some of which was based on reports from the SIS and SOE to which it had direct access. The department was almost overwhelmed in the spring of 1944 when planning for 'Overlord' was at its highest level.

The term 'Technical Intelligence' relates to the monitoring of developments of enemy equipment, including aircraft, tanks and all the weapons carried on such platforms or in the hands of troops on the ground. So-called 'Secret Weapons' and some highly technical subjects were handled by specialists working under the leadership of

Professor R V Jones, the Assistant Director of Intelligence (Science), and they became very involved in the electronics aspect of the war and with monitoring the developments of the V-1 and V-2 rockets.

The branch of Air Intelligence responsible for technical intelligence on the Luftwaffe was AI2(g). The main sources of information open to this branch were POW reports, via the Combined Services Detailed Interrogation Centre (CSDIC); the SIS; captured documents; and the examination of crashed or captured enemy aircraft. By and large AI2(g) detected, in good time, various new German aircraft, including the first jet fighters, the Me 163 and Me 262, and intelligence files of that time are full of incredibly detailed reports on those aircraft. The Branch was not so successful in the matter of the upward-firing cannon, which was fitted to some Luftwaffe night fighters and known as 'Schräge Musik'.

The SOE, although primarily an operational force, acquired increasing importance as a source of tactical intelligence and this led to some friction between themselves and the SIS; in particular, concerning the priorities in allocating aircraft for the despatch and recovery of agents.

Apart from its obvious value in providing detailed intelligence on such subjects as the developments of the V-1 and V-2, the SIS was able to penetrate areas which could not be covered by normal operational intelligence methods. Information on such subjects as enemy morale, the reaction of French civilians to bombing, production

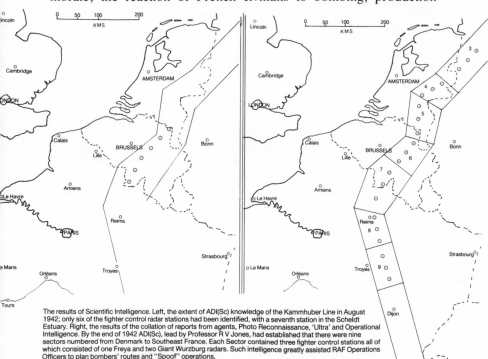

The results of Scientific Intelligence. Left, the extent of ADI(Sc) knowledge of the Kammhuber Line in August 1942; only six of the fighter control radar stations had been identified, with a seventh station in the Scheldt Estuary. Right, the results of the collation of reports from agents, Photo Reconnaissance, 'Ultra' and Operational Intelligence. By the end of 1942 ADI(Sc), lead by Professor R V Jones, had established that there were nine sectors numbered from Denmark to Southeast France. Each Sector contained three fighter control stations all of which consisted of one Freya and two Giant Wurzburg radars. Such intelligence greatly assisted RAF Operations Officers to plan bombers' routes and "Spoof" operations.

figures, and personalities, was obtained from a wide network of agents. They conveyed their messages via coded radio transmissions, written messages, drawings, photographs, stolen documents, and even via the time-honoured pigeon service (operated by the RAF, who dropped the birds in special crates which were designed to open automatically if they were not found by the agents within a given time!).

A branch of Military Intelligence (MI14) was responsible for compiling the Order of Battle of German ground forces, therefore a sub-section of the branch was responsible initially for collating and distributing intelligence concerning German anti-aircraft defences. In July 1943 MI15(AA) was created to take over this responsibility and, like its predecessor, dealt directly with the Air Ministry and continued to work as an inter-Service and inter-Allied organisation.

Much of the intelligence supplied to units prior to the Normandy landings and during the subsequent land-battle was provided by the newly formed Theatre Intelligence Section (TIS), which became part of the intelligence organisation within the Supreme Headquarters Allied Expeditionary Force (SHAEF). To a certain extent, the section duplicated the work of existing intelligence agencies and (as we will see later) some of their conclusions proved to be controversial[2].

In spite of its apparently unwieldy size, the Allied Intelligence structure was generally successful. Parts of Professor Jones's book *Most Secret War* illustrate, very clearly, the manner in which information from the various agencies was put together to create a comprehensive picture of what was happening on 'the other side of the hill'.

It is clear from the foregoing that the Bomber Commands of both the RAF and USAAF Eighth Air Force were well supported by the Intelligence Services, which proved themselves extremely capable of collating and disseminating the mass of information which poured in from all quarters. Without this intelligence both Commands would have suffered additional casualties and wasted a lot of bombs. It does seem, however, that there were times when the principles, if fully understood, of analysing intelligence were not always applied by some members of the intelligence community, who were in the job 'for the duration'. Such intelligence officers left themselves open to criticism by scientists and other academics who had greater analytical skills.

Notes

1 Hinsley, *British Intelligence World War II, Vol 3, Pt 11.*
2 *Ibid.*
  Also, *after many years' experience, I came to the conclusion that some duplication was, and is, inevitable.*

CHAPTER THREE
THE AIR FORCES

RAF Bomber Command

Appendix 1 gives the Orders of Battle for RAF Bomber Command for 9 March 1944 and 1 June 1944. The number of heavy bombers available for operations on any one night fluctuated slightly, but increased generally between January and June. The numbers of serviceable aircraft and type available to the RAF on 31 March 1944 (three weeks after the first experimental raid of the Transportation Plan) were:

Lancaster	536
Halifax	270
Sterling	57
Mosquito	63

In addition, two Special Duties squadrons operated Halifaxes, Hudsons and Lysanders in support of the European Resistance Groups, and a squadron of American B-17 Fortresses, fitted with electronic jamming equipment, was on loan to No 100 Group. Some sixty-eight operational squadrons were involved in the Transportation Plan, including some from the Royal Australian, Royal New Zealand and Royal Canadian Air Forces. Thirteen squadrons of the RCAF comprised No 6 (Canadian) Group. The average squadron holdings against establishment were very high (about 99 per cent) and the rate of serviceability of aircraft held against establishment improved during the early part of 1944 and was approximately eighty-four per cent by June.

Although it was planned that A V Roe and English Electric should produce a total of 250 heavy bombers a month, the production targets were seldom reached[1], and in January 1944 only 160 four-engined aircraft were built. A reduction in the 'missing' rate and the fact that many damaged aircraft were rebuilt and returned to service prevented a crisis of attrition. Nevertheless, Bomber Command was able to mount some 57,000 sorties during the six months from January to June 1944, and still show a net gain, as follows:

Heavy bombers available for operations 1 January	930
Plus new-built and repaired aircraft 1 January–30 June	2059
Less aircraft missing or damaged beyond repair	1779
Aircraft available for operations on 30 June 1944	1210

The narrow margins highlight a point that other authors have made regarding the temporary respite which was created by the bombing of French targets. Had Harris persisted with the big attacks on Germany the losses could have outstripped production and repair, and would have reduced the amount of aircraft available for 'Overlord'.

The great majority of aircraft that went missing during raids fell victim to the Luftwaffe's night fighters. Official German night fighter claims were much higher than those estimated by RAF Bomber Command at the time, and gave rise to speculation about the effects of the oblique-mounted cannon on the Ju 88 and Me 110 twin-engined night fighters. It is possible that some damage attributed to light flak was in fact the result of hits from these cannon, which fired upward into the underside of the bombers. (See Appendix 12).

Over 57,000 sorties were flown by Bomber Command during the first six months of 1944, of which nearly 3000 were day sorties, mostly in June 1944. The table shows how the loss rate came down after the Battle of Berlin during the winter of 1943/44:

Month	Sorties*	Missing	% Loss
January	6315	318	5
February	5057	200	4
March	9410	285	3
April	10,000	202	2
May	11,455	283	2.4
June	15,196	264	1.7

* The numbers of sorties vary a little between the documents available; the figures above are the average.

It has been calculated that for a bomber crew to have had a fair chance of completing a tour of thirty operations, the loss rate had to be below four per cent.

The increasing use of radar together with ground control of fighters by the Germans in 1942/3 resulted in Britain's use of countermeasures and the start of electronic warfare. Initially, many *ad hoc* arrangements were tried, but on 23 November 1943 No 100 (Special Duties) Group was established within Bomber Command. This Group, under the direction of Air Cdre E B Addison, was not only responsible for airborne countermeasures to deceive or jam enemy radio and radar systems, but it also gave support for the night bomber force by attacking enemy fighters in the air and on the ground.

The early results of attacks on enemy fighters by No 100 Group were disappointing, mainly because of a lack of experience with and technical malfunction of the new equipment (twenty-seven German aircraft only were destroyed between December 1943 and April

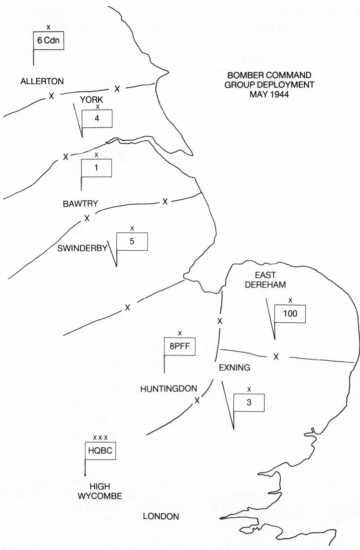

x
6 Cdn

ALLERTON

BOMBER COMMAND
GROUP DEPLOYMENT
MAY 1944

X

X
YORK
x
x
4

X
x
1

BAWTRY
X
X

x
SWINDERBY 5

EAST
DEREHAM

X
x
100

X

x
8PFF
X
EXNING

HUNTINGDON
x
X
3

x x x
HQBC

HIGH
WYCOMBE

LONDON

1944). It was not until May and June 1944 that 'Serrate'-equipped Mosquitos began to obtain better results and were able to give some protection to the main bomber force. As a result of the disastrous Nurenburg Raid at the end of March, Air Marshal Harris asked for ten more fighter squadrons. He received three, one of them (No 23 Squadron) was transferred from Malta.

At that time No 100 Group had three heavy, jamming squadrons only, one of which was on detachment from the USAAF. Another squadron, No 101 (which for some unknown reason never came under the command of No 100 Group), was operating 'Airborne Cigar' (ABC) and accompanied the main force on most raids. As part of No 1 Group, the Squadron was required to carry out normal bombing runs, but there was an eighth member of the crew (known as the Special Operator) who was usually able to speak German, and operated equipment designed to jam enemy night fighter frequencies.

New measures and countermeasures followed in quick succession, and the Germans even tried to give coded directions to their fighters by playing pre-arranged music.[2]

Some mention should be made at this point of the Operational Training and Heavy Conversion Units of Bomber Command. Although not part of the Main Force both units played an important role in creating diversions by dropping leaflets over enemy-held territory and by laying mines in enemy waters.

The Operational Training Units (OTUs), of which there were as many as twenty-two, were equipped mostly with twin-engined Wellington bombers, and OTU instructors were usually drawn from crews who had completed an operational tour. Some 262 Wellingtons from the OTUs took part in the first Thousand Bomber Raid on Cologne, in May 1942, but it was not general policy to use OTUs for that purpose, as it was realised that the inevitable disruption in crew training would lead to a cut in the supply of replacement crews. The leaflet raids, known as 'Nickel' sorties, gave the aircrews a moderate taste of enemy air defences and helped to confuse German radar operators and fighter controllers in their assessments of the likely destinations of the main force.

At their peak there were twelve Heavy Conversion Units (HCUs), equipped with Sterlings, Halifaxes and, eventually, Lancasters. As their title implied, the units provided the necessary step from the OTUs' twin-engined Wellingtons to the four-engined aircraft which the crews would fly when they reached their operational squadrons.

As did the OTUs, the HCUs provided valuable diversions from the Main Force during the Normandy invasion, playing some part in the laying of mines during the so-called 'Gardening' sorties. The threat imposed by the mines resulted in the German Navy having to deploy a predominately minesweeping force in the invasion area — 178 minesweepers together with only one 'Elbing'-class destroyer and thirty E- boats.

By the spring of 1944 Bomber Command had replaced its twin-engined Whitleys, Wellingtons, Hampdens, and the underpowered Manchesters with four-engined Stirlings, Lancasters and Halifaxes. The Sterling (described by some aircrew, with perhaps some recent girlfriend in mind, as comfortable but lacking in performance) was being phased out of Main Force operations. Of the two surviving types the Lancaster was the most successful; although some crews favoured the less sophisticated Halifax, claiming that it could take more punishment.[3] There is some evidence on file which suggests that losses and incidences of 'early return', were higher amongst the Halifax squadrons.

The Mosquito, which with modifications was capable of carrying a 4000-lb bomb to Berlin, was perhaps the RAF's most successful aircraft of the war. It was used by Bomber Command from 1942 as a bomber, fighter, intruder and for pathfinding and pinpoint marking. With a top speed of over 360 mph it could outrun most German fighters; the bomber version carried no defensive armament. The American four-engined B-17 Fortress was considered by the RAF but, although it carried more defensive armament and had a better operating ceiling the bomb load it could carry over a given distance was thirty-five per cent less than that carried by the Lancaster.

Such then was the overall position of Bomber Command with regard to equipment; but what of the men who flew and operated that equipment?

In the year ending September 1944 more than 16,500 aircrew of Bomber Command lost their lives on operations and a further 2,500 were killed in flying accidents. On 31 March 1944 the total number of fully trained crews available, including those from the Dominions, was 1,097. By comparison with the number killed on operations, the number taken prisoner or evading capture after baling out over enemy held territory was very low, and the chances of survival for an airman reported as 'missing' were only one in five.

Of the seventy-one airmen reported missing from a raid on Ternier marshalling yard on 10/11 April, fifty-eight are buried in minor cemeteries in northwest France. A post-war analysis of Bomber Command casualties showed that for every one hundred aircrew: fifty-one were killed on operations, nine were killed in crashes, three were seriously injured in crashes, twelve became prisoners of war, one evaded capture, and twenty-four survived unharmed.[4]

Looking at those figures many years later, it seems almost impossible that Bomber Command was so well-served by its aircrew; yet, apart from the winter of 1943/44, morale seems to have remained remarkably high. How did you do it? I have put that question to a number of those people who were involved, and received similar answers: 'We accepted it as part of the war, and never thought it could happen to us.'

It was evident however that Station Commanders were always on the look-out for a breakdown in morale, and most cases of 'LMF' — Lack of Moral Fibre — were dealt with swiftly and without much sympathy. In the early days the tendency to 'release bombs early and get the hell out of it' was countered by the installation of flash-operated cameras which were used to substantiate the accuracy of crew reports.

Morale, discipline and leadership are all required by any fighting force. During my own service in the Army, I spent a considerable number of years in Joint Service Establishments, and at one time had the privilege of commanding a support wing of RAF personnel. During that time I formed the impression that man-management in the RAF is different to that of the other two Services. That is not so much a criticism, more a reflection of the different nature of air fighting. On land, a whole battalion, including the Commanding Officer, may come under the same shelling; in a ship all the crew are in equal danger; but for every aircrew member of a front-line squadron there was another of the same unit who might never have heard a shot fired in anger. Again, this is in no way a criticism of ground crews, without whose devotion to their duty of servicing aircraft many more aircrew would have died in accidents.

Aircrew training was thorough. The introduction of the Empire Air Training Scheme allowed pilots and navigators to acquire their skills without interruption by the enemy; but they did not get much experience of flying in bad weather. Crews came together at the OTUs and went on together to the HCUs. Both of those advanced training units gave the crews a taste of the things to come, but it all took time. One of my own brothers, a navigator, joined the aircrew recruitment centre in October 1941, but he did not reach his first operational squadron until February 1944. Some crews had the misfortune to lose the pilots with whom they had trained. New pilots, on reaching their squadrons, were required to make at least one trip with an experienced crew; sometimes they did not return.[5]

In training and in squadron service the aircrew lived in a wide range of accommodation. A few were housed in overcrowded but reasonably comfortable buildings on pre-war airfields, but the vast majority lived in the quite primitive conditions of Nissen huts which were situated on the edge of the newly built airfields of eastern England. A call of nature (the result of a night on the beer possibly) often resulted in a long trip in the cold, or having to resort to a wellington boot — preferably not one's own!

Being a mixture of officers and NCOs, most crews were divided into their respective messes. On stand-down nights officers might visit their NCO crew members in their billets for a game of darts, or the whole crew would climb into old cars for a trip to the local pub.

Crews which survived their first six sorties were regarded as having a better chance of survival subsequently, and superstitious gimmicks, based on the fact that nothing should alter their pattern of luck, would creep in. Urinating on the aircraft tailwheel before take-off seems to have been one popular superstition; carrying some sort of lucky charm was another. The crews with the best chances of surviving thirty operations were undoubtedly those that were led by a pilot who maintained discipline and insisted on constant vigilance and checking the equipment. The biggest danger for such dedicated crews was a series of 'quiet trips' which could cause them to drop their guard.

Most of the aircrews overcame their intense and quite natural fears, some claim to have been more afraid of showing fear than of the root causes. Some were 'frozen' onto controls during fighter attacks or periods of intense anti-aircraft fire. For others the worst parts were the waiting and preparation for the operation — tasteless sandwiches being gobbled down in an effort to create some feeling of normality. When airborne, there was usually much to do and, if attacked, a sort of calm set in while they got on with the job in hand.

It is now generally accepted that every person has a varying amount of courage and that once it is expended, fear will creep in. Some were able to rebuild their reserves of courage after a rest. The convalescent home at Matlock in Derbyshire claimed that many men were returned to their units actually wanting to 'have another go'.

In the Korean War eight years later, it was concluded that those who had had the misfortune to be caught and tortured by the Chinese had survived their ordeal best if they had some deep conviction, religious or otherwise. Having spoken with an ex-RAF Padre, it seems that the same criterion applied within Bomber Command during the Second World War.

The immediate after effects of a bad trip were often vented in wild parties and alcohol-assisted pranks, such as chopping down the Station flagpole to the cries of 'T i m b e r!'; or in the arms of a 'popsie' in Lincoln, but the long-term effects were sometimes more serious. Some men became alcoholics, some had an inability to settle down, some had coronary problems, or they just became the local pub bore.

USAAF Eight Air Force-Bomber Command

The full story of 'Bolero' (the build-up of American armed forces in England) can be best read in Craven and Cate's *Army Air Forces in the Second World War*. This book is concerned with just one small part of that operation; namely, the gradual assembly, composition and operations of those American strategic bombers based in England, between mid-1942 and the end of the war in Europe.

A joint American/British directive, issued on 8 September 1942, stated their aim to continue the bombing offensive against the Axis powers. The directive further stated that the primary force for night bombing operations would be RAF Bomber Command, and daylight bombardments would be the responsibility of the USAAF Eighth Air Force. The first American Air Headquarters in Europe (the United States Army Bomber Command) was established under Gen Ira C Eaker on 22 February 1942. Eaker's brief was simple: to go to the RAF Bomber Command's Headquarters at High Wycombe and study RAF procedures; to look around for suitable airfields; and to make recommendations for the equipping, training and deploying of American heavy bomber units in England. A close association with RAF Bomber Command was established from the onset.

The USAAF Eighth Air Force moved to Britain in June 1942. After a bad start, when some B-17s made forced landings on Greenland's icy plateau, a steady stream of bombers, and some escorting fighters, made their way via Greenland and Iceland to Scotland. By the end of August well over one hundred B-17 Fortresses had landed in England via the North Atlantic route. On 17 August twelve of the heavy bombers, escorted by British Spitfires, led by Gen Eaker (in an aircraft called 'Yankee Doodle') attacked the marshalling yards at Rouen-Sotteville.

By the end of 1942 nearly 700 aircraft of varying types, belonging to the USAAF Eighth Air Force, had reached their new bases in England. A year later, the average number of heavy bombers available for operations on a daily basis had reached 1500, of which 870 were B-17 Fortress bombers, the remainder were B-24 Liberators.

Early fighter escorts consisted of P-47 Thunderbolts and P-38 Lightnings; but they had a limited range and, even with the introduction of drop tanks, they were unable to operate beyond a range of about 500 miles. In January 1944 the Eighth Air Force's Fighter Command was comprised of 576 F-47 Thunderbolts and almost 100 P-38 Lightnings. By the end of June the Thunderbolts had been replaced largely by P-51 Mustang fighters, which were being equipped with Rolls-Royce engines and long-range fuel tanks. By that time, there were nearly 900 fighters available to escort the bombers and take independent action against the German fighters, which had been wreaking havoc amongst the large American daylight formations.

At the beginning of 1944, delivery of new heavy bombers to the Eighth Air Force averaged 460 a month[6], most of them being flown to Britain via the route previously described. Set against the enormous production figures, units' losses against holdings for the month of January average almost twenty per cent. (It should be noted that the figure relates to aircraft missing and damaged beyond repair and should not be compared directly with figures given elsewhere for RAF Bomber Command, which were calculated as percentages of aircraft missing to sorties flown; for the Eighth Air Force that figure for January was 3.3 per cent.) As it is for all statistics, much depends on the method of calculation. Serviceability of American aircraft was calculated on a different basis; the Americans included in their figures aircraft which would be serviceable 'within thirty-six hours'. Generally speaking, there appears to have been little difference in the rates of serviceability between the RAF and USAAF (about eighty per cent) but later figures suggested that the RAF rate improved whereas that of the Americans declined as the battle progressed.

Third echelon repairs (those beyond the resources of ground crews) were carried out by Service Squadrons, some of which were mobile; but major overhauls, repairs and conversions were undertaken by Strategic Air Depots (which, in the early days, were linked with the British Ministry of Aircraft Production) and they employed British civilians. One of the earliest and largest of these depots was located at Burtonwood in Lancashire, but advanced depots, such as those at Troston and Neaton in East Anglia, were soon established near to the bomber wings.

Between January and June 1944 there was a further increase in the number of B-17s, and two additional bomber groups were added to the Eight Air Force's ORBAT (Order of Battle). At the same time the number of B-24s held rose dramatically from 138 to 864, and the number of B-24 groups was increased from eight to nineteen. Each bomber group had approximately forty-eight aircraft, and by the time of the Allied invasion Eighth Air Force Bomber Command had approximately 2000 aircraft allocated among forty-one bomber groups.

At this point it becomes necessary to discuss the American approach to the problems of strategic bombing. It will be remembered that Gen Eaker (the first commander of the Eighth Air Force[7]) had persuaded Churchill, at the Casablanca Conference in January 1943,[8] that his bombers should be used in compliance with the directive of the previous September: in daylight only. The opposite view, taken by the British, was based on the results of early Bomber Command daylight attacks in 1940 and 1941, and on experience gained during the Battle of Britain, when, although outnumbered, RAF fighters had forced the Luftwaffe to operate under cover of darkness. The Americans, whose aircraft carried more defensive armament, believed that their 'box' formations could fight their way to the targets, which

COMBAT BOX

PLAN VIEW   SIDE VIEW

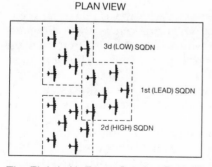
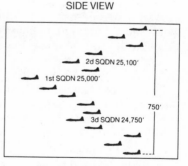

The Eighth Air Force Combat Box. The formation consisted of 18-20 bombers, stacked in such a way as to give mutual support from as many top and bottom turrets as possible. (*US Air Force*)

would then be bombed visually, using the somewhat superior Norden bombsight. Both the B-17 and the B-24 had been designed for this type of battle. However, Gen Eaker realised that they would not be able to carry out their task to full effect unless the numbers of German fighters could be reduced drastically. Also, his bombers would have to be escorted by Allied fighters for most, if not all, of the way to and from the targets.

On 17 August 1943 the Eighth Air Force celebrated its first anniversary of operations in England by attacking the large Messerschmitt aircraft works at Regensburg, and the ball-bearing plants at Schweinfurt. The aircraft detailed to attack Regensburg flew on to newly established bases in North Africa. Of the 376 B-17s despatched, thirty-six were lost on the Regensburg mission and twenty-four on the Schweinfurt mission; a total of sixty aircraft, representing sixteen per cent of the force. It appears that the Regensburg mission could have resulted in a greater loss of aircraft had it not taken the Germans by surprise by flying on to North Africa. The Luftwaffe unleashed every trick in the book, Focke-Wulfe 190s and Messerschmitt 109s attacking from all directions, singly and in large groups. Despite the ferocity of the battle the bombers did a very good job, and the Germans were forced even more onto the defensive and therefore concentrated on the production of fighters rather than bombers.[9]

On 20 February 1944 sixteen combat wings of the three air divisions of the Eighth Air Force, numbering over 1000 bombers, took off in heavy weather to bomb twelve aircraft plants throughout Germany. The force was escorted by seventeen groups of fighters from the USAAF's Eighth and Ninth Air Forces, and by sixteen RAF fighter squadrons. It was the start of Operation Augument ("Big Week" as it became known) and it marked the beginning of an upward turn in the fortunes of American bomber crews.[10]

Of the two types of heavy bomber in use with the Eighth Air Force the B-17 was considered by most to be the better aircraft. The B-24 Liberator was equatable in some ways with the Halifax and crews would meet disparaging remarks from Fortress crews about 'Pregnant Cows' with cries of 'Pansy' and would defend their aircraft on the grounds that it could take more punishment. The maximum permissible take-off weight for the B-24 (71,000 lb) reflected a greater range rather than bomb load, and it was this fact that led to the aircraft being used for maritime reconnaissance by both the American and British Air Forces.

Many modifications were made to both types during the course of the war. One particular version of the B-17, known as the YB.40 Protection Ship, had extra gun turrets and carried no less than fourteen .50in calibre heavy machine guns — it was not a great success.[11]

One of the major problems for the planners of the raids was the safe assembly of large aircraft formations in the somewhat limited airspace over East Anglia. Special brightly painted 'assembly ships' were used to help the bombers formate with their correct squadrons, and aircraft markings were larger than those on RAF aircraft.

Aircraft were given names more widely in the USAAF than in the RAF, and some veteran bombers and assembly ships were never referred to in any other way. For example, the bright yellow B-24 assembly aircraft of the 44th Bomber Group was always known as 'Lemon Drop'.

The average bomb loads carried by the Eighth Air Force were less than those carried by the RAF, and the bombs were smaller; although the smaller bombs proved to be inadequate for attacking some industries and shipping, they were an advantage when attacking troop concentrations, and they were less likely to fail to explode.

One Allied answer to the requirement for a bomb to penetrate German U-Boat pens and to smash massive concrete gun emplacements, was the 4500-lb, rocket-assisted 'Disney Bomb', which was developed by the Royal Navy and carried by American B-17s. The bomb was released at 24,000 ft and was boosted at 5000 ft by rockets fitted to its tail. The bombs, which reached a terminal velocity of 2400 fps, were used against the E-boat pens at IJmuiden in Holland. Napalm was introduced in 1944, during Operation Cobra[12] and in early 1945 against coastal defences in the Bordeaux area, which had been holding out since the previous August.

An unusually bad patch of weather in September 1943 led General Eaker to order the first radar-assisted mission undertaken by the Eighth Air Force. Much of the airborne radar and electronic countermeasures equipment was of British origin, and American Pathfinder aircraft were fitted with H2X, the American version of the British H2S radar, which had worked so well during the battle of Hamburg. In the autumn of 1943 the Eighth Air Force's bomber formations began to counter German radar-controlled guns by using 'Chaff' (the American name for 'Window', see glossary) and they developed their own airborne transmitters which were capable of jamming German ground radar. Known as 'Carpet' the equipment was introduced and used to good effect from October 1943.

The living conditions for American bomber crews based in Britain were very similar to those of the RAF; except that their food was better and they operated during what was considered to be a man's normal working day.[13] Some forty-one airfields in England were occupied by Eighth Air Force units, flying American heavy bombers. A few of these (e.g. Bassingbourne) were pre-war RAF stations. Hastily constructed wartime airfields were built to a set pattern, with aircraft dispersal pens, mess halls and accommodation areas set up to a mile or more apart. In the early days most American aircrews were issued with standard RAF bicycles for personal transport, but Jeeps were soon in general use. Rain, fog and winds 'straight from Siberia' were features that most crews had not experienced before, and which are still talked about amongst veterans when they visit their wartime bases.

In spite of the weather and periods when they sustained very heavy casualties, morale amongst the aircrews remained fairly high. Having survived and surmounted initial troubles they pressed on with dogmatic faith, and the American superiority complex drove them on to try and succeed where others had failed. The chances of completing a tour of twenty-five operations unharmed were much the same as those in the RAF (twenty-five per cent), and if the 'missing' rate went above four per cent there was little chance.

Fortress and Liberator crews experienced the same tensions as their cousins did in the RAF, the worst time again being in the preparatory stages of a mission. Mascots, lucky charms and pre-flight rituals were, if anything, more in evidence. One of the disadvantages of operating in daylight was that they could see their friends going down in flames. A study of available statistics shows that, once hit, more crews were able to bale out of American bombers than out of RAF Lancasters and Halifaxes.

Like many RAF crews who had done their initial training in the colonies where the weather was fair, the American crews got a shock when they arrived in England and reported to either of the two

8th USAAF BOMBER GROUP LOCATIONS
6 JUNE 1944

Approximate Air Division Boundaries   —X X—

803 Sqn (PFF)

combat replacement centres located northwest of London. The CCRCs equated with the RAF's OTUs, and combat-experienced crews taught the new arrivals the latest tactics employed by Luftwaffe fighters.[14] Total flying hours before reaching operational bomber groups averaged 250 hours.

From the first hesitant steps in August 1942 the Eighth Air Force grew both in strength and stature. During the winter of 1944/45 the average daily number of heavy bombers actually available for operations seldom fell below 2000. Like their RAF counterparts, they were nearest defeat in the winter of 1943/44 but, with the help of fighter escorts, they went on to take much of the credit for the complete destruction of German aircraft and oil industries, and defeating those Luftwaffe squadrons which had threatened the successful outcome of 'Overlord'.

The USAAF Eighth Air Force will be remembered for many more years with pride and admiration, not necessarily because it was technically superior, but for the determination and bravery shown by all who served in it.

The Luftwaffe

While reading this section it should be borne in mind that some of the information available on the Luftwaffe is possibly inaccurate, this is particularly so in published material where it has been discovered that dates of events, nomenclature of units, and statistics do not always agree. Some excuse for these anomalies is to be found in the great number of changes made to the Luftwaffe's Command and Control Systems and the apparently illogical and confusing subordinations of formations in parent Commands.

The following is a brief summary of the organisation, capabilities and reactions of that part of the Luftwaffe which faced Allied heavy bombers during the critical months prior to the invasion of Normandy in June 1944. I have also included a brief account of the Luftwaffe's somewhat limited operations against Allied shipping and ground forces at the time of the Normandy landings.

The basic command system of the Luftwaffe followed a pattern devised in 1939:

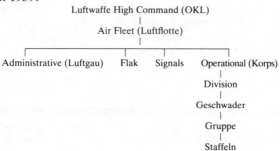

Luftwaffe High Command (OKL)
|
Air Fleet (Luftflotte)
|

| Administrative (Luftgau) | Flak | Signals | Operational (Korps) |

Division
|
Geschwader
|
Gruppe
|
Staffeln

The Staffeln consisted mostly of nine or ten aircraft, but some had that number increased to sixteen. There would be three or four Staffeln to a Gruppe (equivalent roughly to an RAF Wing), and three or four Gruppen to a Geschwader (equivalent to an RAF Group). A Korps consisted of a varying number of Geschwader, according to its operational requirements, and these were sometimes broken into Divisions. When referring to Staffeln or Gruppen it was usual to show the Geschwader to which they were subordinate, thus 111/NJG 1 indicated No 3 Gruppe of N 1 Nachjagdgeschwader (Night fighter Geschwader).

At the beginning of the war the Luftwaffe relied mainly on anti-aircraft guns and searchlights to combat night attacks, but in October 1940 Oberst Joseph Kammhuber was given the task of organising a night fighter force, which he began by forming a defensive system which became known to the British as the Kammhuber Line. Early versions of the line (which lay across northern Germany and the Low Countries) consisted of sound locators, searchlights and guns. Later, the sound locators were replaced with radar and the Himmelbelt System was established with radar guiding night fighters towards the attacking bombers which were illuminated by radar-controlled searchlights.

In 1942 the airborne radar 'Lichtenstein' was fitted to the night fighters which were directed by ground control to a position from whence their own radars took over. The ground control stations were set up under the direction of chief fighter controllers (Jafues). Together with the introduction of the improved dish aerial 'Wurzburg' radars, the whole system began to help the Luftwaffe to achieve success against the Allied bomber streams.

During that time Kammhuber (then a Generalleutenant) had been steadily building up his force from Divisional strength to become No XII Fliegerkorps which controlled three Fighter Divisions, three Radar Regiments and two Searchlight Divisions.

In 1943 it became apparent that the weight of Allied bomber attacks would soon overwhelm the German defences; but by then it was already too late. Earlier pleas by Kammhuber for more fighters had been ignored and terrible losses on the Russian front were adding to the problems. Arguments ensued within the German High Command. Partially trained pilots were being used in operations. Then, on 24 July, as the Americans put the pressure on with massive daylight raids, the RAF hit Hamburg.

The raid on Hamburg marked the first use of 'Window'. Some 92,000,000 strips of tin foil were dropped, creating a fog of echoes that rendered German fighter and fire control systems useless[15]. The best the German controllers could do was to direct their fighters into the Hamburg area, with instructions to search for the bombers. In fact this raid was the first big test for the Wilde Sau (Wild Boar)

System which was then under development. It was based on the idea of talking fighter aircraft into a general area and letting them find their targets, using light from fires and flares. 'Wilde Sau' provided a temporary respite to the problems caused by 'Window', but when the RAF changed ther tactics, the success rate of the German fighters began to fall again until better airborne electronic devices led to the Zahme Sau (Tame Boar) System, whereby fighters were directed into the bomber streams.

After another devastating attack on Kassel in October 1943 Generalfeldmarschall Milch[16] called a conference to discuss the reasons for the Luftwaffe's failures. Later that month XII Flieger-korps was disbanded and was replaced by Jagdkorps (Fighter Corps) I, which controlled three fighter Divisions, and Kammhuber was banished to Denmark. The resultant shuttling around of units went on into the spring of 1944, and created an extraordinarily complicated chain of command. By March 1944 a second Jagdkorps was established in France, within the Luftflotte III area. From its headquarters near Paris it controlled 4 and 5 Jagddivisions.

Although many new types of piston-engined aircraft were under development,[17] and some (including the Heinkel 219, and the Messerschmitt 210 and 410) did get into night fighter units, the mainstay of the fighter force consisted of updated versions of well-tried, single-engined Messerschmitt Bf 109s, Focke-Wulf Fw 190s, and twin-engined Messerschmitt Bf 110s and Junkers Ju 88s. A few units were equipped with fighter versions of the Dornier Do 217 and, after many delays[18]. the Messerschmitt 262 jet fighter began to reach operational units in the early summer of 1944.

The escalation in electronic warfare resulted in many versions of Airborne Intercept (AI) radars being fitted to Luftwaffe night fighters, and improved versions of the Fu 220 'Lichtenstein' SN2 were being produced in large numbers in September 1943. The Fu 220, which had a range of about three miles, was fitted to many of the twin-engined fighters; the smaller FuG 216 'Neptune', which had a range of two miles, was fitted to some single-engined aircraft employed in the night fighting role. When the Mosquitos of RAF Bomber Command's No 100 Group became a threat, the Luftwaffe began to fit tail warning radars, and some fighters were equipped with sets to detect emissions from Bomber Command's H2S and other electronics.

The superior armament of Luftwaffe fighters seems to have compensated for many of their disadvantages. Of the seven different guns in use, four were of a heavier calibre than any carried by Allied heavy bombers. The 20mm Oerlikon MGFF and the 20mm Mauser MG/151/20 seem to have been prominent in most offensive armament packs, the 30mm Rheinmetal MG 108 came into service with the later types of aircraft. It has been estimated that fifteen rounds of explosive ammunition from an MG 108 was all that was required to bring down a four-engined bomber, and that fifty 20mm rounds was equivalent in effect to 250 rounds of 7.9mm bullets.

Although the American aircraft carried .50in (12.8mm) guns, most of the Lancasters and Halifaxes of Bomber Command had to rely on turrets fitted with two or four .303in (7.76mm) machine guns.[19] Reports of attacks by air-to-air and ground-to-air rockets, particularly in daylight, grew more frequent during the summer of 1944, but such weapons never replaced the excellent armoury of machine guns and air cannons in use with the Luftwaffe.

Local improvisation led to many improvements in the performance and armament of Luftwaffe aircraft. One such improvement was made in mid-1943, when pilots were complaining of the difficulties in attacking Lancasters from below, the natural quarter because most were not fitted with ventral turrets. An enthusiastic fitter at a Luftwaffe night fighter station devised a mounting and sight for a pair of cannon, located behind the pilot and angled to fire upwards and forwards into the fuel tanks of the enemy. This deadly arrangement (known as 'Schräge Musik' — Jazz Music) must have accounted for many RAF Bomber Command aircraft from mid-1943 until its existence was noted in an Intelligence Summary in September 1944. (Because I believe that one of my brothers was shot down by this equipment, I have conducted some research into the matter and the results appear in Appendix 12.)

In spite of 'Point Blank' and, in particular, Operation Argument (Big Week) in February 1944 (when more than 3000 American heavy bombers delivered nearly 10,000 tons of bombs on the German aircraft industry), German fighter production began to actually rise during the early part of 1944.[20] Between 1 March and 30 June, 750 Ju 88s and 550 BF 110s came off the assembly lines. During the same period, deliveries of new single-engined fighters amounted to 3600 BF 109s and 1700 Fw 190s. The monthly output of fighters reached a peak in September 1944, when no less than 3375 aircraft were produced,[21] but there was a vast difference between the production and the availability of aircraft. The table below shows the overall position on 31 March 1944, three weeks after the start of Transportation Plan:[22]

Type	Number established	Number on charge	Number serviceable	Percentage serviceable
Night fighters	1047	565	361	64
Single-engined fighters	2320	1696	1188	70
Other twin-engined fighters	?	251	148	58

Of the total number of fighters available, it was estimated that sixty-five per cent were allocated to the Western Front but, although poor delivery and serviceability (reflected in the table above) caused problems, the worst problem was the lack of trained pilots which had been caused by terrible combat losses and cuts in training.

The average number of Luftwaffe pilots for the months January to May 1944 was 2280; but losses during the same period amounted to 2262 (ninety-nine per cent).[23] New pilots of day fighters were taking on an increasing number of Mustang escort fighters, and night-fighter crews (if they were not writing off themselves and their machines in accidents) were being chased by an increasingly effective force of Mosquitos from No 100 Group.

In May 1944 Luftwaffe fighter pilots received only 60-80 hours' training in operational aircraft, whereas their opposite numbers in the RAF and USAAF logged an average of 225 hours in combat types before joining operational squadrons. During a conference with Goering in May 1944,[24] the Inspector of Fighters, Generalleutnant Adolf Galland, reported that Luftflotte 3 had lost twenty-four per cent of its fighter strength, and the Luftwaffe had lost 489 pilots and received only 396 replacements during the previous month. He added that he proposed to use some night-fighter pilots for day fighting, and that he was 'weeding out' trained pilots from schools and staff jobs.

Each part of the problem was interrelated, which created a knock-on effect. A vicious circle began wherein increased losses led to heavier demands for pilots, which in turn led to less pilot training, and ended inevitably with even heavier losses through combat and accidents. When some sort of order was finally restored, there was such a severe shortage of fuel that advancing Allied ground forces found new, serviceable aircraft which had never taken part in the fighting.

There was plenty of evidence via 'Ultra' that the German High Command soon became aware of the significance of the heavy attacks on the railways in northwest France and Belgium. During the early part of the campaign, Germany's night fighters were being held back on the German border, in case the attacks should turn out to be directed at the Ruhr and southwest Germany; but a signal from Luftflotte III, at the beginning of May, seemed to confirm the fact that the Germans realised that rail centres had to be protected. The signal, which requested the subordination of three Jagddivisions met with strong opposition from Luftflotte Reich, but a compromise was achieved whereby some night fighters were transferred south and west: II/NJG 1 and I/NJG 5 to St Dizier, where they joined part of II/NJG 4; and III/NJG 1 to Laon/Athies. Some single-engined fighters of I and II/KG 51 and I/SKK 10 were also deployed to France for possible use in Wild Boar operations. Later in May, III/NJG 5 was deployed to Laon/Athies also.

Further problems for Luftflotte 3 came in May, when Allied Tactical Air Forces, prompted by intelligence reports of repairs to German airfields in France, stepped up their attacks on these installations. They had been earmarked as forward bases from which to attack Allied land forces when they arrived. These attacks were so successful that many of Germany's plans for dealing with the invasion had to be revised, and some fighters were actually withdrawn to airfields further east. When they were called forward again in June, they had to operate from new and inadequately prepared airfields[25]. The map on page 31 shows the deployment of fighter Geschwader in France and the Low Countries at the end of March and June 1944.

Although the primary concern is the Luftwaffe's defensive effort during the Allies' preparations for 'Overlord', it would be remiss of the author if no mention was made of other Luftwaffe units which were gathering in France and the Low Countries in order to meet the expected onslaught from the Allied Armies.

As mentioned previously, the Germans had already been forced onto the defensive. Although some bomber production was maintained, the bulk of these aircraft were being sent to the Russian Front, to be used in the tactical role. Therefore, there was little threat to the invasion forces, gathering in southern Britain, from bombers, ground-attack and even photographic reconnaissance aircraft. There was, however, a potential threat from the V-1 pilotless flying bomb (which will be discussed later in this book).

Partly because of a lack of foresight and partly because an impending Russian offensive was feared, nearly all the Luftwaffe's ground attack aircraft were on the Eastern Front. In fact, Luftflotte 3 (on whose shoulders the burden of D-Day would fall) had seventy-five ground attack aircraft only, and no more than 300 bombers, most of which had been detached to anti-shipping units of Fliegerkorps X, based in the extreme southwest of France. As has been pointed out already, the majority of the fighter aircraft in the area came under the control of Jagdkorps I and II.

When D-Day arrived, Luftlotte 3 was able to mount about 100 sorties only against the beaches, and the effort was described by Allied Commanders as barely perceptible. Some slight improvement occurred during the night 6/7 June when 175 sorties were mounted by the bombers of Fliegerkorps IX. A further improvement occurred between 7 and 10 June during which time 300 additional fighters had been transferred from the East.

Additional reinforcements did not reach Fliegerkorps X until 13 June, by which time the total number of aircraft of all types available to Luftflotte 3 had risen to 1000. Lack of specialist ground-attack aircraft led to single-engined fighters being used in that role, but they proved to be so unsuccessful that it was not long before orders came directly from Berlin for the fighters to revert to their correct role within Jadgkorps II.

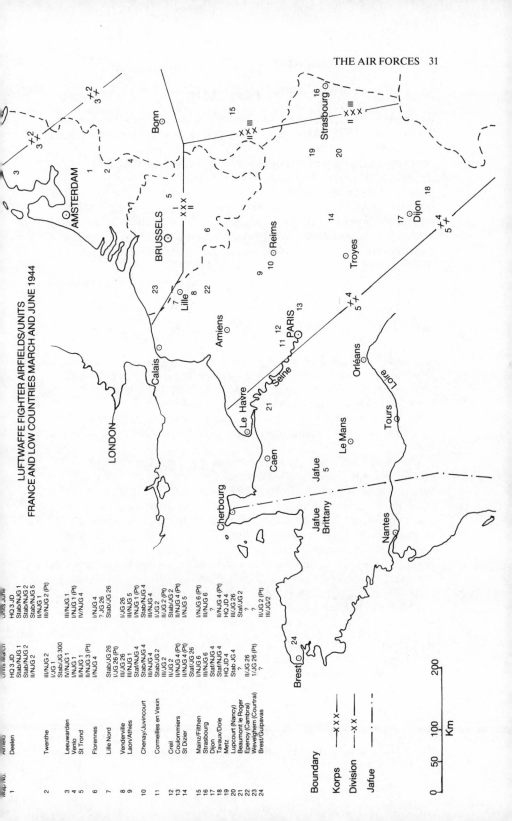

**LUFTWAFFE FIGHTER AIRFIELDS/UNITS
FRANCE AND LOW COUNTRIES MARCH AND JUNE 1944**

Map No.	Airfield	Units March	Units June
1	Deelen	HQ 3 JD; Stab/NJG 1; Stab/NJG 2; II/NJG 2	HQ 3 JD; Stab/NJG 1; Stab/NJG 2; Stab/NJG 5; II/NJG 1; III/NJG 2 (Pt)
2	Twenthe	III/NJG 2; I/JG 1	II/NJG 1
3	Leeuwarden	Stab/JG 300; IV/NJG 1	III/NJG 1
4	Venlo	I/NJG 1	III/NJG 1 (Pt)
5	St Trond	II/NJG 3 (Pt)	IV/NJG 4
6	Florennes	I/NJG 4	I/NJG 4
7	Lille Nord	Stab/JG 26; II/JG 26 (Pt)	? JG 26; Stab/JG 26
8	Venderville	III/NJG 1	I/JG 26
9	Laon/Athies	Staf/NJG 4	III/NJG 5
10	Chenay/Juvincourt	Stab/NJG 4	I/NJG 1 (Pt)
11	Cormeilles en Vexin	III/NJG 4	Stab/NJG 4; III/NJG 4
12	Creil	Stab/JG 2	I/JG 2
13	Coulommiers	III/JG 2	II/JG 2 (Pt)
14	St Dizier	II/NJG 4 (Pt); II/NJG 4 (Pt)	Stab/JG 2; II/NJG 4 (Pt); I/NJG 5
15	Mainz/Filthen	I/NJG 6	I/NJG 6 (Pt)
16	Strasbourg	III/NJG 6	III/NJG 6
17	Dijon	Staf/NJG 4	II/NJG 4 (Pt)
18	Tavaux/Dole	Stab JG 4	HQ JD 4
19	Metz	?	III/JG 26
20	Lupcourt (Nancy)	?	Staf/JG 2
21	Beaumont le Roger	II/JG 26	?
22	Epenoy (Cambrai)	1/JG 26 (Pt)	II/JG 2 (Pt)
23	Wevelghem (Courtrai)	?	III/JG/2
24	Brest/Guipavas		

Boundary — — —

Korps —×××—

Division —×x—

Jafue —··—··—

0   50   100   200
Km

The Flak Arm

Germany's initial defense against the night bombers was mostly detailed to the Flak Arm, but when the task was reallocated the guns were not entirely replaced by fighters. On the contrary, Hitler believed that his people would take heart from the sound of guns and the appearance of searchlights whenever the bombers came.

In 1940 there were approximately 250,000 men in the Flak Arm. By 1942, approximately 450,000 men were manning 12,000 heavy anti-aircraft guns and 3000 searchlights all of which were being controlled increasingly by improved Wurzburg radars. Intelligence estimates in January 1944 showed the distribution of guns and searchlights as:

	Guns	Searchlights
Germany and the Western Front	20,500	7000
Other Fronts	9500	1000

The figures illustrate vividly the value of the Combined Bomber Offensive in drawing off guns and ammunition from other theatres of war, and reflects the German view that a greater threat was posed by both the RAF and the USAAF than by the Russian Air Force.

Production of heavy flak guns increased annually and in 1944 some 8200 of these were produced in Germany against 200 produced in the UK!

The main gun in service with the Flak Arm was the 88mm Flak 18. An outstanding weapon, which could be used in the ground role against tanks, it had an effective ceiling of 26,000 ft and a rate of fire of fifteen rounds per minute. A later version, the Flak 41, had a ceiling of 35,000 ft, and although the rate of fire was increased also to 20 rpm, the gun had to be cooled off after every twenty-five rounds. Other heavy guns included the 105mm Flak 28 and the 128mm Flak 40. Lighter calibre guns, often seen as multiple-barrelled versions, included 37mm and 20mm, the latter having a rate of fire of 7-800 rounds per minute and a ceiling of approximately 7000 ft.

The basic flak unit was the Abteilung (Battalion) of which there were four types:

Heavy	— 4/5 batteries of six guns
Light	— three batteries of three guns (mostly 37mm)
Mixed	— usually three heavy and two light batteries
Searchlight	— 3/4 batteries each having between nine to sixteen 150cm lights, 200cm 'master' lights were usually located at three mile intervals.

In 1940 the Luftwaffe calculated that nearly 2500 rounds of heavy shells and the same number of light shells were expended before one bomber was brought down, but many aircraft were damaged so severely by shell splinters that they were written off on returning to their base. This was particularly so of USAAF Eighth Air Force aircraft which, operating in daylight, suffered more from flak than their counterparts in the RAF.

Before leaving the subject of flak the reader should be aware of an interesting difference of opinion over the existence, or otherwise, of 'Scarecrow' shells, fired by the Germans. One view was that the sight of the shells simulated that of exploding aircraft and would thereby lower the morale of the bomber crews. Max Hastings in his book *Bomber Command* stated that there were no such projectiles, but Alfred Price in his *Luftwaffe Handbook* noted that experiments with 'Scarecrow' shells fired by 88mm guns were withdrawn after a short period. I certainly found many references to 'Scarecrows' in Squadron Operations Records. It may be that the two accounts are connected, a large number of Allied aircraft hit by flak or machine-gun from night fighters did actually explode in the air, and it is very easy to understand that rumours of 'Scarecrows' might have been allowed to circulate in order to provide a calming effect on the nerves of those aircrews who witnessed such horrific incidents.

In conclusion: mishandling, poor coordination and Hitler's inter-ference, all played a part in the demise of the Luftwaffe, which started the war in a favourable position. A lack of trained aircrew consequent upon heavy losses, and a shortage of fuel both led to the Allies gaining air superiority. Yet, in spite of everything, the Luftwaffe came near to defeating both the RAF and the USAAF, and Allied losses in the closing stages of the war are proof enough that the defensive side of the Luftwaffe remained a force to be reckoned with — to the very end.

Notes

1 It is regrettable to record that bomber production was delayed on several occasions by industrial action.
2 For example, a waltz might have meant 'Proceed to beacon A'.
3 Statistics do not bear this out, but the escape hatches were better placed in the Halifax, resulting in a crew having a better chance of survival when an aircraft was hit.
4 Martin Middlebrook, *The Nuremberg Raid*.
5 In tracing the fate of the aircrews reported missing in the narratives in Part 2 of this book, I have been amazed at the number of such incidents. I imagine that carrying an extra crew member, for whatever reason, must have been very unpopular amongst crews who were near the end of their operational tours.
6 Almost twice the UK output of Lancasters and Halifaxes.
7 Gen Ira C Eaker was replaced by Gen James H Doolittle in December 1943. Although given command of the Mediterranean Allied Air Forces Gen Eaker was disappointed in having to leave the Eighth Air Force, which he had built up from scratch.
8 See Introduction.
9 Ibid.
10 Hansell, *The Strategic Air War Against Germany and Japan*.
11 Craven and Cate, Part 2, p680.
12 See Chapter 19.
13 Although true to a degree, ground crews worked in the dark preparing aircraft for dawn take-offs, and in the summer aircrews were often awakened at about 0300 hr.
14 RAF Meteor jet fighters were used later to simulate attacks by German Me 163 and Me 262 jets.
15 On 9 May 1943 the crew of a Ju 88 defected. The aircraft was fitted with the latest airborne radar, which later revealed that antiaircraft and air radars all worked on the same frequency, therefore a single jamming system could neutralise both the Flak and Fighter Control Systems.
16 Generalfeldmarschall Erhard Milch. Inspector General and Deputy Commander of the Luftwaffe and Deputy Air Minister.
17 Aders, *History of the German Night Fighter Force*.
18 For the arguments that occurred over the production of the Me 262 see pp 263-364 of *Inside the Third Reich* by Albert Speer.
19 The Rose-Rice tail turret with twin .50in guns began to enter service in the early part of 1944.
20 Aders, *History of the German Night Fighter Force*.
21 Webster and Frankland, *The Strategic Air Offensive Against Germany*, p 495.
22 Ibid. Based on Table XXVIII and AHB Translation VII/107. It should be noted that the figures have been accepted as the most accurate. Quite large variations are to be found in books, due, I think, to the fact that some authors have mixed figures for aircraft established, held and serviceable.
23 Williamson Murray, *Luftwaffe*.
24 AHB Translation VII/71.
25 AHB Translation VI/19.

CHAPTER FOUR
PRECISION BOMBING

The problems of finding a small target in the dark and bombing it accurately in any weather became very evident at the outset of the war. In 1941, amid alarm over the apparent inability of most bomber crews to locate their targets, Lord Cherwell,[1] Churchill's scientific advisor, asked D M Butt of the Cabinet Secretariat to conduct an investigation into the results of RAF Bomber Command's attacks on targets in France and Germany. Butt's report did more than confirm Lord Cherwell's fears, it shocked everyone concerned.

It seemed that on an average raid in 1940/41, one-third of the crews had returned having failed to bomb their primary targets. Of the remaining two-thirds, one-third only had come within five miles of the aiming point, and against heavily defended targets, such as the Ruhr, the proportion that achieved even that degree of success was one-tenth. The report reached Churchill in September 1941 and prompted him to send a copy of the report and a personal note to the Chief of the Air Staff, Sir Charles Portal: 'This is a very serious paper and seems to require your most urgent attention, I await your proposals for action.'

The report raised doubts not only about the value of the raids on Germany but also about the whole future of Bomber Command. Arguments raged, but the desire to hit back at Germany prevailed and, backed by Churchill, the Air Staff went on to propose further increases in expenditure for Bomber Command.

It was recognised that inaccurate bombing could not always be vindicated by so-called area bombing, the main supposition being that any bomb dropped on Germany was of some value. If Bomber Command was to continue to receive support, better navigation and target location techniques would have to be introduced. As Sir Charles Webster and Noble Frankland stated in their official history of the Strategic Bombing Offensive, 'The problem was target marking and not bomb aiming'.

The first priority, therefore, was the ability to find the target, navigating over a blacked-out Germany, in all weathers. The difference between forecast and actual winds, sometimes combined with violent course deviations caused by taking evasive action, was inclined to make 'dead reckoning' very inaccurate. In the spring of 1942 a new batch of navigational aids began to appear in Bomber Command's aircraft. The first of these, codenamed GEE, was based on radio pulses from three widely separated ground stations; when related to special charts, they provided the navigator with a position 'fix', the accuracy of which was dependent on the distances from the ground stations. At short range the results were very good, and GEE was sometimes of more value to crews trying to find their own base in the UK than to those navigating east of the Ruhr.

In November 1940 Coventry had been bombed by Luftwaffe aircraft using 'blind bombing' systems, known as 'Knickerbein' and 'X-Great'. The value of a system that not only directed an aircraft to its target but also told it when to release its bombs was obvious enough, and British scientists soon came up with a similar radio aid.

Codenamed 'Oboe', the British device relied on two ground stations: one tracked the aircraft and emitted a dot or dash signal, which warned the pilot of any deviation from the planned course; the other (the releasing station) measured the ground speed of the aircraft, warned the navigator at two or three minute intervals of the time to bomb release and gave the release signal. Early versions caused difficulties in the planning and execution of a raid when a large number of aircraft were taking part because they all had to take the same path to the target; later versions incorporated a multi-approach system. Like GEE, 'Oboe' was limited in range to an arc from Lincoln, cutting through Nantes, Cologne and Emden. Efforts to extend its range by using airborne repeater stations were largely overtaken by the introduction of the airborne radar 'H2S'[2] which gave a screen picture of the ground beneath the aircraft.

There were no range limitations, but navigators had to learn a whole new art: interpreting a screen picture which was being built up by differing degrees of response from normal ground features. Water and coastlines were particularly well 'painted' onto the radar screens and this made Hamburg more easy to relate to the chart than Berlin.

Another beam system under development was G-H, which was similar in concept to but the reverse of 'Oboe', in that the interrogating transmitter was carried in the aircraft, and presentation was visual rather than aural. Stirlings of No 3 Group used G-H during the very successful attack on the rail depot at Chambly (a point which will be discussed later in this book).

Problems with the production and serviceability of the new equipment led Portal to conclude that since only a small proportion of the bomber force would be equipped in time for the coming bomber offensive, some interim solution had to be found to the problem of getting the whole force onto targets in Germany. Advised by the Deputy Director of Bomber Operations, Grp Capt Bufton, he came down in favour of setting up a special force, equipped with the electronic aids that were available, which would guide the Main Force to the target by marking it with flares and other pyrotechnics. Air Marshal Harris, whilst agreeing with the requirement, was against the idea of setting up any sort of special force, claiming that such a solution would lead to loss of flexibility within his Groups. He proposed that each Group should have its own target finding and marking squadrons.

After several meetings and the exchange of some fairly acrimonious letters, Harris was overruled and ordered to set up a force of Pathfinders, consisting of four squadrons: No 7 (Stirlings), No 35 (Halifaxes), No 83 (Lancasters) and No 156 (Wellingtons), all drawn from existing operational Groups. To command the new force Harris chose Wg Cdr D C T Bennett, who had served under him in 1932. Bennett, promoted to Group Captain, set up his Headquarters at RAF Wyton in August 1942. By February 1943 the special force had increased to become No 8 (PFF) Group and Bennett had been promoted to the rank of Air Vice Marshal.

The cardinal problem of leading the main force to the target had been largely overcome, but there remained the difficulty of persuading the crews not to drop their bombs 'somewhere onto fires' (which to them was the target) or worse still, onto decoy fires set up by the Germans.

Early experiments with pathfinding techniques came to fruition during the opening phases of the Ruhr campaign, which was the first real test for the PFF. In March 1943, eight 'Oboe'-equipped Mosquitos led the main force to the Krupps armaments factory in Essen, by dropping a line of yellow flares along the selected line of approach to a point fifteen miles short of the target. The Mosquitos then flew to the target where they dropped red target indicators onto the aim point. Lancasters of No 8 (PFF) Group followed the Mosquitos, along the line of approach flares and dropped green target indicators onto the target indicators already dropped by the Mosquitos. Following the line of flares, aircraft of the main force flew timed approaches from the last flare and dropped their bombs onto the red or green target markers, thereby reducing the possibility of bombing decoy fires. The raid was a great success and the marking techniques used formed the basis of future procedures within No 8 (PFF) Group.

In May 1943 No 617 Squadron carried out its well-known, low-level attacks on the Möhne and Eder Dams. A study of the Squadron's training for and execution of these attacks revealed the exacting requirements and problems of low-level flying and precision marking, which had to be overcome before attacks could take place against relatively small French targets without the danger of killing Allied civilians. Two members of the Squadron co-pioneered low-level marking in Lancasters, Leonard Cheshire and Mick Martin. A third member, the original CO, Guy Gibson, had used VHF radio during the Dambusters Raid to control the attacks, and it was his experience which led to the introduction of the 'Master Bomber' technique, a major feature in the success of many future operations.[3]

An attentive reader will have detected by now further evidence of Air Marshal Harris's ability to get his own way. Having conformed to the Chief of the Air Staff's request to form the PFF Group under Bennett, he had No 617 Squadron (part of No 5 Group commanded by Air Vice Marshal Cochrane) experimenting with ways and proving their ability to find, mark and bomb targets with great accuracy, flying at very low level.

Flying Lancasters at heights of 50-60 ft formed a major part of No 617 Squadron's training and, in spite of the heavy Lancaster's limited manoeuvrability, Martin was quite convinced that it was safe to fly at these levels because 'night fighters could not get beneath, and anti-aircraft gunners hardly had time to take a shot before the aircraft disappeared behind the trees'. The threat from balloon cables could be kept to a minimum by following railways. However, after the disastrous low-level raid on the Dortmund-Ems Canal in September 1943, the Squadron was withdrawn from operations to begin training for dropping the then current Barnes Wallis invention — the 12,000-lb armour-piercing 'Tallboy' bomb.

To obtain maximum penetration the bomb had to be dropped from high altitudes, and a number of technical problems needed to be overcome before the necessary accuracy could be obtained. Cochrane decreed that the bombing error, using practice bombs, would have to be less than 100 yd from a height of 20,000 ft before 'Tallboys' could be used economically. In spite of the use of the new stabilised bomb sight (SABS), errors in thermometers, altimeters and boost guages resulted in unacceptable margins of bomb misplacement. When all the instruments had been checked and replaced the Squadron's average bombing error was less than ten yards from a height of 20,000 ft!

Although No 617 Squadron had changed to high-level precision bombing, Leonard Cheshire, its new CO, and Martin were still in favour of low-level flying for marking techniques. In February 1944 Cheshire and Martin marked the Gnome-Rhone Aircraft Factory in France, using a dive-bombing technique they had devised together.[4] The Squadron then bombed on the markers from a normal height with such accuracy that there were no French casualties.

Later that month Cheshire, again accompanied by Martin, led an attack on the Antheor Viaduct, close to the French-Italian border. The target lay in a steep ravine and low-level approaches were limited (a point in favour of the anti-aircraft defences). Both marking Lancasters were hit, Martin's so badly that he only just made a landing on the island of Corsica, which had only recently fallen into Allied hands. Efforts to persuade Martin to give up operational flying were unsuccessful; although posted to HQ No 100 Group, he was soon flying Mosquitos on night-fighter intruder operations with No 515 Squadron. Cheshire, in a thoughtful mood, went off in search of a few Mosquitos in which to carry on low-level marking.

The success of the Mosquito as a fast and manoeuvrable aircraft at low-levels was to prove vital to pinpoint marking and subsequent bombing accuracy by the main force. Different procedures were used, depending on the weather conditions over the target, and it became almost standard practise for the Master Bomber to assess the initial markers, issue instructions to back-up markers, and direct the main force onto the better placed markers. Later innovations included the use of offset markers, which overcame the problems caused when aiming points were obscured by smoke. (A table containing the code names and descriptions of the various marking techniques in use in May 1944 can be seen in Appendix 3.)

No 5 Group's experience and success in low-level marking and bombing led Harris to transfer a Mosquito squadron (No 627), and two Lancaster PFF squadrons (Nos 83 and 97) from No 8 (PFF) Group to No 5 Group (not a popular move as far as Bennett and his crews were concerned). In spite of the moans, the newly transferred squadrons went on to mark not only for No 5 Group but for other groups in the Command also. There was, and still is, some professional rivalry between aircrews of these two Groups: but it was not always unhealthy rivalry. No 5 Group's markers were generally used on targets outside 'Oboe' range; other targets were attacked using a combination of No 8 (PFF) Group's 'Oboe' Mosquitos, operating at 30,000 ft, and No 5 Group's low-level marking. There was always an interchange of ideas between the groups.

No 617 Squadron continued to put its bombing accuracy to the test by carrying out precision attacks with 'Tallboy' bombs on targets such as the V-1 and V-2 sites in the Pas de Calais area. Later, they isolated the German Army Divisions in the Bordeaux area by closing the Saumur rail tunnel.

Such was the background against which the Transportation Plan was born. It is not surprising that some of the arguments put forward by Air Marshal Harris, and detailed in Chapter 6, fell on deaf ears. The scene was set for a new type of bombing offensive which could yet prove to have been the Army's saviour in the battle for Normandy.

Notes

1 Previously Prof Sir Frederick Lindemann.
2 Several accounts exist about the origin of the name. I prefer the more humorous, if probably less accurate, one: apparently, Lord Cherwell, irritated by delays in production, remarked 'this whole business stinks, you had better call it H2S'!
3 The idea was first put forward by Flt Lt E W Anderson in 1942, but was turned down on the grounds that it was far too dangerous!
4 In straight and level flight the markers tended to bounce, creating positional errors. Martin solved the problem using the dive-bombing technique.

CHAPTER FIVE
THE GERMAN ARMY
IN THE WEST

The dilemmas facing the German High Command during the winter of 1943/44 began to make themselves known in October when Field Marshal von Runstedt, Commander in Chief West, indicated that the Allies' main invasion of the mainland of Europe would take place via either the Channel coast or the Bay of Biscay, or even the French Riviera. (Perhaps he should have been a weather forecaster because he certainly knew how to hedge his bets!)

Following these vague predictions and the gloomy reports about the state of the so-called 'Atlantic Wall' from the Chief of Operations, Field Marshal Jodl, Hitler, in his capacity as Supreme Commander and Commander in Chief of the German Army, issued Directive 51. It stated that Germany was then in more danger from the West than from the East, that the Russian Front should no longer be manned and equipped at the expense of the West, and that a greater proportion of tanks and guns should be allocated to Runstedt's command.

The directive was equally vague about which sector of the Western Front should have priority, and although it resulted in some Divisions being transferred from the East, most of these were equipped poorly and were really resting from the Russian onslaught. Furthermore, increasing pressures in the East soon forced Hitler to moderate his policy and, three months before the Normandy landings, he agreed to transfer the 2nd SS Panzer Korps (two divisions) from Holland to the Russian Front.

In November 1943 it became clear that Field Marshal Erwin Rommel was not to be given command of the Italian Campaign, and Jodl came to the aid of a somewhat embarrassed Hitler by suggesting that Rommel should be given the task of reviewing the defences in the West. The formal directive instructed Rommel to inspect the defences along the entire coastline from Denmark to Brittany. As Rommel went about his task he propounded his theory that the only way to prevent an invasion was to destroy the enemy on the beaches or landing grounds or even before they landed. His report was highly critical of the defences and the efforts of the commanders in preparing them, and on 15 January 1944 he was given command of Army Group B, which comprised the 7th and 15th Armies which were to take the full brunt of the Allied assault. As soon as he had executive powers, Rommel ordered a massive increase in the laying of minefields and the erection of thousands of obstacles designed to thwart any invasion by sea or air. The beaches along the entire coastline became littered with armed spikes, steel tetrahedra and 'can openers' designed to rip the bottom out of the Allied landing craft.

In spite of Rommel's energetic attempts to improve the defences in the West, two basic intelligence problems remained: where and when would the enemy land? Unlike his counterpart in the East, the head of the Foreign Armies West[1] Col Baron Alexis von Roenne, was either incompetent or, as has been suggested by some authors, was deliberately misleading German operations staff, in the belief that in so doing he might shorten the war and so save German lives. It should be noted, however, that at the time the Luftwaffe was only capable of a token effort regarding photographic reconnaissance. Had the German intelligence services received a fraction of the number of reports that the Allies obtained daily from that valuable source, things might have been very different.

Hitler was reported to have been privy to information obtained via the renowned agent 'Cicero', who is supposed to have obtained the code name 'Overlord' and information about the proposed landing area, but mistrusting his commanders, he passed on the information saying that it was a 'hunch'.[2] However, Hitler was generally consistent in his choice of Normandy as the most likely landing place. Others, including Rommel, seemed to have been influenced either by the Allied deception plan 'Fortitude', or by the advice from German naval experts. They declared the coast of Normandy unsuitable for landings because it had rocky shoals offshore. They thought that the attack would come in the Pas de Calais area. Runstedt, who listened to the advice of von Roenne, remained undecided, even after the landings, and it was weeks rather than days before he released some of the 15th Army divisions from guarding the Calais area.

Rommel's theory led to another dilemma and arguments amongst the senior commanders and staff about the deployment of tank Divisions and the tactics to be used when the invasion came. Rommel was in favour of moving all the tanks close enough to the beaches to be able to mount counter-attacks as soon as any enemy troops set foot on French soil. Among those opposed to this idea was Hitler's chief tank advisor, General Guderian, and one of Rommel's own Army commanders, General Dollman, but the most violent opposition came from Gen Gehr von Schweppenburg, who was Runstedt's own tank expert and the somewhat covetous commander of the Panzer Group West. This group was to field no less than eight of the eleven armoured Divisions which were committed to the battle before the Allied breakout from the beachhead.

The map on page 42 shows the positions of the German Army in the West at the time of D-Day, and reflects the results of those dilemmas which faced German commanders: the even distribution of the so-called Limited Employment or Static Divisions from Brest

THE GERMAN ARMY IN THE WEST
Dispositions 6th June 1944

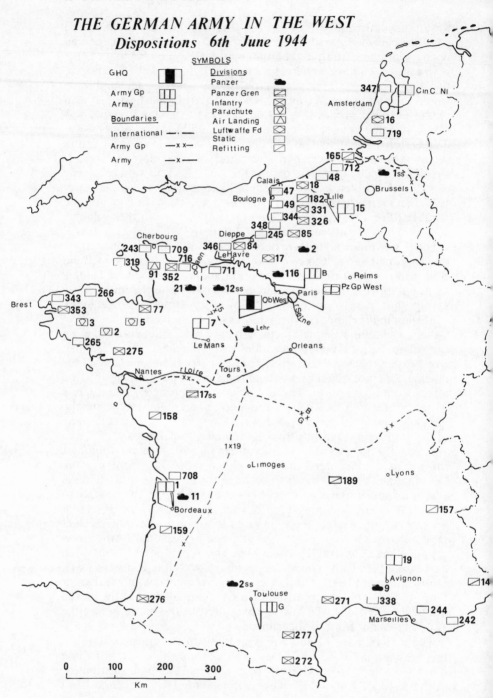

to Ostend, and how these were supplemented by Parachute, Field Infantry and Luftwaffe Field Divisions should be noted; also, the wide dispersal of the tank (Panzer) Divisions and that only the 21st Panzer Division was near enough to the coast to be brought into action on D-Day.

Of the forty-six infantry divisions (including Para and Luftwaffe) shown on the map, twenty-six only had been in action in Normandy by the time the Allies broke out from the beachhead at the end of July, and of those twenty-one had to make significant journeys before reaching the battlefield. The journeys ranged in distance from 50-750 miles and averaged more than 300 miles. Of the nine tank (Panzer) Divisions and one motorised rifle division (Panzer Grenadier) all, except 11 Panzer Division[3], were in action by the end of July. The two Divisions of II Panzer Korps, which had been transferred to the Russian Front in March and April, were recalled and joined the battle at the end of June.

The general feeling in the German High Command was that the only way of avoiding complete catastrophe would be by destroying the Allied armies first, then to deal, once and for all, with the Russians. In spite of Directive 51 most commanders were unhappy about the quality and strength of the infantry Divisions in the West. Most of the static Divisions consisted of nine battalions of over-aged and medically downgraded men, who were recuperating from nasty experiences on the Russian Front. The total strength of each of these divisions was approximately 12,500 men, who were equipped with a mixture of artillery and other weapons, much of it captured during earlier and more successful campaigns. There was little or no motor transport[4] and guns and carts were horse-drawn. However, many of the men had been in battle and therefore had some advantage over their mostly untried opponents, who waded ashore into the unknown.

The Field Infantry Divisions (some of which had been moved into the area as a result of Hitler's directive) were of little better quality and were up to their reduced establishment of 8000 men. The hard core of the infantry Divisions consisted of the 91st Air Landing Division and the three Parachute Divisions of II Para Korps. Each of the Para Divisions consisted of about 12,000 men and they had some motor transport. Motorised (Panzer Grenadier) Divisions had no tanks but they did have a battalion of forty-five assault guns, mounted on tank chassis, and almost 3000 other vehicles.

Top priority for men and equipment was always given to the Panzer units, particularly the Waffen Schutzstaffel (Waffen SS), the military element of the Corps d'Elite of the Nazi Party, which provided the men for the dreaded SS Panzer Divisions. They contained almost twice as many men than did the infantry Divisions and they were equipped with a variety of motor transport and some of the most dangerous tanks: the Mark VI (Tiger) and the Mark V (Panther).

A breakdown of the 2nd SS Panzer Division (Das Reich) is shown on page 238 and provides some insight to the logistical problems which faced the Germans as they tried to move and re-supply these divisions over rail and road systems which were not in full working order.

The Corps' Headquarters are not shown on the map. They were situated between the Divisions and the Army Headquarters.

The grouping of divisions under Corps was subject to change when Divisions were moved about the battlefield, or were subordinated directly to Army Headquarters to be used as reserves. There were two Panzer and eight infantry Corps Headquarters at the time of the Allied landings, the largest (and the one which took the full weight of the assault) was the LXXXIV (84th) with its headquarters at St Lô. It was commanded by General Marcks,[5] a one-legged and highly professional veteran of the Russian Front. An 'Ultra' report on May 1944 credited the Corps with having eight Divisions in its area, including the 91st Air Landing Division; a letter from Marcks to his wife in May mentioned a total strength of 100,000 men.

Field Marshal von Runstedt seemed to have been well aware of the likelihood that Allied bombing would prevent supplies from reaching the forward areas and there was no shortage of dumps of fuel and ammunition in the 7th Army area. All were within 150 miles of Caen, and records compiled by the Transport Officer and Quartermaster Branch of the 7th Army showed that no less than twenty-five tank off-loading ramps had been earmarked for use within the same area, twenty of which were considered to be capable of handling the heaviest tanks.

On 1 May the War Diary of the 7th Army recorded that there was a total of nearly 18,000 tonnes of ammunition in the Army's nine munitions dumps,[6] the largest of which was located near Vire (code named Michel) and contained over 3000 tonnes. However, most of the dumps were not operating to their full capacity, and a report dated 12 May indicated that most dumps were only half full. Fuel dumps in the same area consisted of ten Army and three 'Fuhrer Reserve' dumps. On 1 May the Army dumps contained a total of 1400 cubic metres of petrol and 400 cubic metres of diesel,[7] while the 'Fuhrer Reserve' dumps contained a total of over 2000 cubic metres of petrol and 300 cubic metres of diesel. A map showing the locations of the tank off-loading points and the ammunition and fuel dumps can be found on page 45.

What is clear from the foregoing, is that the lack of firm intelligence about the area chosen by the Allies for their landings, together with internal squabbles about tactics, resulted in the Germans keeping their divisions so widely dispersed that rapid movement became an essential factor in their plans to meet and keep pace with the Allied build-up of forces on the Normandy beaches.

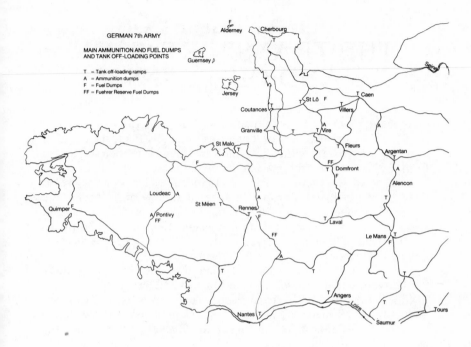

Notes

1 Foreign Armies West was the intelligence department responsible for producing reports on Allied capabilities and intentions in northwest Europe.
2 See Hinsley, *British Intelligence in the Second World War*, Vol 3 Part 2.
3 11 Panzer Division had its move to Normandy cancelled by Hitler. It was ultimately used against the Allied landings in the South of France.
4 An 'Ultra' report mentioned that 363 Division joined the battle from Denmark but had no motor transport and only 800 sick horses.
5 General Marcks was killed on 12 June 1944 by Allied aircraft near Carentan. It was reported that his artificial leg prevented him from getting out of his car and taking cover.
6 BA MA RH20-7/294.
7 1000 cubic metres = 220,000 galls = 727 tonnes.

CHAPTER SIX
THE TRANSPORTATION
AND OIL PLANS

One of the pre-conditions of a successful invasion of Normandy, as prescribed by the planners of 'Overlord', was, in effect, the creation of a 'railway desert' within 150 miles of Caen. The idea emanated from the realisation that it would be essential to delay the arrival in Normandy of the German Panzer Divisions, which were scattered throughout northwest Europe. In spite of short-term setbacks, the Italian Campaign was steadily turning in favour of the Allies, and some commanders believed that this was due, in no small measure, to the bombing of Italian railways, upon which the German Army was largely reliant for reinforcements and supplies.

The man responsible for the Italian Rail Plan was Prof Solly Zuckerman, scientific advisor to Air Marshal Tedder, the Commander in Chief of the Middle East Air Force. Tedder was back in England and about to be made Deputy Supreme Commander for the Allied assault on Normandy. He arranged for Zuckerman to assist Air Marshal Leigh-Mallory's team, which had been charged with the responsibility for producing the overall air plan for Operation Overlord.

It was always Zuckerman's contention that the problem was of a strategic rather than a tactical nature, and that attacks on locomotives, rolling stock and repair facilities would not only create a greater and more lasting problem for the enemy but would drive the Germans onto the roads, where they were already showing signs of fuel and transport shortages, and along which they could be attacked by medium and fighter bombers of the Tactical Air Forces.

On his arrival at the Headquarters of the Allied Expeditionary Air Force (AEAF) Zuckerman was shown a plan which had been drafted by a joint Army/AEAF Planning Committee. The plan was anything but strategic in nature and Zuckerman considered it to be totally inadequate. He was accordingly invited to produce a plan similar to the one that had been successfully tried out in Italy.

When considering the Rail Plan for 'Overlord' Zuckerman contacted a number of railway experts: Capt C E Sherrington, who was the head of the Railway Research Service; his colleague, E D Brant, who had extensive pre-war knowledge of the French railway system; and V M Barrington Ward of the Railways Executive Committee. Two important factors, not present in the Italian Campaign, had to be considered: the close proximity to the target areas of friendly civilians, and the need to avoid giving the Germans any indication of the area chosen for the actual landing of Allied ground forces in Normany. Both these considerations created problems of target selection and the former very nearly prevented the plan from being implemented.

Strangely enough, Zuckerman did not appear to have been made aware of those limitations until the end of March. In fact, in a conversation between himself and the author it became apparent that he did not receive any formal brief or guidelines before he set about creating the plan.

Apart from a poor and controversial estimate from the JIC on the number of locomotives available and required by the Germans, the intelligence available to the architects of the plan seems to have been quite accurate, with clear statistics on volumes of traffic using the comprehensive French and Belgian railway systems, and precise locations of locomotive and rolling stock repair facilities. Most German Army supply dumps had been located as had the major troop formations, largely as a result of 'Ultra'. The locations of tank off-loading points in Normandy were also reasonably well known, when compared with the available German records,[1] and that information was to be of more value to the Tactical Air Forces, when battle had been joined. 'Ultra' also provided good forecasts of moves and transfers of German Army Divisions to northwest France (in accordance with Hitler's Directive 51).

Most of the intelligence branches had made estimates of the numbers of trains required to move the various types of German Division, and those of AI3(c) compared very favourably with the actual records of the German 7th Army Transport Officer. For example: it required eighty-one trains to move the Panzer Lehr Division from Budapest to Le Mans in May 1944 and AI3(c) estimates at the time were:

Infantry Division (15,000 men)	60-66 trains
Tank Division	77-82 trains
Motorised Division	Probably as for tank
Low Grade Division	44-48 trains
Light Division	53-58 trains

Rates of movement were estimated as between 95-125 miles per day for a motorised column, and the average train speed was put at 288 miles in twenty-four hours.

It should be noted at this point that although armoured units have more motor transport than their infantry counterparts, tracked vehicles are subject to sudden and embarrassing track failures if they are driven on metaled roads for any great distance. The author has vivid memories of losing both tracks simultaneously whilst travelling quite fast along a road across the Jordanian desert in a Bren Gun Carrier, and heading for a deep ravine without any means of stopping or turning. A tank crew losing one track in the middle of a battle would probably not be lucky enough to survive.

Armed with what they considered to be all the necessary background information for target selection, the next problem the planners had to overcome was to estimate the type and weight of bombs to be dropped, and the number of aircraft required to put the targets out of action for a given period of time. The total potential bomb lift available in the three months 1 March to 31 May 1944 was estimated to be 186,000 short tons,[2] 151,300 of which could be expected from both Bomber Commands of the RAF and the USAAF Eighth Air Force, the remainder to be provided by Leigh-Mallory's Tactical Air Force, the planners estimated also that about half of that total might be required for specific Overlord targets during those three months, and of that approximately 40,000 tons would be needed for the Railway Plan.

The estimate was based broadly on four assumptions:

1 That sufficient damage could be caused by landing four 500-lb bombs per acre in the target area.

2 That the accuracy of visual day bombing by the USAAF Eighth Air Force and night bombing by the RAF could be maintained at January 1944 levels.

3 That only 500-lb bombs would be used.

4 That fifty per cent of the targets would be within 'Oboe' range.

Apart from the problem of the possible heavy loss of life amongst French and Belgian civilians, there were other political pressures developing because the Rail Plan was clearly in breach of the existing Point Blank directive. In an attempt to allay the criticism, consideration was given to the inclusion in the target list of a number of German rail centres, which, if attacked, would produce a further strain on the industries of the Ruhr and Rhineland. An alternative solution, along the lines of the plan that Zuckerman had already rejected, was that bombing at the time of the invasion only would seriously delay the German Divisions from reaching the Front.

In the end several ideas were considered and some counter arguments were anticipated before the first draft of the Plan emerged. When it did appear, there were two concepts for consideration, and they became known as the Tactical and the Strategic Plans. (Later, the terms 'Interdiction' and 'Attrition' became widely used.)

The Tactical Plan had a number of obvious disadvantages. The first was that any sudden onslaught on the rail facilities in the Normandy area would jeopardise the element of surprise which was vital for a successful landing. The second was that to block and keep blocked for days, or even weeks, a number of points in a previously unimpaired railway system presupposed the availability of a large number of heavy bombers which, once battle had been joined, might be needed for emergency tactical targets. There was the weather factor also, which could prevent operations during the critical period.

The aim of the Strategic Plan was not so much the direct cutting or blocking of lines, more the widespread destruction of the very means of maintaining the railway system. It was never suggested that this would stop all traffic for any length of time because it was realised that the enemy could probably reinstate one or two lines fairly quickly, but reduction in the number of trains actually running would make the task of complete annihilation by the medium and fighter bombers that much easier. Apart from meeting the requirements of security, the Strategic Plan also had the advantage that the Germans, in appreciating the effects of the bombing of the rail centres, would be forced to think in terms of additional road transport and build up its forward stocks of ammunition and fuel, all of them very suitable targets for Allied tactical aircraft. Also, in making the same appreciation, the German High Command would be faced with an even more acute dilemma — whether to keep their tank reserves together, or move them up to the Front while the trains were still running.

The first draft of the Plan, entitled 'Air Attacks on Rail and Road Communications'[3], was considered by the newly formed AEAF Bombing Committee on 10 January 1944, under the chairmanship of Air Cdre E J Kingston-McCloughry. Although the immediate reaction of the committee was that some of the targets were too small to be bombed without hitting the surrounding houses, the general outline of the Plan was accepted and the list of targets was amended in harmonious discussion between Zuckerman and Kingston-McCloughry. The Committee was further encouraged to accept the Plan after a letter was sent by the Air Staff to Leigh-Mallory, requesting that his planners take note of the conclusions and recommendations of a report by Zuckerman on the bombing of the Italian railways in support of the landings in Sicily and Italy. The general conclusions of the report supported the strategic concept.

Two lists of targets were then drawn up. One, known as Plan A, consisted of seventy-six rail centres between Normandy and the Rhine, of which thirty-two were in west Germany and the remainder in northwest France and Belgium; the second, Plan B, comprised seventy-eight centres, of which six only were in Germany. The targets in both lists had been selected because they contained extensive repair and maintenance facilities. Bomber Command was encouraged to accept the lists by placing each target in a 'Weather Zone' to be attacked when weather conditions did not permit deeper penetration raids into Germany.

On 22 January Leigh-Mallory presided over the sixth meeting of the AEAF Bombing Committee. The Committee considered a second draft plan which was sent to the Supreme Allied Commander, General Eisenhower. Apart from querying some of the targets, on the grounds of security, Eisenhower accepted the general concept of the plan, even though it was quite clear strategic bombers would be required in its implementation.

In the meantime, Harris had already 'got wind' of the plan and on 13 January had written a letter to the Chief of the Air Staff, stating that his crews were not trained for the sort of operations envisaged, and that the best way that Bomber Command could help in the coming invasion would be to carry on and even intensify its attacks on German industries.

Zuckerman and Kingston-McCloughry decided to counter Harris's letter by writing detailed counter-arguments to his assertions in the form of a table.[4] The document was sent to the Air Staff who added their own column of replies. A further column of remarks was added by the Air Staff, *after* the Normandy landings, showing that events had proved that Harris's original letter had contained many inaccuracies and misconceptions. The table, which is produced in full in Appendix 6, does much to capture the general atmosphere of the argument. Relations between Harris and the Air Staff were not at their best during that time, and the signs were that the Air Staff would support the AEAF's plan. However, on 19 January, Portal and

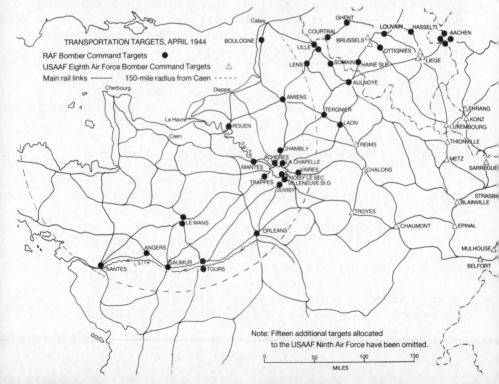

TRANSPORTATION TARGETS, APRIL 1944

RAF Bomber Command Targets ●
USAAF Eighth Air Force Bomber Command Targets △
Main rail links ——— 150-mile radius from Caen - - - - -

Note: Fifteen additional targets allocated to the USAAF Ninth Air Force have been omitted.

0   50   100   150
MILES

Leigh-Mallory both joined the Commander of the US Strategic Air Forces, General Spaatz, in sending a signal to the Joint Chiefs of Staff, affirming their continued support for the Point Blank Directive.

Harris was backed, to some extent, by Spaatz, although the American was to fight the AEAF plan on the grounds that oil should be the primary target. A more prolonged series of equally strong attacks came from the Director of Bomber Operations in the Air Ministry, Air Cdre Sidney Bufton, who fought the Plan on a variety of issues which included the inability of Bomber Command to attack all the targets listed in the time available, through the 'tactical rather than strategic' concept. Together with the Americans, he argued that the destruction of the enemy's oil and its airfields was more important to the success of 'Overlord', and that such subjects should be regarded as alternative targets when weather conditions prevented operations in accordance with 'Point Blank'. Contemporary files on the subject contained many letters and memos from Bufton which attracted some forthright comments from those who were supporting the AEAF plan.

On 3 February 1944 the third draft of the Plan, titled 'The employment of bombers in relation to the outline plan', was circulated prior to a meeting which took place on 15 February, which was attended by Harris and Spaatz. The first public confirmation that heavy bombers would definitely be used to carry out the Plan was revealed during the meeting. Harris and Spaatz exploded! Harris washed his hands of any responsibility for the consequences and complained of the 'fallacious estimates' of the bomb lift from his command. Spaatz complained that the plan was inconsistent with his current directive, and the meeting was left with the impression that he would not take orders from Leigh-Mallory. According to Zuckerman, the meeting marked the end of 'rational discussion' about the Plan, and all those opposing it joined forces in an attempt to defeat the apparent threat to the independence of the Strategic Air Forces.

Two groups led the attacks on the Plan. The first group, which Zuckerman was surprisingly invited to join, was a sub-committee of the Joint Technical Warfare Committee, chaired by Prof Charles Ellis, scientific advisor to the Army Council. The second, and perhaps more formidable, was known as 'The Committee of Four' and included D L Lawrence, from the Objectives Department of the British Ministry of Economic Warfare; and C P Kindleberger from the Enemy Objectives Unit (EOU) of the American Economic Warfare Department, which had already pronounced its disagreement with the AEAF plan, and was pushing the case for attacks on oil.

Zuckerman attended most of the meetings held by Professor Ellis but disagreed with the findings of the committee on the grounds that it had applied 'rigid, quantitive estimates of the weight of attacks required to produce cuts in railway lines and the delays caused'.

After two unsuccessful attempts to get Zuckerman to change his mind, the committee's findings were passed on, in draft form, to a limited number of senior officers whose staff quoted from it and so passed on 'groundless speculation' according to Zuckerman.

The main argument put forward by the Committee of Four was that crippling motive power and damaging rolling stock in northwest Europe were of no consquence because the enemy had vast reserves of locomotives and wagons. The Committee also argued that military rail traffic formed a very small proportion of the total, and summed up its views by saying that it would take at least twelve months for the AEAF plan to have an appreciable effect.

All the arguments were aired again at a further meeting, called by Leigh-Mallory on 25 February, the minutes of which consisted of forty-three pages of detailed argument and counter-argument — but no further decisions. However the meeting did produce additional support for the Plan in the form of Major General Napier, who was head of the Movement and Transportation Branch at SHAEF. The day after the meeting, Napier wrote to the AEAF saying that he believed that attacks on the railway systems would either force the Germans back to the Rhine, after about six weeks of battle, or, by moving their locomotives and rolling stock to France, weaken their rail transport position on other fronts — or even within Germany's industrial areas.

On 5 March General Spaatz forwarded to Eisenhower his plan for extending his current 'Point Blank' directive to include attacks on the German petroleum industry. He claimed that his plan would

1 Assure air supremacy at the time of the Allied assault.

2 Progressively reduce fuel supplies for the German Army.

3 Bring about a further reduction in the production of all fuels.

4 Provide some direct tactical air support.

Spaatz proposed thirty-seven major attacks and that the targets should include fourteen synthetic oil plants in the Ruhr and eastern Germany, and thirteen refineries in north Germany. It was claimed that the attacks would reduce supplies of fuel to the German forces by fifty per cent over a period of six months. W W Rostow, who was a member of the EOU, claimed in his book *Pre Invasion Bombing Strategy* that Spaatz weakened the case for oil by confining his plan to the oil industry. The EOU's plan had included attacks on bridges, and fuel and ammunition dumps, in addition to the refineries. Rostow suggested that had Spaatz put the full EOU plan to Eisenhower, it might well have taken precedence over the AEAF's Rail Plan. The oil plan was certainly given very serious consideration.

Meanwhile, the interdiction versus attrition argument was getting into full swing. Bridges over the Seine were seriously considered for inclusion in the Transportation Plan; but Zuckerman, calling on his experiences in the Italian Campaign, was able to get these targets deferred to the tactical air forces, on the grounds that attacks by heavy bombers on bridges was a very costly business. His views were actually backed by Spaatz, who had just made a visit to his units in Italy and had seen for himself that Zuckerman was right.

With only three months to go before the Allied assault, AEAF staff were becoming very impatient. In spite of the fact that Eisenhower and Tedder were both committed to the strategic plan, none of the targets could be attacked until the entire Plan had been cleared by the Combined Chiefs of Staff who, at that time, still controlled the activities of the heavy bombers. After repeated requests for action it was agreed that Bomber Command should carry out a few experimental attacks on rail centres in France. The first of these took place against Trappes near Paris on the night of 6/7 March, and was closely followed by attacks on Le Mans and Amiens.

The success of the experimental attacks confounded Harris, and convinced Eisenhower and Tedder that the AEAF Transportation Plan was probably the most likely way of preventing German reinforcements reaching Normandy in the early and critical days after the Allied landings.

On 20 March the Chief of the Air Staff, ACM Sir Charles Portal, decided that no useful purpose could be served by allowing the controversy to drag on any longer. Accordingly, he invited Eisenhower and Tedder (both strategic air commanders), the Director of Bomber Operations, and representatives from the MEW and the War Office to a meeting on 25 March. At the meeting, Eisenhower again supported the Transportation Plan; but he agreed that the Oil Plan had great attractions also, and that serious consideration should be given to adopting that plan as soon as the critical stage of 'Overlord' was over. During the same meeting, most of the original arguments were repeated. Bufton made a strong stand but, in the face of Eisenhower's strong support for the Transportation Plan, the opposition began to crumble. Portal summed up the meeting by saying that, in his view, there was no suitable alternative.

The decision was passed to the British Combined Chiefs of staff on 27 March and they immediately agreed that control of the strategic air forces should be transferred to Eisenhower. He in turn delegated Tedder to coordinate all of the bomber forces in northwest Europe. Harris and Spaatz both continued to battle on for another three weeks before Eisenhower was cleared to issue his first directive to the commanders of the heavy bombers. In broad terms the directive stated that their mission was: to carry on destroying the German Air Force, and to disrupt enemy rail communications, particularly those affecting the enemy's ability to move towards the Allied beach-head.

The reader could be forgiven for believing that 'that was that', but further and potentially more serious opposition to the Plan was to follow. Churchill and the British War Cabinet were both extremely wary of authorising the attacks and, when the Plan was considered by the Defence Committee on 5 April, there were moves to eliminate some of the targets that might lead to the heaviest civilian casualties. Zuckerman became involved again, regarding the estimates of those casualties. It transpired that the original figures of 40,000 dead and 120,000 seriously wounded had been incorrectly derived by the Operational Research Section of Bomber Command from a formula worked out by Zuckerman at the time of the German raids on England. The figures had been further exaggerated by Bomber Command, who had multiplied estimates of the bomb loads required by an operational factor of three. Churchill was enraged by the fact that incorrect estimates had been passed to the Chiefs of Staff and blamed, quite wrongly, AEAF planners. It fell to Zuckerman to try and explain that the AEAF had played no part in preparing the figures, and he was asked to produce new estimates.

The new estimates suggested that some 16,000 civilians could be killed, but the experimental attacks on Trappes, Le Mans and Amiens had shown that the casualties could be even less than 16,000. In spite of intelligence reports that the number of casualties appeared to be less than even the revised estimates, Churchill remained unconvinced. On 27 April he called another meeting of the War Cabinet, after which Eisenhower was asked again to limit the number of targets to be attacked.

At that stage, Eisenhower was ready to call the whole thing off. He had agreed already that attacks in which heavy casualties could occur should be left as near as possible to D-Day, because Churchill thought it would be easier then for the French to accept the casualties as being incidental to their liberation. Fortunately, Leigh-Mallory persuaded Eisenhower to stay with the Plan.

Even the Defence Committee's conditions, imposed on 3 May, that the casualties should be limited to 10,000 dead, did not satisfy Churchill. On 7 May he outlined his fears in a cable to President Roosevelt. The President replied:

> *I share fully with your distress at the loss of life among the French population incident to our preparations for "Overlord". I share also with you a satisfaction that every possible care is being and will be taken to minimise civilian casualties. No possibility of alleviating adverse French opinion should be overlooked, always provided that there is no reduction of our effectiveness against the enemy at this crucial time.*
>
> *However regrettable the attendant loss of civilian lives is, I am*

> *not prepared to impose from this distance any restriction on military action by the responsible commanders that, in their opinion, might militate against the success of "Overlord", or cause additional loss of life to our Allied forces of invasion.*[5]

Churchill remarked in his book *The Second World War*:

> *This was decisive. Meanwhile the rate of casualties to French civilians continued to be less than feared. The sealing off of the Normandy battlefield from reinforcements by rail may well have been the greatest contribution that the bomber forces could make to "Overlord". The price was paid.*

In the same way that Harris had been told to carry out the experimental attacks on the French rail centres, General Spaatz had been authorised to test his bombers against oil targets deep into Germany and the Balkans and the USAAF Eighth Air Force did not join in the attacks on the rail targets until 27 April — the date of Eisenhower's first directive. As had the experimental attacks on the rail targets, the attacks on oil (long-feared by Albert Speer, the German Minister for Production) proved to be very successful. They led to a combined offensive by American and British heavy bombers, which proved to be complimentary, not contradictory to the Transportation Plan.

Notes

1 MABA RH 20-7/294. See Chapter 5 also.
2 One short ton = 2000 lb.
3 Several titles for the plan existed. The one most widely used was the 'Transportation Plan'.
4 See Appendix 6.
5 PRO PREM 3/334.

Part Two

Introduction

In writing the following, I have drawn upon the very detailed information contained in the official Operations Records of the Groups and Squadrons involved, and I am grateful to those members of Bomber Command and Squadron Associations who have given me much help and encouragement in obtaining personal accounts from ex-aircrew who took part in the raids.

Considerations of time and space (and probably the patience of the reader!) dictate that I should limit these accounts to but a fraction of the total raids carried out. In deciding which ones to describe, I have foresaken a strict geographical and chronological balance, in order to illustrate extremes of success or failure, or to describe some special event which could help the reader to visualise the problems encountered and the action which followed.

Most of the raids were masterpieces of organisation, good communication and precision bombing, the remainder the exact opposite. All the raids were important to those who flew on them, and I apologise in advance if I have omitted to mention a particular raid which the reader considers to have been the most memorable.

CHAPTER SEVEN

Trappes Marshalling Yards — 6/7 March 1944
RAF Bomber Command Target No. Z431

Doubts about bombing accuracy and fears of heavy casualties amongst friendly civilians both resulted in Bomber Command being ordered to carry out a series of experimental attacks on rail targets in France and Belgium in the early part of March 1944. Although it was one of six key rail facilities in the Paris area, Trappes was chosen to be the first target, not so much on account of its importance, but because it lay in relatively open country and there was less risk of heavy civilian casualties.

Situated in flattish terrain, sixteen miles west-southwest of the centre of Paris, the target consisted of two eliptically shaped sidings, set end-to-end in a northwest/southwest direction; the sidings were joined by a number of through lines, which also served the main passenger station. The northeast group of sidings contained a locomotive depot which, at the time of the attack, was estimated to contain forty-eight electric locomotives, which operated on the electrified Paris-Le Mans section. The whole complex covered an area of about 160 acres, and was an important centre through which German troop trains, originating from the east and south of Paris, would normally pass on their way to the Normandy area.

The area to the south of the target consisted of open fields and small woods, with well-scattered farms, but the north side contained two built-up areas. The first bordered the southwest sidings, and was separated from them by the N10 road only. The second and larger urban area sat more astride the N10, in the area immediately north of the main passenger station. A large lake, elongated in an east-west direction (which became the water sports centre of the Etang de St Quentin) was situated approximately half a mile northeast of the centre of the target, and provided a good reference point for both visual and radar identification.

RAF Bomber Command Operation Order No A/C 763 instructed that the target should be attacked in two phases. The aiming point (AP) for the first phase was the centre of the southwest group of sidings; crews in the second phase were to aim at a point just south of the sheds on the northeast sidings. 'Zero hour' was set as 2045 hr (GMT), and the 8th (PFF) Group was directed to send six Mosquitos to mark the target, using 'Musical Parramatta'.[1]

The Main Force consisted entirely of Halifax bombers of Nos 4 and 6 (Canadian) Groups. The latter was to form the first wave and attack between 'zero' and 2051 hr; No 4 Group was to follow between 2111 and 2117 hr. Each aircraft was ordered to carry a mix of 1000- and 500-lb High Explosive bombs and seventy-two bundles of 'Window' which was to be released, when the enemy coast was crossed, at the rate of one bundle every minute. The route out and back was Bases – Dungeness – Target – a point some thirty miles West of Paris – Selsey Bill – Reading – Bases. Aircraft were to attain a bombing height of between 12,000-15,000 ft before crossing the French coast.

The Operation Order concluded by stating that all crews were to be briefed about the proximity of friendly civilians and the need for extreme bombing accuracy. Bombs were to be brought home if the target could not be positively identified.

On receipt of the Bomber Command order, each of the three groups involved issued their own orders for the attack to the squadrons involved. In all, 266 Halifax aircraft and six Mosquitos were fuelled, bombed-up and generally made ready for take-off.

With the prospect of a round trip of approximately 850 miles, the maximum bomb loads could be carried, which, together with the fuel required, brought the take-off weight of each aircraft to almost its maximum of 65,000 lb. The Operations Diary of No 419 (Moose) Squadron noted that those aircraft detailed for the attack carried the largest bomb load lifted in a single night from its base at Middleton-St-George. A typical bomb load was that carried by No 51 Squadron's "C" Charlie (piloted by Flt Lt Johnson): nine 1000-lb and six 500-lb bombs. All were fused to .25 of a second so that when the bomb aimer, Flt Sgt Moroney, released them they could create a good combination of blast and cratering. Altogether 1980 1000-lb and 1650 500-lb bombs were taken to Trappes that night, of which about one-third were required to land in the target area, if Solly Zuckerman's calculations were right.

There was less tension than normal among the crews as they prepared themselves for what was considered to be an 'easy one — not much more than a 'Nickle' raid with bombs instead of bumph'. Certainly, the thought of a five-hour trip, with less than three hours spent over enemy territory, seemed a much better prospect than some of the recent long flogs to Berlin with the sky full of enemy fighters and radar-predicted flak. Even the 'Met' man was fairly encouraging, forecasting reasonable conditions and moderate visibility, lasting at least until most of the crews should be safely back on their own airfields.

The first wave of Halifaxes from No 6 Canadian Group began taking off just before 1800 hr when Flt Lt Stewart of No 419 (Moose) Squadron lifted "P" Peter off the runway at Middleton-St-George. The larger, No 4 Group contingent took off a little later. By

1925 hr all those aircraft taking part in the raid had left their Yorkshire bases. Five Halifaxes of No 6 Group had to be left because of technical problems; a further two of its aircraft had to return early. Plt Off Rawlinson of No 429 (Bison) Squadron 'got in on the show', however, by swapping his aircraft, which had developed a flat tyre, for one of No 427 (Lion) Squadron's (which presumably had been made ready as a reserve).

At 1841 hr Plt Off Cameron of No 158 Squadron, flying one of the new Mark III Halifaxes, did well to overcome the shock of having the escape hatch blow open just as he was taking off from Lisset — it took the crew an hour to fix the hatch while en-route to the target. Similar determination was shown by two pilots of No 10 Squadron, Plt Off Simmonds and Sgt Cartright, who both suffered the loss of one engine when outbound, but carried on to bomb the target and return against a headwind on three engines.

As forecast, the weather on the way was quite good. There was some stratocumulus during the early part of the trip and most crews experienced a tail wind of 30-40 kt, which helped them from the English coast all the way to the target.

The first No 8 (PFF) Group marker to attack was a Mosquito of No 109 Squadron, piloted by Sqn Ldr Stephens. Approaching from the north, in the light of an eleven-day moon and in a cloudless sky, Stephens' navigator released two red target indicators, using Oboe, at 26,000 ft. They landed, one 70 yd, the other 140 yd south of the first AP. The time was 2042 hr and the attack had started.

Within a minute of the first markers going down Plt Off Pratt, at the controls of "D" Dog of No 434 (Bluenose) Squadron, ran in from the north and the bomb aimer, Plt Off Snelgrove, released his bombs from 13,000 ft. By 2048 hr the first part of the attack had reached a crescendo, almost twenty-five aircraft a minute dropping their bombs onto the first red markers. In the middle of it all a Mosquito of No 105 Squadron. Piloted by Sqn Ldr Austin, released two further red target indicators, which landed 470 and 580 yd northeast of the original AP.

By 2054 hr things were beginning to quieten down a little and most of No 6 Group's crews were on their way home, but two further sets of red markers, put down at 2055 and 2059 hr, created a secondary climax to phase one of the attack and the rate of aircraft bombing rose again to six per minute before dying away again to isolated attacks by three aircraft, until the start of the second phase.

With six minutes to go before reaching the target No 4 Group's crews were able to see the fires started by the Canadians in the first part of the attack, and identification of the northeast aim point was helped further by the lake, which showed up quite clearly in the moonlight. As with the first phase, all the aircraft in the second wave approached the target from the northwest, most crews reporting aircraft headings at the time of bomb release of between 120 and 180 degrees. The wind at 14,000 ft above the target was from the northeast and 40 kt — almost at right angles to the line of approach.

Sqn Ldr Stephens of No 109 Squadron started the second phase of the attack. Exactly at the planned time of 2114 hr his navigator released the last of his red markers, which fell, one 180 yd south, the other 260 yd southwest of the second AP. Almost immediately No 4 Group's aircraft pounced. At this point the available records were a little confusing: one report stated that a No 77 Squadron aircraft recorded 'bombs gone' at 2113 hr, but credit for the first flash photos went to Halifax "P" of No 76 Squadron, piloted by WO Jenkins, whose bomb aimer released his load at 2115 hr (which undershot the target by quite a distance). Within five minutes the rate of attack had built up to an incredible twenty-seven aircraft per minute — one salvo of bombs every two seconds, creating an almost continuous sound of explosions which lasted for about four minutes. No wonder some crews complained, on debriefing, of congestion over the target!

Enemy opposition in both phases of the attack was generally regarded as slight, the aircraft encountered some accurate but spasmodic, heavy anti-aircraft gunfire, but no searchlights. One or two enemy aircraft were reported but there was no combat.

No 8 (PFF) Group's plan had been to supplement the red target indicators with green ones, but No 105 Squadron's two Mosquitos, both carrying the green TIs suffered problems on the chosen 'Oboe' channels and no green markers were dropped as a result. In spite of that failure the average radial error for the red TIs on both APs was only 354 yd, and the consensus of opinion amongst crews was that the Pathfinders had done a very good job. In fact, the accuracy of the marking and the good visibility prompted one experienced No 4 Group pilot to remark that he thought that some bomb aimers had been rather careless in not getting all their bombs onto the target! Several aircraft experienced bomb 'hang ups' and six aircraft of No 425 (Alouette) Squadron, based at Tholthorpe, had one 1000-lb bomb at least that would not 'go away'. Most of the 'hang ups' were jettisoned into the sea on the return journey.

The last crew to bomb was that of Fg Off Edwards, of No 77 Squadron, who pulled "A" Able away to the northwest at 2135 hrs, fifty-three minutes after the first markers had gone down. In all, 3650 bombs (over fifty per cent of which were 1000-pounders) had been dropped in near perfect conditions, and crews seemed well pleased with their efforts, as they headed for the first turning point to the west of Paris on the first leg of their homeward journey.

Although the sky was still clear over France, the expected warm front was moving eastwards over England more quickly than had been forecast and the smoke haze, which had been affecting bases since 2300 hr, was being replaced by low cloud, drizzle and generally poor visibility. By 0100 hr it had spread over the whole of Yorkshire and aircraft had to be diverted to airfields in the south of England. Harwell, where No 15 OTU had just disbanded to make way for the gliders of No 38 Group, acted as temporary hosts to aircraft from Nos 428 (Ghost) and 419 (Moose) Canadian squadrons, bringing to sixteen the total number of crews so received in a month. Plt Off Johnson took "V" Victor of No 431 (Iroquois) Squadron to Chipping Warden, where he claimed to have received a most unusual and less than warm reception, which became the subject of a subsequent enquiry. Others landed at Topcliffe, and Wing. All the aircraft landed somewhere, without too much damage, and crews, on debriefing, spoke enthusiastically about the success of the raid — which was described, in the vernacular of the day, as 'a wizard prang'.

Early in the morning of Tuesday 7 March a No 541 (PR) Squadron Spitfire took off from Benson to photograph the results of the raid.

Flying at 24,000 ft, Flt Sgt D Gravensted switched on his F52 cameras, fitted with 36 in lenses, and produced good pictures of the southwest part of the target, but only a high oblique of the locomotive sheds to the northeast.[2]

A second sortie, on 9 March, produced good pictures of the whole area and enabled the photographic interpreters at Medmenham to issue a supplementary report, which completed the picture of devastation. The two reports listed the damage as being:

> Engine sheds 75% destroyed, water tower destroyed, small railway buildings 35% destroyed, extremely heavy concentrations of craters throughout the sidings and all internal lines blocked, at least six locomotives completely destroyed, more than 50 bombs on lines of rolling stock, 34 hits on electrified lines and the marshalling "hump" and points near it had received direct hits.

It was reported also, that there appeared to be quite severe damage to the residential area north of the first AP, and that there was some damage to houses and business premises north of the passenger station.

A detailed report from Bomber Command's Operational Research Section, issued on 15 March, credited the bombers with having landed 288 bombs in the target area (7.9 per cent of the total dropped, which was a little less than the expected 10.1 per cent). The actual number of hits per acre of target was above that estimated as being the minimum required. The attack was considered to have been completely successful and gave much encouragement to the supporters of Zuckerman's Transportation Plan.

The following night, the bombers went to Le Mans.

Notes

1 See Appendix 3.
2 Gravensted was possibly distracted by a Dornier 217 which approached him and made off in a hurry on recognising the Spitfire!

CHAPTER EIGHT

Aulnoye Marshalling Yards and Workshops
25/26 March 1944
RAF Bomber Command Target No Z599

RAF Bomber Command's raid on Aulnoye on 25/26 March 1944 followed a smaller raid made ten days earlier by twenty aircraft of USAAF Ninth Air Force Bomber Command. Subsequent reconnaissance had shown that the American bombers caused little or no damage to the railway tracks or facilities, and it was clear that a larger and much more concentrated attack was necessary.

Aulnoye was situated on the east bank of the River Sambre and some thirty miles northwest of St Quentin in northern France. The main railway line ran northwards from St Quentin, passing through Aulnoye, to the border town of Maubeuge, where it divided: one line going to Mons, the other Charleroi and thence to Liège and Germany. An important east to west line, connecting Metz to Lille, passed close to the southwest of Aulnoye, where it formed a right-angled junction and crossing point with the line from St Quentin. Disrupting that junction would have caused serious delays to German reinforcements for Normandy, not only from Belgium and Holland but from Germany itself via Saarbrucken.

Quite apart from its importance as a major junction, Aulnoye also contained vital locomotive, wagon and carriage repair shops, and, at the time of the raid, it was estimated that more than 100 locomotives would be housed at the running sheds, located near to the locomotive repair shops. The whole target area covered approximately 170 acres, and was more difficult to attack than Trappes because of its widely dispersed layout and the fact that the marshalling sidings and repair facilities were separated by domestic housing.

Unlike the first raid on Trappes, which was carried out by two Groups only, equipped with Halifax bombers, RAF Bomber Command sent aircraft from each of its six operational Groups. They detailed thirty-four squadrons who amongst them used all three types of four-engined bombers (Halifax, Lancaster and Stirling). Out of a total of 193 aircraft detailed originally, some squadrons provided one aircraft only, and it appeared that the planners intended to give as many squadrons as was possible some experience in that type of attack.

Bomber Command's warning order AC 843[1] of 25 March stated that zero hour would be 2145 hr, and that the attack would be in two phases. The first was timed to commence at zero hour; the second was to start twelve minutes later, at 2157 hr. A six-minute reserve period for anyone late on target was to begin at 2209 hr. The bombers were to be allocated equally between the two waves, both numerically and by type. The Aim point for the first wave was in the vicinity of the locomotive repair shops, south of the target area, and crews in the second wave were to aim at a piont near to the marshalling sidings and wagon repair shops, in the northern half of the complex. Bombing, using a mix of 1,000-lb and 500-lb bombs, was not to take place above 15,000 ft altitude. The orders concluded with the, by then, standard warning about the proximity of friendly civilians and the need for accuracy.

The orders issued by No 8 (PFF) Group detailed Nos 105 and 109 Squadrons each to provide eight 'Oboe'-equipped Mosquitos for target-marking using 'Musical Parramatta'. Two Mosquitos plus two reserves were to drop red target indicators, using each of the 'Oboe' channels 1, 3 and 11; two more aircraft and their reserves were to drop green TIs, using channel 12.

The planned route to and from the target took all the aircraft away from England, via Selsey Bill; across to the French coast, between Fécamp and Dieppe; east, towards St Quentin; and north, to the target. After the target the route continued north for a short distance; before turning southwest, to a point south of Amiens, then joined what had been their outward track over the French and English coasts. Depending on the location of their home bases, the crews would be covering between 800 and 1100 miles, and would be in the air for an average of 5 hr 20 min.

The usual preparations took place during the afternoon of 25 March. Crew briefing for No 77 Squadron, based at Elvington, was scheduled for 1530 hr, which was probably representative of the timing of that event for all of the thirty-four squadrons involved.

Standard tables were used to calculate the amount of fuel required and the permissable bomb load (see Appendix 8). A typical calculation was that for a Mk 2 Halifax of No 4 Group:

$$\frac{980 \text{ miles} + 200 \text{ gal}}{0.83} = 1380 \text{ gal} = 9936 \text{ lb}.$$

Disposable load of Halifax Mk 2 = 20,200 lb.
Weight available for bombs: 20,200 − 9936 = 10,264 lb.

Each bundle of 'Window' weighed approximately six pounds, and the total bomb load would then have been reduced to less than

10,000 lb. Other variations occurred due to the availability of bombs and having to carry special equipment.

The Lancasters of Nos 1 and 5 Groups carried the greatest weight of bombs that night, and it was interesting to compare the 14,000 lb carried by each No 1 Group aircraft which had 920 track miles to cover, with the Stirlings of No 3 Group which, having only 800 miles to fly, could only manage just over 9000 lb of bombs per aircraft.

Allowing for some fuel being left in the tanks, it was probable that a total of something like 200,000 gallons of petrol were dispensed from bowsers around the airfields of eastern England during the afternoon of the raid. Given that a round trip averaged 900 miles, and that 176 heavy bombers were involved, the figures provided some insight into the vast logistical effort required to mount a thousand-bomber raid, deep into the heart of Germany.

The Halifaxes of No 6 Group, which had further to fly than most, were among the early starters that evening. Sqn Ldr Dyer of No 419 (Moose) Squadron took off from Middleton-St-George in Co. Durham at 1824 hr. He would be airborne for almost six hours, a little above the average for his Group. To the south, at Ludford Magna in Lincolnshire, Air Commodore Cozens, the Senior Air Officer of No 1 Group, took the controls of No 101 Squadron's Lancaster "X2". His crew included Special Operator Plt Off Blair, who was to work the radio jamming equipment 'Airborne Cigar', with which most of No 101 Squadron's aircraft were equipped. At about the same time, AVM C M McEwen, the newly appointed commander of No 6 (Canadian) Group, was climbing aboard a Halifax of No 431 (Iroquois) Squadron, to act as second pilot to Sqn Ldr Higgins.

All the aircraft destined to take part in the first phase of the attack were airborne by 1920 hr; except the Mosquitos of No 8 (PFF) Group which, because of their greater speed and having less distance to travel, did not begin to take-off from their bases in Huntingdon-shire until 2000 hr.

The weather, which had been a little cloudy in the afternoon, began to clear soon after dark, and apart from some stratocumulus near Rouen, the route out was clear; there was some ground haze near the target. Mosquitos "W" of No 109 Squadron and "G" of No 105 Squadron were one minute ahead of schedule when they approached the target from the north. At 2143 hr they released a total of three red target indicators from an altitude of 32,000 ft. The mean point of impact (MPI) of the three markers was in some fields, approximately 550 yd east of the southern aim point. There was no "Master Bomber" to issue any corrections, and within two minutes Flt Lt Pritchard, the bomb aimer aboard Halifax 'E' of No 77 Squadron, approaching from the south and against the wind, pressed his bomb release to send bombs crashing down onto the markers. The raid had begun.

At 2147 hr a Mosquito of No 105 Squadron released two green target indicators from an altitude of 28,000 ft, but they too fell well to the southeast of the aim point. By this time, Main Force aircraft were arriving from the south, dropping their bombs accurately from 8,000 ft onto the markers, at a rate of eighteen aircraft per minute. That rate of intensity lasted for nearly a minute before it tailed off to leave a single aircraft attacking at 2155 hr. In fact, five aircraft from the second wave bombed in the first phase, giving a total of eighty-six bombers attacking between 2145 and 2156 hr.

A lull of about one minute preceded the start of the second phase. At 2155 hr the navigator, flying in aircraft 'D' of No 105 Squadron, pressed his release button to drop two red TIs onto the northeast aim point. At 2157 hr, exactly as planned, Flt Sgt Chappele's bomb

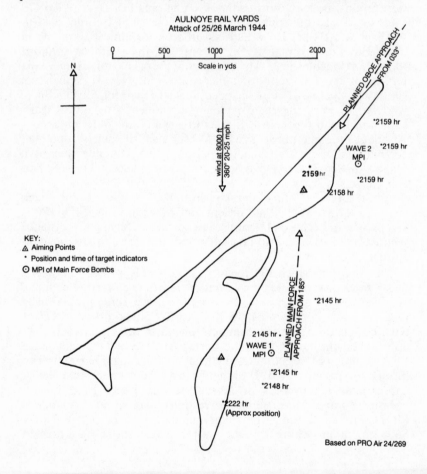

AULNOYE RAIL YARDS
Attack of 25/26 March 1944

Scale in yds

KEY:
△ Aiming Points
* Position and time of target indicators
⊙ MPI of Main Force Bombs

wind at 8000 ft
360° 20-25 mph

PLANNED OBOE APPROACH FROM 033°

*2159 hr
WAVE 2   *2159 hr
MPI
⊙
*2159hr   *2159 hr
△   2158 hr

PLANNED MAIN FORCE APPROACH FROM 185°

*2145 hr

2145 hr •
WAVE 1
MPI ⊙   △

*2145 hr
*2148 hr

*2222 hr
(Approx position)

Based on PRO Air 24/269

aimer, lying in the nose of Chappele's Stirling 'S' of No 9 Squadron, placed his bombs onto the markers. Additional red and green target indicators released by the Mosquitos resulted again in an MPI which was nearly 600 yd northeast of the planned aim point. What followed was a prime example of the bombing (which was done from approximately 8000-9000 ft), being too accurate for the marking which, because of the requirements of 'Oboe', was done at about 30,000 ft.

The error in marking was blamed afterwards on a combination of the poor calibration of 'Oboe' equipment, and incorrect estimates of wind drift, which had been based on a forecast of a surface wind of 18 kt from the northeast. In fact it was probable that conditions at the surface were almost calm. The ease with which the target indicators were identified, together with little or no ground opposition, and the fact that the bombs were released against the wind, created such ideal conditions that most bombs fell very close to the markers and so missed the target. (See Plan on page 66).

The peak of the second phase occurred around 2159 hr when eighteen aircraft per minute attacked the target. The rate was held for at least a minute, and it was a further two minutes before it fell to less than fifteen aircraft per minute. As a result, fifty of the seventy-eight bombers which attacked the north part of the target dropped approximately 850 bombs in the space of three minutes (over four bombs per second). Most of the second-phase crews reported a huge explosion at 2204 hr, which was thought to be a factory southwest of the marshalling yards.

Nine of the bombers attacked in the later 'reserve' period, between 2209 and 2222 hr, but generally speaking the raid was notable for its precision timing and concentration. It was a great pity about the errors in marking, which resulted in only 116 bombs falling in the designated target area (4.4 per cent and less than half the number planned or expected). A Spitfire, piloted by a Canadian, Fg Off Lott, took off from Benson on the following morning. Lott brought back pictures showing that, in spite of these errors, the bombs that did find their mark had caused considerable damage to the carriage and wagon repair facilities, and had blocked several through-lines and sidings.

Looking back over Stirling 'G's port quarter as it approached Amiens on its way home, Plt Off A A Lange's crew from No 90 Squadron, reported that they could see large fires burning in the area of the target some fifty miles to the northeast (possibly the aftermath of the large explosion reported earlier).

The Bomber Command night raid summary credited the German defences with having had a small mixed force of fighters in the area; one Ju 88 had dropped flares in the vicinity of Fécamp when the bombers were crossing the coast on their homeward run. Flt Sgt

J P O'Neill reported that his mid-upper gunner, Sgt R B Laroche, had frightened off an enemy fighter when it attacked their No 51 Squadron Lancaster. Although some of No 10 Squadron's crews reported having seen searchlights in the target area, the summary did not mention the fact. However, it did record that one heavy and several light anti-aircraft batteries were in action in the target area, and that two Halifaxes of No 6 Group received slight flak damage. One aircraft was damaged by machine-gun fire from another British aircraft.[2]

Smoke haze in Nos 5 and 6 Group's area began to clear when the aircraft returned to their bases, and all returned without diversion; with one exception. With only two engines working, Plt Off Eyjulfsen of No 419 Squadron jettisoned his bombs off the French coast and crash-landed aircraft 'L' whilst trying to get into Ford. Fortunately, none of the crew were seriously hurt, but the aircraft was a write-off.

Of the 179 Main Force aircraft planned for use in the attack, 176 took off, and 173 bombed the target. A total of 2636 bombs were dropped of which sixty-three per cent were 500 pounders, the remainder were 1000-lb MC or GP bombs. Most of the bombs were released from heights of between 7000 and 9000 ft whilst the aircraft were flying at indicated air speeds of between 165 and 200 mph.

That first attack on Aulnoye gave a few crews their first experience of that type of precision attack. It was unfortunate that the results were not better, and that a further two attacks were necessary, later in April, before the target became classified as 'A' (no further attack required). Regrettably, several of the crews which took part did not live to see the later, more successful attacks, because the disastrous attack on Nuremberg on the night of 30/31 March intervened.[3]

Notes

1 PRO Air 24/267.
2 Not an unusual occurrence. It was often too late if gunners waited to obtain positive identification of some dark shape which appeared to be closing on their own aircraft.
3 For one of the best accounts of the Nuremberg Raid of 30/31 March 1944 see Martin Middlebrook's book on the subject.

CHAPTER NINE

Lille/Delivrance
9/10 March 1944
RAF Bomber Command Target No Z751

Being surrounded mainly by business and domestic premises, La Delivrance was one of the targets which the British War Cabinet would have liked to delete from the list of Transportation Targets. It was a little surprising therefore that it was attacked so early in the programme, and within a week or so of an attack on a similar target using both the Master Bomber and the new low-level marking techniques, which were being developed for the very purpose of attacking targets surrounded by friendly civilians.

The pear-shaped target area measured 2500 yd long in a northeast-southwest direction, by an average of 600 yd wide, the narrowest part being at the southwest end. The whole facility was confined on its north, east and west sides by the suburbs of Lomme, Le Marais and Delivrance, respectively. At the time of writing the marshalling yards are bordered on their southern side by Autoroute A25, which runs between Lille and Dunkerque.

In addition to the traditional three groups of sidings for the reception, sorting and forwarding of trains, the area contained extensive wagon and locomotive repair workshops, and, being close to the border with Belgium, was an important junction for the lines running southwest from Gent to Rouen and Paris, and from Dunkerque to the Strasbourg area. Lille contained the headquarters of the German 15th Army, and the destruction of the rail network in that area was to add to the confusion which resulted in the 1st SS Panzer Division having to take fourteen days to cover the 300 miles from Belgium to Normandy.

Bomber Command Orders, issued on 9 April 1944 detailed a twin-phase attack again, with zero hour set at 2310 hr the same day. The first wave, consisting of 115 Halifaxes of No 4 Group, was to attack between Z and Z+6 hr and this was to be followed by a mixed force of 53 Halifaxes of No 6 Group, 22 Stirlings of No 3 Group and 40 Lancasters of No 8 (PFF) Group. The Pathfinder Group was also required to provide twelve 'Oboe'-equipped Mosquitos for marking the target, using 'Musical Parramatta'. At the same time as these orders were issued, another set of orders was sent to Nos 1, 3, 4, 6 and 8 Groups for a parallel attack on the marshalling yards at Villeneuve St George near Paris.

9 April was a typical British Easter Sunday, and the afternoon rain and drizzle caused the 'Met' man to recommend that zero hour be put back by ninety minutes, so that the weather front might have more time to clear the target area by midnight. In the event, it began clearing from most of the Bomber Command bases by tea-time, and at 1715 hrs, No 77 Squadron, for one, was briefing its seventeen crews for the operation. The weather forecast for the expected times of return to bases was reasonable, except for the possibility of smokey haze in No 4 Group's area.

One of the first Main Force bombers to take off on the raid was that piloted by Flt Lt Stewart, who took Halifax 'O' (one of thirteen No 419 Squadron aircraft) into the air at 2130 hr. The aircraft was carrying seven 1000-lb and eight 500-lb bombs, and some 1100 gal of fuel for the 550-mile round trip, which was to take it out of England via Selsey Bill, across to the French coast near Dieppe, where it would continue east before turning north towards the target. Having bombed, the plan was to make for home via the southern part of the North Sea, to Orfordness, hopefully to land back at Middleton-St-George some time around 0230 hr.

Fourteen crews reported having sighted enemy fighters on the way to the target, and five combats took place at that stage.[1] The sky was largely clear and there was a nearly full moon. The level of enemy fighter activity was high, in comparison with earlier raids, and was indicative of the growing concern with which the Germans were beginning to view the attacks on the railway centres of northern France and Belgium. Air Intelligence reports indicated that the Luftwaffe could be reinforcing their 4th Fighter Division in the Amiens area already.

The first target-marking Mosquito to reach the area was flown by Fg Off Deighton of No 105 Squadron, but a technical failure prevented his navigator from releasing the red target indicators. One minute later, but still three minutes before the planned time of 0038 hr, Mosquito 'R' of No 109 Squadron came in from the northeast and released two red target indicators, which cascaded down approximately 800 yd north-northeast of the northern Aim Point. A further two pairs of red indicators were delivered, one pair at 0039 hr, the other pair at 0040 hr, and the mean point of impact of all the markers dropped up to that time was 320 yd north of the first Aim Point — well within the prescribed target area.

The first photograph taken, activated by the bomb release of a Main Force aircraft, was timed at 0037 hr, and was attributed to Fg Off Baer, flying Halifax 'N' of No 578 Squadron. The photograph indicated that the bomb aimer was a little hasty, and that the quite strong westerly wind at the altitude of 14,000 ft probably carried the bombs into the relatively open countryside southeast of the Aim Point, narrowly missing a heavy flak battery. Another No 4 Group crew, obviously eager to get on with the job in hand, was that of Plt Off Viner of No 77 Squadron, who recorded 'bombs gone' at 0038.30 hr. Within three minutes, and exactly at the new zero hour of 0040 hr, there were twenty-one aircraft per minute, flying in from the south and attacking the northern Aim Point. They dropped their bombs from approximately 14,000 ft onto the well-positioned target indicators. At that time there were some sightings of enemy fighters, but no combats were reported. A number of searchlights were active, and some slight but accurate, heavy anti-aircraft fire came up from a battery located in the southwest outskirts of the town. A few light anti-aircraft guns opened up but the bombers were mostly out of range.

Several crews reported having seen a large explosion at 0042 hr, and subsequent reports suggested that an ammunition train had blown up in the reception sidings. By 0046 hr the first part of the attack was dwindling, and the rate was down to five aircraft per minute. Although some did not bomb until 0049 hr, most of the 111 Halifaxes of No 4 Group were already setting course for home. Bomber Command's Operational Research Section noted in its report that four aircraft, despatched to bomb in the second phase, had bombed *before* the second phase markers had been put down,

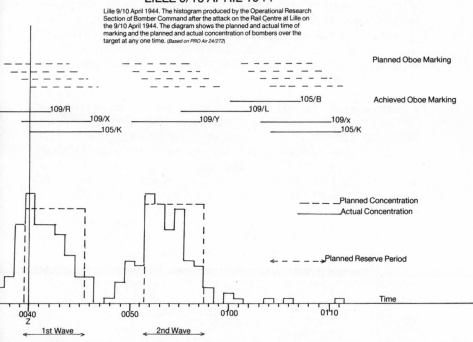

LILLE 9/10 APRIL 1944

Lille 9/10 April 1944. The histogram produced by the Operational Research Section of Bomber Command after the attack on the Rail Centre at Lille on the 9/10 April 1944. The diagram shows the planned and actual time of marking and the planned and actual concentration of bombers over the target at any one time. (*Based on PRO Air 24/272*)

and that these aircraft must have added their bombs to those dropped onto the northern Aim Point.

The second phase should have opened with a No 105 Squadron Mosquito dropping red target indicators onto the southern Aim Point at 0049 hr, but its 'Oboe' failed. Consequently, No 109 Squadron put down the first four red markers at 0050 hr. These were extremely well placed, being only seventy yards north of the second Aim Point (which was in the middle of the sorting sidings). It set the scene for some very concentrated bombing by the mixed force of heavy bombers attacking that part of the target.

One of the first bombers to spot the new target indicators was probably a Lancaster of No 156 Squadron which was based at Upwood. From the same Squadron, Sqn Ldr Davies made three runs over the target before his bomb aimer was satisfied that his bombs would hit the target. Seconds after his bombs had been released, another Lancaster came up from below and the two aircraft actually touched, fortunately without too much damage. With concentrations of more than twenty aircraft per minute over some targets, such incidents were not uncommon, and, when viewed in the light of modern air traffic control regulations, it highlighted the dangers of wartime flying, even when enemy opposition was slight.

In spite of the smoke generated by the first phase of the raid, most crews in the second phase were able to see the TIs, although some did use G-H or H2S radars to confirm their positions. Two massive explosions were reported by many of the crews at 0052 and 0053 hr, the first of these was accompanied by a rush of orange flame, rising several thousand feet and lasting a number of seconds. At first, it was thought that particular explosion was associated with hits on the Paul Bernard Chemical Works, situated just north of the target area, and which was later reported by the photographic interpreters as having three large buildings completely destroyed, but a later intelligence report suggests that it was another ammunition train blowing up.

The peak of the second phase of the attack came just before the planned time of 0052 hr. Within a minute, twenty-one aircraft each released their load of 1000- and 500-lb bombs so that approximately 300 bombs per minute were raining down on the southern part of the target. That intensity was maintained for nearly four minutes before dying away to just eight aircraft per minute. Excepting three aircraft which bombed the northern Aim Point in the 'Reserve' period between 0104 and 0110 hr, some 219 heavy bombers had attacked the target in the twenty-four minutes between 0037 and 0101 hr. According to Bomber Command's Operational Research Section, 875 of the 3335 bombs dropped had fallen into the designated target area. The official summary of the raid described it as the best centred of all the marshalling yard attacks to date. Even so, there was no disputing the fact that over 2000 bombs fell into predominately urban areas, inhabitated by civilians whose friendly cooperation was to be an important factor in the forthcoming Allied invasion.

Although the raid was generally described as 'quiet' by most crews,[2] there were a few problems. Of the 227 aircraft that actually took off on the raid, six developed problems with their engines or other vital equipment, and were forced to jettison their bombs over the east end of the English Channel. Also, Lancaster ND701, piloted by Fg Off R J Bordiss of No 35 Squadron, took off from Gravely at 2311 hrs and was not seen again.[3] The last crews home were those of No 6 Group, who had attacked in the second phase, and who did not reach their bases until approximately 0330 hr. Several crews reported that fires could be seen in the area of the target as they headed out over the southern part of the North Sea — at least fifty miles into their homeward flight.

Subsequent photo-reconnaissance, by a Spitfire of No 542 Squadron, from Benson, confirmed that all the rail tracks had been cut at least once, and that many wagons had been destroyed. However, in spite of a density of 2.7 bombs per acre, the important locomotive and wagon repair shops and the engine sheds lay in small gaps in the crater plot and had survived with only partial damage. The CIU report also mentioned considerable damage to industry and housing, especially in the areas north and east of the target.

In a memo, dated 13 April[4], to the Prime Minister, the Chief of the Air Staff, Sir Charles Portal, reported that in the ten attacks on French railway targets since 6 March it was estimated that nearly 800 French civilians had been killed, of which about 150 deaths were attributed to the attack on Lille. On the same day, however, Lord Cherwell, Churchill's Scientific Advisor, who was opposed to the Transportation Plan, drew the Prime Minister's attention to a Vichy Government broadcast on 12 April. During the broadcast it had been claimed that 400 civilians had been killed and 900 injured at Lille, including fifty French railway workers and their families.

German propaganda sources claimed that 600 civilians had been killed. Having seen the aerial photographs of the area myself, a mean figure of 380 killed would have seemed quite possible.

Notes

1 One of these resulted in Plt Off McCullough of No 434 Squadron reporting that his gunners had fired on a twin-engined enemy fighter, which was seen to explode in the air.

2 Up to that time, the highest Bomber Command casualties connected with the Transportation Plan had occurred during the night of 15/16 March when three aircraft had been lost while attacking Amiens.

3 Both Fg Off Bordiss and his navigator, Flt Sgt Talbot, were buried at Abbeville. The rest of the crew baled out; the wireless operator, Sgt O'Brien, arrived home eventually after being interned in Switzerland.

4 PRO PREM 3/334/2.

CHAPTER TEN

Tergnier Marshalling Yards
10/11 and 18/10 April 1944
RAF Bomber Command Target No Z572

Although the Tergnier marshalling yards were attacked by a small force in February 1944, the first attack of the Transportation Plan took place on 10/11 April, when 144 Halifaxes of No 4 Group dropped 690 tons of high-explosives onto markers laid down by 'Oboe'-equipped Mosquitos of No 8 (PFF) Group. Unfortunately, of the 2237 bombs dropped, only 236 fell onto the target area, the vast majority of them falling onto a housing estate immediately west of the marshalling sidings. It was not surprising, therefore, that a second attack was called for a week or so later.

A glance at the map on page 50 illustrates the importance of Tergnier as a railway junction. Not only did it lie on the important Liège-Paris line, but it was located on a good east-west route, some seventy miles north of Paris, which would have provided an alternative, albeit more northerly, route for German units moving towards Normandy from Metz and southwest Germany.

In addition to the marshalling facilities, Tergnier contained very large carriage and wagon repair sheds, transhipment sheds and a locomotive depot which, at the time of the first raid, was estimated to contain ninety engines. The attack of 10/11 April took place in two phases, each within a planned period of six minutes, with a gap of six minutes between the attacks. Zero hour was set as 2350 hr, and crews were instructed to bomb from heights between 9000 and 11,000 ft. The approach to the target was from the southwest. The weather at the time of attack was moderate to good, with some ground haze and a 25-30 mph westerly wind at the bombing height.

The attack was planned to start three minutes before zero hour, when an 'Oboe'-equipped Mosquito of No 105 Squadron was to drop red TIs onto the northern Aim Point. That aircraft and a Mosquito of No 109 Squadron both had technical failures, and the first red TIs to be dropped were those from a second No 109 Squadron aircraft, whose pilot released his markers at 2348 hr. By zero hour another Mosquito of No 105 Squadron had dropped two more red TIs which, together with the earlier ones, created a mean point of impact (MPI) about 600 yd southwest of the northern Aim Point — just outside the western boundary of the target area.

The timing of the first wave of Halifaxes was exceptionally good, and at zero hour seventeen aircraft per minute were dropping mixed loads of 1000- and 500-lb bombs. In all, seventy-two Halifaxes bombed in the eight minutes between zero hour and 2358 hr and, with good conditions at 9-10,000 ft, the bomb aimers could hardly miss the red TIs.

The marking for the second phase began when a Mosquito of No 105 Squadron dropped four green TIs, using 'Oboe', onto the southern Aim Point. In fact, those target indicators created an MPI approximately 2500 yd north-northwest of the target. Two minutes later, at 0002 hr, another No 105 Squadron Mosquito dropped four red TIs to give an MPI of approximately 400 yd southwest of the centre of the target area, and 150 yd only from the concentration of bomb craters created by the first wave. Right on cue, seventy-two Halifaxes flew in from the southwest; the first fourteen of those were attracted by the badly placed green TIs, but the majority bombed on the red TIs, creating further devastation among the houses to the west of the target.

Bomber Command's Operational Research Section drew attention to the similarities between the raid and the one on Aulnoye on 25/26 March, and put most of the blame onto the poor serviceability of 'Oboe' equipment. However, they also discovered that the position of the southern Aim Point had been incorrectly calculated because of an error in the photographic scale which had accompanied the Target Illustration Print. The result of the latter mistake led to both phases of the attack being centred mostly around the same Aim Point. The Research Section pointed out that, had the bombing taken place from 15,000 ft, the spread would have been greater and more bombs would have fallen in the target area.

Accurate figures for the number of casualties amongst French civilians were not calculated easily from the reports available, but the best estimate seems to have been: eighty killed and 200 wounded. The night was also costly for Bomber Command. No 4 Group lost ten Halifaxes (almost 7 per cent), including no less than four of the twenty despatched by No 158 Squadron. Most of them were lost in combat with enemy night fighters in the Poix and Montidier areas. A further two aircraft of No 158 Squadron, 'M' (flown by WO Collins) and 'K' (Flt Sgt Wright), were also attacked by twin-engined night fighters after leaving the target. Collins and Wright, together with crews of No 466 Squadron, reported having seen several aircraft going down in flames in the same area. There was little anti-aircraft fire at the target, but heavy, predicted flak was encountered while the bomber stream passed between Amiens and Poix, and again when they recrossed the French coast near Dieppe.

The Operational Research Section attributed the greatly increased enemy air activity to the fact that the Germans thought that the bombers were heading for southern Germany but, as mentioned in the account of the raid on Lille, the Germans were beginning to take the raids on railway centres very seriously. In addition, Tergnier was dangerously close to the Luftwaffe fighter bases at Laon/Athies and Montidier.

There were several minor mishaps that night. Flt Lt Silverman, piloting aircraft 'O' of No 102 Squadron (based at Pocklington), had to order the release of his four 1000-lb and eleven 500-lb, just short of the target because of a fire in the bomb bay. A further two aircraft had to jettison their bombs over the English Channel, one because of hydraulics failure which prevented the flaps and undercarriage from retracting, the other because of engine trouble. A further three aircraft never got off the ground because of engine problems.

The CIU's Immediate Interpretation Report of 12 April recorded that, in spite of the lack of bombs in the target area, the wagon repair and transhipment sheds had been partly destroyed, that many wagons had been destroyed and several lines had been cut. However, it was not good enough, and it was clear that another attack would be required.

Mindful of the poor results of the 10/11 April raid, marking instructions for the 18 April raid included the use of twenty-four Lancasters of No 8 (PFF) Group for visual marking, illuminating, support and back-up. A Master Bomber (one of three visual markers of No 7 Squadron, with the, somewhat unglamorous, radio callsign of Stinkbow) was to control the raid using VHF radio. The initial marking was to be carried out once again by 'Oboe'-equipped Mosquitos of Nos 105 and 109 Squadrons. One Aim Point only was chosen for the attack, which was to take place in two phases between zero hour (2330 hr) and 2336 hr, each phase being planned to last three minutes. The Main Force consisted of 142 Halifaxes of No 4 Group, which were to approach the target from the southwest, bomb from approximately 15,000 ft, then fly north for a few miles before turning west to recross the French coast, just north of Dieppe.

The weather over Tergnier on 18 April was good, with cloudless skies, no moon and very light winds; there was, however, some slight ground haze in the target area.

The attack commenced as planned, but again the Mosquitos suffered poor serviceability of their 'Oboe' equipment, and of the eight detailed to attack, three only actually released their TIs, creating an MPI further to the west of those of the previous raid. With the help of hooded flares from four of No 405 Squadron's Lancasters, the visual markers of No 7 Squadron (including the master bomber, Wg Co T F Barron of the RNZAF) went in with additional red and green TIs — Barron's markers cascading nicely over the wagon repair shops.

Barron then called in the back-up from Nos 7 and 405 Squadrons, telling them to add to the better placed TIs. In spite of that, the main concentration of TIs remained outside the western edge of the target area, and Barron was heard clearly by many Halifax crews to order them to bomb to the east of the markers; most crews claimed to have responded to this instruction. Further valiant attempts by Wg Co Barron to minimise the effects of the poor marking were of no avail, and the bombing drifted away increasingly towards the southwest. Only 126 of the 2315 bombs dropped fell into the target area; most had fallen onto the town, southwest of the marshalling yards. The attack had failed again, and only the presence of the master bomber prevented an even bigger fiasco.

Of the 171 aircraft that took off for Tergnier, only 156 reported to have attacked the target between 2324 and 2340 hr. Six Halifaxes were missing, of which four fell to night fighters apparently between the target and the French coast, one to flak between Dieppe and Treport, and one was unaccounted for. Four aircraft returned to their bases early with technical faults, and Sgt J Saynor and his crew, in aircraft 'W' of No 10 Squadron, had to land away from base at Stradishall because of a fuel shortage. On the plus side: No 76 Squadron claimed an Fw 190, and an Me 110 was claimed by a No 100 Group Mosquito, which was flying in support of the bombers.

In a brief report on the raid, Bomber Command's Operational Research Section calculated that the combined number of hits from the two attacks amounted to only sixty-four per cent of that originally required, and a third raid was recommended.

The third raid took place on 31 May and was successful enough for the planners to class Tergnier as Category A — no further attacks required. However, the third raid cost Bomber Command two aircraft and their crews, bringing to eighteen the total number of aircraft lost on the three raids. Imperial War Graves Commission Registers recorded that of the 113 aircrew that went missing on the first two Tergnier raids, no less than ninety were buried in minor cemeteries, located in the area between the target and the French coast near Dieppe.

The table in Appendix 11 summarises the fate of those crews involved.

CHAPTER ELEVEN

Chambly Depot
1/2 May 1944
RAF Bomber Command Target No Z836A

The Chambly attack by eighty-two Lancasters and sixteen Stirlings of No 3 Group was supported by 'Oboe' target-marking Mosquitos and fourteen Lancasters of No 8 (PFF) Group. The sixteen Stirlings of No 18 Squadron were making their second attempt at bombing, using G-H equipment. Their first attempt took place on 20/21 April when, as part of a much larger force attacking other rail targets in northern France and Belgium, only two aircraft had G-H equipment that worked well enough for their pilots to attempt a bombing run.

Chambly was described by Intelligence departments as one of the most modern and important permanent way depots in northern France. However, in spite of its importance and location in relatively open countryside, approximately twenty-two miles north of Paris, the depot did not appear in the early list of targets cleared for attack as part of the Transportation Plan. Bomber Command Executive Order AC504, which detailed the two Groups for the attack,[1] stipulated that zero hour would be 0020 hr on 2 May, and that the main bombing force would attack in two waves, each lasting four minutes, from zero to 0024 hr, and 0024 to 0028 hr. The more specific No 8 (PFF) Group Form B, issued at 1330 hr on 1 May, detailed four Mosquitos from each of Nos 105 and 109 Squadrons to be prepared to drop red and green 'Spot Fire' markers using 'Oboe' from 0014 to 0017 hr; and fourteen Lancasters from No 7 (New Zealand) Squadron to act as illuminators and as back up from 0015 to 0022 hr. A master bomber and his deputy, also from No 7 (NZ) Squadron, were to be on the scene from 0015 hr, and all crews were to act on his instructions. Known by the call sign 'Little John' the master bomber was to operate below an altitude of 7000 ft.

No 3 Group's Form B detailed for the raid the sixteen Stirlings of No 218 Squadron, based at Woolfax Lodge, twenty-nine Lancasters from 32 Base and fifty-six Lancasters from 33 Base. The two types of aircraft were given different routes over France, the Stirlings being directed to take a more westerly course to the target, then home via a more easterly track. Then they were to join the Lancasters at the

French coast, northeast of Dieppe, from whence all the aircraft were to make for home via Dungeness and Bradwell. The average distance for the trip was 500 track miles. No 3 Group also detailed the composition of the two waves; each wave was to contain similar proportions of squadrons and aircraft types. Bombing height for the Stirlings, using G-H, was set at 14,000 ft,[2] and that of the Lancasters at 7-10,000 ft.

The Stirlings of No 218 Squadron began to take off at 2210 hr, the ill-fated 'P' Peter, piloted by Fg Off Jones, and 'G' George, piloted by Plt Off Elliot, taking off at 2214 and 2217 hr respectively. The Lancasters, which were faster than the other aircraft, left their bases a little later; Sqn Ldr J M Dennis, the master bomber, who had to be on target before the main force, taking to the air above Oakington at 2214 hr. Most of the Stirlings were each carrying eighteen 500-lb bombs and were destined to be in the air for almost four hours. The Lancasters, which were more powerful, were carrying approximately 12,000 lb of a mix of 1000- and 500 lb bombs and were expected to be airborne for three-and-a-half hours.

The weather forecast for the night, both at the bases and in the target area, was fair, except for the possibility of some broken stratocumulus over northwest France; there was a half moon also. The 'Met' man was correct; most crews reported good visibility all the way to the target.

At Kingsdown, Signals Intelligence operators heard the first conversations between the fighters of both NJG 1 and NJG 4 and their controllers at 2349 hr. They seemed to be flying in the area of Florennes, approximately 150 miles northeast of the target area, and the conversations indicated that the fighters were being held back, in case the raid developed against a target in southern Germany.

Although well on time and within range of their 'Oboe' ground stations, only two of the eight target-marking Mosquitos could get their equipment to work satisfactorily. Sqn Ldr R C E Law and Flt Lt R A Palmer, both of No 109 Squadron, released their target indicators; but even these appeared to have been affected by some sort of technical malfunction because they landed some distance to the north of the selected Aim Point.

Just before 0015 hr — five minutes before the Main Force were due to begin the attack — the master bomber was heard, over the radio, to instruct the illuminators from his squadron to release their flares over the ground markers. Drifting over the target in the northerly wind, the flares made it possible to identify the Aim Point. At 0018 hr the master bomber released his yellow target indicators, which cascaded accurately over the Aim Point. Sqn Ldr Dennis then instructed the Main Force to ignore the spot fires and bomb on his yellow markers.

Some very accurate and concentrated bombing then occurred. The

Stirlings of No 218 Squadron had rid themselves of the 'gremlins' which had dogged their earlier attempts, and the night flash plot showed that their bombing, using G-H from 12-14,000 ft, matched that of the Lancasters from 7-9000 ft. In fact the bombing was so accurate that the markers put down by Sqn Ldr Dennis were soon obscured by smoke and dust; at 0025 hr he ordered his deputy, Flt Lt H C Williams (also a New Zealander, flying in 'P' Peter) to re-mark the Aim Point. On hearing this, Sqn Ldr H Tiles (piloting Lancaster 'H' of No 622 Squadron) made a second orbit of the target area whilst waiting for the new markers. Williams placed his markers with equal accuracy at 0025 hr and the second wave of aircraft carried on with the attack. At 0028 hr Sqn Ldr E G B Reid went in to attack from 5000 ft, then descended to 2000 ft for the return home (he was obviously a fan of Mick Martin).[3]

There were a few ill-controlled searchlights in the target area, and some spasmodic heavy flak came up from an area to the south of it. At 0029 hr listeners at Kingsdown heard clearly a call of 'victory' from a German night fighter,[4] and it was clear that the fighters, probably from Laon and Juvincourt, had reached the area during the attack. All the crew of No 7 Squadron's Lancaster 'B', except the pilot who survived and evaded capture, were buried in the small churchyard in the village of Nointel, just across the river from the target.

Attacks by twin-engined fighters (Ju 88s and Me 110s) continued all the way along the route back to the French coast. Crews of No 218

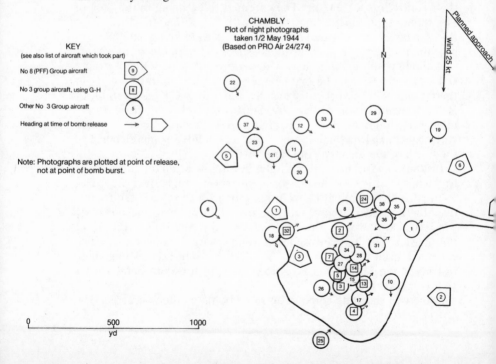

CHAMBLY
Plot of night photographs
taken 1/2 May 1944
(Based on PRO Air 24/274)

KEY
(see also list of aircraft which took part)

No 8 (PFF) Group aircraft

No 3 group aircraft, using G-H

Other No 3 Group aircraft

Heading at time of bomb release

Note: Photographs are plotted at point of release, not at point of bomb burst.

Squadron reported not only their own combats, but that they saw four aircraft go down in flames after leaving the target. Ten of the two missing crews from No 218 Squadron,[5] together with New Zealander Sqn Ldr E Sachter and his crew of No 75 (NZ) Squadron Lancaster ME 689, were buried in the churchyard at Poix, a small town south-west of Amiens, which lay less than ten miles from the planned track of the homeward bound aircraft. One of the Stirlings attacked, flown by Plt Off R Scammell, crash-landed at Woodbridge and the flight engineer, Sgt R E Lodge, was killed.

No 514 Squadron was equally hard pressed on the way home. Flt Sgt C F Proules (flying aircraft 'O') reported one combat, Flt Sgt Watkins (piloting in 'F2') was attacked six times, and Flt Sgt J B Topham arrived home with holes in the wings and fuselage of his aircraft 'K2' (caused by flak over Dieppe). All these terrifying experiences must have been capped by that of Flt Sgt C J Medland and his crew, flying in 'A'.

Soon after leaving the target, at approximately 0025 hr, Medland was attacked by a Ju 88, which literally blew away his starboard inner engine. His two gunners (Canadian Sgt C E Rose, and Sgt B R Williams) chased off the attacker, but excessive vibration from the port inner engine demanded that it be feathered. At 0034 hr, with their speed down to 140 kt, they were attacked again by an enemy fighter, which came at them from the port bow, opening fire from a range of 1500 yd. In spite of the loss of speed, Medland corkscrewed and evaded the attack. Nine minutes later, another fighter came in again, from the port side, firing from 700 yd. Notwithstanding the loss of power in the turrets, the gunners returned the fire and no further damage was sustained.

The final attack came at 0048 hr, from dead astern, but was repelled again. Although Medland had prepared the crew to bale out, he recrossed the French coast at 6000 ft and decided to press on for Woodbridge, where he landed safely at 0200 hr. The aircraft was later declared a write-off.[6]

Flt Lt R J Curtis and his crew in 'H2' were not so lucky. Their aircraft was caught by a night fighter, and was seen to fall vertically, then explode near the village of Chaumont en Vixien. All the crew are buried in St Sever Rouen cemetery.

Excepting some low stratus cloud in the Midlands and in the proximity of No 8 (PFF) Group's bases, the weather was reasonable for the returning aircraft, and all those able to return to their bases did so by approximately 0230 hr.

Later in the day of 2 May, two Spitfire X1s of No 541 (PR) Squadron took off from Benson to photograph Chambly and other targets in northwest France. Particularly good pictures of Chambly were obtained by Flt Lt L H Scargill, and they allowed photographic interpreters to assess the damage done as:

1 Points and crossing shop. One large building destroyed, two others 75 per cent destroyed by direct hits.
2 Sleeper impregnation plant. Four buildings 50 per cent gutted.
3 Stores yards. Craters saturating the access lines.
4 The main double track Paris-Le Treport line south of the target severed in five places.
5 Six other medium sized buildings completely gutted.

The photograph 'Chambly Rail Depot' in the photo section shows not only the damage but, in conjunction with the night photograph plot on page 80, also illustrates the accuracy of the attack. The raid was both well planned and executed, but the loss rate (4.2 per cent) should perhaps have given some warning of what was to happen at Mailly le Camp, two nights later.

Notes

1 In addition to the attack on Chambly, Bomber Command aircraft were also attacking rail targets at Tours, Malines and St Gislen.
2 The Stirlings had some difficulty in obtaining higher altitudes with full bomb loads and on that occasion Flt Lt J McAllister, piloting aircraft 'J', had to jettison four of his 500-lb bombs in order to gain the altitude prescribed.
3 See Chapter 4.
4 At his debriefing Sqn Ldr Reid reported having seen a fire at that time, to the south of the target. He thought it was either a crashed aircraft or some jettisoned bombs.
5 See Appendix 11.
6 There was some discrepancy in the records at this point. Medland was reported earlier as having been an 'early return' because of engine failure.

CHAPTER TWELVE

Multiple Attacks — 19/20 May 1944

An analysis of the attacks on rail facilities in North France and Belgium during April, showed that it was possible to confuse German night fighters by hitting two or more targets in one night. However, the key to success lay in choosing targets which were separated as widely as possible.

For example, on the night of 10/11 April, four of the five targets to be attacked lay within a radius of fifty miles of each other, and the aircraft loss rate was 3.2 per cent. On the night of 20/21 April, four targets were attacked within the larger radius of eighty miles, and the loss rate fell to 1.2 per cent. Confirmation of this trend came on the 10/11 May when, during an attack on four targets within the smaller radius of sixty-five miles, the loss rate rose again to 2.5 per cent.

As will be explained later in this book, there were other reasons for the heavy losses during the attack on Mailly le Camp on 3/4 May, but matters were not helped by the fact that only two targets were attacked in northern France and that both forces attacking used much the same route.

On the night of 19/20 May almost 600 heavy bombers were despatched to attack five rail centres in northern France, all of which lay within a radius of 150 miles from Caen. On the same night a further 180 bombers attacked radar and coastal defence installations on the Normandy and Picardy coasts, and another 120 took part in a wide range of tasks which included a Mosquito attack on Cologne, minelaying and intruder operations. Of the total of 900 aircraft only seven failed to return, of which two almost certainly collided over the target, bringing the loss rate through enemy action down to 0.5 per cent.

Of the five rail targets that were attacked, three (Le Mans, Orléans and Tours) were severely damaged; Boulogne was damaged but many of the bombs fell wide of the target, and Amiens was so covered in cloud that most of the bombers were withdrawn before they had bombed, in order to preserve the lives of the French civilians.

Five of the heavy bomber groups were involved, including No 8 (PFF) Group. That Group distributed its forces in order to mark four of the five targets, using 'Oboe'. No 5 Group carried out its own marking, using the low-level techniques which were proving to be generally successful.

On 19 May the weather was terrible: low cloud, mist and fog covered most of the bases during the morning; but a forecast of a temporary respite at least in the early part of the evening, and reasonable conditions over France, led to a decision to 'go'. In the event, low cloud and rain affected most of Yorkshire again before midnight and the more southern bases by approximately 0130 hr. The French targets were covered by varying amounts of cloud having a base of 5-8000 ft.

The times set for the attacks ranged from 0025 hr for Le Mans to 0120 hr for Amiens, and the routes out and back were so arranged that those returning from attacks should not clash with those on their outward run.

The reader might be forgiven for thinking that those precautions were elementary and routine, but the point is made because it should be fully understood that the planners, and all those connected with mounting those multiple attacks, had very little time in which to work everything out and issue the necessary orders. Because the lives of the crews were at stake, the tension amongst ground crews and Headquarters Staff must have approached that within the crew rooms. No conscientious officer or fitter could help but worry in case he had forgotten some vital point that could lead to disaster. If modern-day psychiatric theories are to be believed, it is a constant wonder to the author how those so-called 'stress related activities' did not result in all those who were involved becoming jibbering idiots.

In addition to the five aircraft that were missing from the attacks on rail facilities, two others crashed on returning to England, and one was so badly damaged by flak that it had to be written off. A further six aircraft received varying degrees of damage as a result of enemy action, and five were damaged in minor incidents, including a collision over the target.

On the morning following the attacks, Spitfires of Nos 541 and 542 Photo-Reconnaissance Squadrons took off from Benson to photograph the damage. Boulogne and Orléans were clear, but it was not until 23 May that Le Mans and Tours were eventually photographed successfully in hazy conditions. When analysed by the Photographic Interpreters at Medmenham, they confirmed the enthusiastic claims made by the bomber crews at their debriefings.

Extracts from the Immediate Photo Interpretation Reports (IPIRs) are included in the more detailed and individual narratives contained in this chapter. Prior to reading these more comprehensive accounts the reader may benefit from consulting the following brief summary of the night's work.[1]

Target	Group Nos	No of aircraft sent	No of aircraft attacking	Time on target	No of aircraft reported missing
Orléans	1, 8	122	112	0037–0058 hr	1
Le Mans	3, 8	116	110	0017–0040 hr	3
Tours	5	117	107	0036–0102 hr	0
Boulogne	4, 8	143	134	0058–0111 hr	0
Amiens	5, 8	121	40	0111–0133 hr	1

Le Mans — 19/20 May 1944
Bomber Command Target Z444

The first and most westerly of the rail targets attacked on 19/20 May were the marshalling yards and repair shops situated on the south side of Le Mans, between the rivers Sarthe and Huisne. The area presented a satisfactory objective because the marshalling yards were surrounded by other attractive targets, which included the aero-engine plant of Gnome and Rhone, a Junkers aircraft repair facility, a Renault factory producing tank components and an airfield. Therefore, if they missed the actual target the bombers would still have some effect on the German war effort.

The attack was to take place in two waves each lasting three minutes, and was timed to start at 0025 hr on 20 May. 100 Lancasters of No 3 Group, and 11 Lancasters of No 8 (PFF) Group were mostly airborne at 2230 hr on 19 May; four 'Oboe'-equipped Mosquitos, two from each one of Nos 105 and 109 Squadrons, took off at approximately 2345 hr, the same day.

The route out went via the Sussex coast, then almost due south to the target, which took the aircraft close to Le Havre. From Le Mans the bombers flew west for a while before turning northwest to the base of the Cherbourg peninsula, close to the Channel Islands, and then north to cross the coast of Dorset near Bridport.

As they headed out over the Channel most crews reported that the weather showed some improvement, but as they approached the target there was more cloud and navigators were busy preparing timed runs from points picked out by H2S radar.

No 8 (PFF) Group's plan for the marking was that the Mosquitos would drop red and green TIs, using 'Oboe', starting at 0017 hr, and that the Lancasters of Nos 7 and 156 Squadrons would illuminate the target with flares starting from 0019 to 0021 hr. Having identified the Aim Point, the Master Bomber was to drop yellow and white TIs, assess the accuracy of all the indicators and direct the Main Force accordingly.

The marking started on time, but only two of the Mosquitos (one piloted by Sqn Ldr Blessing of No 105 Squadron, the other by Sqn Ldr Cobb of No 109 Squadron) coped with the problems caused by having to operate at the extreme range of 'Oboe'. Unable to see any ground detail, or the TIs, the Lancasters dropped their flares using radar, some having to make a timed run from the more easily identified town of Alencon, approximately thirty miles to the north.

The experienced Master Bomber, New Zealander Wg Cdr T F Barron flying aircraft 'Charlie' of No 7 Squadron, soon realised that no one was going to see either the target or the markers unless they got under the cloud base, which was at approximately 8000 ft. He then ordered the Main Force to do just that. Although most of No 3 Group's crews heard and complied with the order, there were a few who claimed that they did not hear it owing to too much "chat" over the radio. Sqn Ldr W G Devas, piloting aircraft 'B' of No 514 Squadron made no less than five runs over the target before abandoning the mission, but Flt Sgt Peck, flying aircraft 'D' from the same squadron did hear the order and produced the first recorded photograph which was timed at 0025 hr — exactly on time. The Aim Point was clearly visible on the photograph[2].

The attack progressed well, in spite of the cloud and the quite heavy anti-aircraft fire from the Luftwaffe's Flak Arm, who had suddenly found targets within range of their lighter guns. As the marking died away the Master Bomber was heard to order his deputy, Sqn Ldr J M Dennis, flying aircraft 'Roger', to re-mark the target at the centre of the TIs with more white markers. Dennis had successfully controlled the Main Force at Chambly three weeks earlier, and was equally 'on the ball' with his marking at Le Mans. It was presumed that the two planes collided during this phase of the attack because the order was the last that anyone heard from either Barron or Dennis.[3] Consequently, without the necessary directions the bombing became rather scattered; but although many of the bombs fell outside the actual railway facilities some found the alternative targets already mentioned and there were some large explosions on the ground between 0030 and 0040 hr.

As well as the loss of the Master Bomber and his deputy, it is almost certain that Plt Off S S Atkin and his crew of No 115 Squadron's aircraft 'F' fell to light anti-aircraft guns, whilst pulling away from the target, and the aircraft crashed to the south of it. Unfortunately, it was carrying a second pilot, Fg Off J V Hayward, making the loss in terms of aircrew that much worse. Several other aircraft were hit, including those of Flt Lts Gray and Choppin of No 514 Squadron and aircraft 'E' of No 622 Squadron. Flt Lt Morrison of No 405 Squadron and one of the illuminators, had his aircraft damaged slightly just prior to bombing. There were no attacks by fighters over the target, however Flt Sgt Topham, piloting aircraft 'F' of No 514 Squadron had an encounter on the homeward run with a Ju 88, about thirty miles from the target. His gunners both claimed hits on the enemy aircraft.

It was hardly No 514 Squadron's best night. As well as the incidents recorded above Plt Off Greenwood was one of those who could not see the target, forcing him to abandon the mission. Flt Sgt Cossens had to return early with technical failure; Plt Off Delacour narrowly missed another Lancaster over the target; and Flt Sgt Shearing's aircraft crashed at Newmarket. He was killed together with his crew, except the air bomber, Fg Off Peake (a Canadian who baled out successfully)[4] and the rear gunner, Sgt Smart, who was thrown clear in the crash.

For some reason, yet to be discovered, three aircraft of No 15 Squadron acted as hosts to pilots of No 90 Squadron — probably not a popular event amongst the more superstitious crews. All the crews complained at the debriefing of too much chatter over the radio, which interfered, they said, with the instructions given by the Master Bomber.

No 622 Squadron seemed to have had a fairly uneventful night. All its aircraft had taken off from their base at Mildenhall by 2210 hr and had returned by 0300 hr, having bombed within their allotted time span. No 75 New Zealand Squadron had a reasonable night also at Le Mans. Its crews reported good results and no special incidents, and all twenty-four aircraft had returned to their base at Mepal by 0340 hr. They had been in the air for an average time of 4 hr 55 min, and each one had dropped 12,000 lb of high-explosive bombs.

The attack led to much re-routing of German troop trains from the South of France, and to delays during the early part of the Normandy Campaign.

At the time of the attack the German night fighter control of Jagddivision 4 was concerned more with the protection of the routes into southwest Germany, and although a new beacon had been established as far west as Orléans (code named Venus), the majority of the night fighters were called away to the St Quentin area, thus leaving Le Mans to be defended primarily by the Luftwaffe's Flak Arm.

Attempts by No 541 (PR) Squadron to photograph the results of the raid were thwarted by cloud which persisted until 23 May when Fg Offs Darling and Hill, both of 'A' Flight at Benson, managed to obtain some rather hazy pictures. However, an attack by the Canadian No 6 Group which took place during the previous night had added to the devastation and masked the effects of the earlier raid. Nevertheless, the Photographic Interpreters noted from Hill's photographs that there had been several very large explosions amongst what had been concentrations of wagons in the reception and forwarding sidings, and the observation gave rise to some speculation about the presence of ammunition trains. The IPIR[5] also recorded that serious damage had been caused to the carriage and wagon repair sheds, that all but one building in the Junkers repair plant had been destroyed completely, and that the Renault and Gnome Rhone factories had been hit badly.

In four attacks between mid-March and 22 May, RAF Bomber

Command despatched 760 heavy bombers against the railway centre at Le Mans. The aircraft had dropped more than 3500 tons of bombs and five aircraft only had been reported as missing. Two nights after the attack of 20 May, most of the No 3 Group crews were to find themselves back in 'Happy Valley' attacking Duisburg.

Orleans (Les Aubrais) — 19/20 May 1944
Bomber Command Target No Z432

Situated at the extreme range of 'Oboe', Orleans formed an important junction between the lines from Paris to Tours and the Loire Valley, and those from Troyes and Vierzon to Chartres and Normandy. An important rail bridge over the River Loire was situated south of the target area, and was critical to the movement of those trains which ran in a southeast/northwest direction, via Châteaudun, to Normandy. The railway yards and bridge lay on the route attempted by the 9th SS Panzer Division in June as they struggled from the Eastern Front, via Strasbourg to Normandy. (The delays imposed on that Division will be discussed in some detail later.)

The plan of attack was that four 'Oboe'-equipped Mosquitos of Nos 105 and 109 Squadrons were to drop red and green TIs at H-9 and H-7, followed by illuminating and marking by Lancasters of No 635 (PFF) Squadron. The Master Bomber, Wg Cdr W T Brooks, and his deputy, Flt Lt Smith, both of No 635 Squadron, were to direct the attack which was to take place between 0045-0050-H hr to H+5 hr. No 8 (PFF) Group's Lancasters were to aim their flares at the TIs at H−6 to H−4 hr, then orbit the target and make their own bombing runs.

Carrying the minimum load of 1320 gallons and a mixture of 1000- and 500-lb bombs, No 1 Group's Lancasters took off from their Lincolnshire bases in poor weather. Several aircraft reported icing, and at least one aircraft, of No 626 Squadron, had to abandon the trip for that reason.

In its unusually chatty Operational Records Book, No 550 Squadron recorded that fifteen of its aircraft took off in the space of fourteen minutes, led by its new CO Wg Cdr Connolly. It was the first trip of Plt Off Dunkelow and his crew who, sadly, went missing over Duisburg two nights later. Heading out over the Channel, via Beachy Head, the Squadron's aircraft experienced the same clearance as those of No 3 Group who had taken much the same course to Le Mans. Approaching Dieppe, a proportion of the crews began to drop their bundles of 'Window' then, while the weather was improving still further south of Paris, the force swung round to attack the target from the northeast.

While the last of the No 3 Group Lancasters were pulling up from the flak-infested skies above Le Mans, No 8 (PFF) Group's Mosquitos and Lancasters were positioning themselves to mark Orleans. Again, the target was at the extreme range of 'Oboe' and none of the four Mosquitos was able to release its markers. Consequently, the illuminators opened the attack by dropping the first flare at 0038 hr. In clear weather, with only a little ground haze, the deputy Master Bomber was able to identify the Aim Point, and at 0039 hr he released the first white TIs. A minute later, the Master Bomber dropped a yellow TI which fell approximately 400 yd northeast of the Aim Point. He gave instructions, over the radio, for the Main Force to bomb on that with a slight undershoot.[6]

The first bombs to be released by the Main Force were those of Plt Off Jones, flying Lancaster 'U' of No 550 Squadron. Taken at 0044 hr, one minute ahead of schedule, the photograph showed the area of release, rather than the point of bomb impact. The bombers were approaching at 180 mph, from the northeast, against a 10-15 mph southwest wind and at an average height of 10,000 ft, and most of the photographs taken recorded ground detail some distance northeast of the Aim Point (which would seem reasonable, given the factors involved).

Early radio instructions by the Master Bomber were not received too clearly, but crews of No 12 Squadron reported that things improved after a change of frequency had been made. He was then heard clearly by most crews, except one from No 103 Squadron which still could not hear the necessary directions. As a result, they complied with their standing instructions and took their bombs home. As the attack developed, the Master Bomber corrected the tendency to undershoot and re-directed the bombers to different markers on several occasions; this could have caused some confusion. However, at approximately 0047 hr heavy smoke, originating from an earlier huge explosion, rose to 5000 ft and obscured the markers. At that point Wg Cdr Brooks gave the instruction to bomb the centre of the fires. Fg Off A J Hiscock of No 156 Squadron, who had made two earlier approaches without identifying the aiming point, was able then to make his third and finally successful bombing run.

In spite of being classed as 'a quiet trip' by most of the crews, there were several incidents of early returns because of one problem or another, and Plt Off J H Booth and his crew, from No 166 Squadron, failed to return home. From observations made by several other crews there was little doubt that they had fallen victims to a German night fighter southwest of Paris. The speculation is supported by the fact that Booth is buried in a French graveyard at Dreux, and one of his gunners, Sgt J Terry is buried at Thiroy, sixteen miles northwest of Versailles.

The Main Force included six Lancasters of No 300 (Polish)

Squadron, based at Faldingworth. Five of them attacked the target between 0045 and 0048 hr with good results. The sixth aircraft returned early with a failure of its navigational equipment. On the outward trip, some of its crews reported to have seen an unidentified aircraft using a powerful red searchlight.

Although the sixteen Lancasters of No 101 Squadron were carrying their special operators, no report of the success or otherwise of their jamming activities that night can be found; but the spread of their take-off and landing times suggested that they were engaged both in jamming and bombing. Each aircraft dropped eleven 1000-lb and four 500-lb bombs onto the target.

Between 0037 and 0058 hr 112 Lancasters of Nos 1 and 8 (PFF) Groups had dropped nearly 1500 bombs (including two 4000-lb 'cookies' carried by No 635 Squadron), which totalled 615 tons of HE. At their debriefings, crews talked enthusiastically about the large fires and the general success of the attack.

The reactions of the Germans revealed the problems that confronted their fighter controllers. Three groups of fighters were 'scrambled', mainly to the Paris-Caen area, but at 2345 hr some of the crews were ordered to fly to the St Quentin area (presumably in case other bombers, which at that time were making for Amiens and Boulogne, were heading for southwest Germany). Nine sightings of enemy aircraft were reported by No 1 Group but there were no combats other than that, presumably, of the No 166 Squadron aircraft which was missing. The enemy fighters were ordered to land at 0202 hr.

On returning to their bases, via Beachy Head, between 0230 and 0300 hr, No 1 Group's squadrons found that mist was forming on the Lincolnshire Wolds, and a number of aircraft were diverted to airfields further to the south, including some of those from No 166 Squadron who landed at an American airfield in East Anglia. The weather at Elsham Wolds, No 156 Squadron's base, was particularly bad, and four of the Squadron's aircraft spent the rest of the night away from their base.

Just over five hours later, a No 541 Squadron Spitfire XI, piloted by Fg Off Lott, a Canadian, was over Orléans to photograph the devastation. Shortly afterwards, the Photographic Interpreters at Medmenham peered, almost unbelievingly, through their unsophisticated, type 'D' stereoscopes to see the smoke still rising and appearing to come out of the lenses. Their Immediate Photographic Interpretation Report noted 200 craters in the marshalling sidings, a large number of wagons destroyed and some still burning.[7]

Tours (St Pierre de Corps) — 19/20 May 1944
Bomber Command Target No Z434A

At much the same time as the No 1 Group squadrons were pounding Orleans, those of No 5 Group were carrying out a self-contained attack on Tours, approximately seventy miles to the southwest and out of the range of 'Oboe'. It was through the important junction of Tours that both the 17th Panzer Grenadier and the infamous 2nd SS Panzer Divisions were to try to reach the battlefield from their pre-invasion bases in southwest France.

Although Tours is generally regarded as located on the River Loire, there were two other smaller rivers which ran close by the southern part of the town and which also ran in an east-west direction. The old town, its main railway station and the rail complex of St Pierre de Corps were located between the Loire and the middle river, the Cher. Six miles to the south, the River Indre formed another barrier to travel in a south-north direction. The two smaller rivers ran into the Loire a few miles west of the town.

The target area was comprised of extensive marshalling yards, running in an east-west direction; wagon repair sheds of both the SCNF and CIMT; goods transhipment sheds; and a depot which housed more than 100 electric locomotives. Scattered to the south and east of the main area were the rail stores depots, goods depots, the main passenger station and locomotive workshops. The total area covered by all the facilities amounted to approximately 300 acres[8].

Working to the criteria of Zuckerman's plan, the planners were presented with the problem of how to deliver the required equivalent of nearly 10,000 500-lb bombs (2500 short tons) onto the target area to make it a Category A target.

The following account describes the third attack on Tours by Bomber Command since 10 April. In the first attack 173 heavy bombers had dropped nearly 800 tons of high explosives. During the second and smaller raid on 1/2 May, fifty aircraft dropped 186 tons of high explosives.

The plan for the third attack was that the target would be illuminated with flares, by the light of which 'Red Spot Fires' were to be dropped onto the marking points, and, if necessary, they were to be supplemented or cancelled by the Master Bomber and his deputies. The plan also contained some fairly complicated instructions regarding the use of offset markers and the release of bombs on the Aim Points. Over the first Aim Point the bombs were to be released so that the first bomb of each 'stick' was aimed at the markers. For the second Aim Point, the bombsights were to be set so that the centre bomb of each 'stick' was to be aimed at the markers. In both cases the bomb distributors were to be set so that there would be twenty yards between the craters. The average bomb load carried by the Lancasters of No 5 Group was ten 1000-lb and four 500-lb bombs, and each aircraft carried 1400 gallons of fuel, putting each aircraft within the limits of its all up take-off weight of 65,000 lb.

Amid some fierce argument, the Mosquitos of No 627 Squadron and the Lancasters of Nos 83 and 97 (PFF) Squadrons had been transferred from the Pathfinder Group to AVM Cochrane's Group. No 627 Squadron was learning quickly the art of low-level marking, using dive-bombing techniques which had been developed by Leonard Cheshire's No 617 Squadron. The latter squadron had been withdrawn from operations after the Mailly Le Camp attack of 3/4 May, and was preparing for its special 'spoof' operations in the forthcoming invasion. Fourteen aircraft of No 83 (PFF) were used to illuminate the target, and the Master Bomber and his deputy came from the same Squadron; No 627 Squadron sent four Mosquitos as target markers.

The Lancasters began taking off from their Lincolnshire bases at approximately 2200 hr. Nos 463 and 467 (Australian) Squadrons were seen off from Waddington by John Curtin, the Australian Prime Minister, who had been dining in the Officers Mess during a visit to the base.

The weather was not good at the time of take-off, but it did improve over the English Channel. The route to Tours was similar to, but a little more to the east than that taken to Le Mans. The bombers crossed the English coast near Seaford and the French coast near to Fécamp before going straight to the target and attacking it from the north.

The first flare to be released was probably that of Flt Lt Hellier, piloting aircraft 'O' of No 83 (PFF) Squadron, which was timed at 0036.30 hr — eight and a half minutes before zero hour. By 0039 hr the target was well illuminated. Shortly afterwards two No 627 Squadron Mosquitos, piloted by Flt Lts Peck and Grey, dived from 5000 ft to 1500 ft to deliver their 'Red Spot Fires'; these were assessed by the markers as having a mean point of impact (MPI) about 500 yd west of the two Aim Points.

Wg Cdr Taite, the Master Bomber piloting aircraft 'N', was having problems with his VHF radio, and the Main Force was anxiously awaiting a broadcast giving the wind to which the bombsights could be set. Taite handed over control to his deputy, Wg Cdr Jeudwine, flying aircraft 'A'. Jeudwine's navigator quickly worked out the wind, but most crews claimed they did not receive this until after zero hour, which was 0045 hr.

The initial marking by No 627 Squadron had been so accurate that the two other Mosquitos were not required, consequently Fg Off 'Benny' Goodman[9] and Sqn Ldr Mackenzie took their markers home. No other markers appeared to have been released by the Master Bomber or his deputy.

The late receipt of the wind information for bombing caused some delay in the bombing by the Main Force. The first recorded photograph was that taken by Plt Off Bowman, flying aircraft 'D' of No 463 Squadron, and was timed at 0049 hr. The rate of bombing reached a peak two minutes later. The plot formed by the centrepoints of the photographs showed two groups, one to the north of the northern Aim Point, the other quite close to the southern Aim Point. Because the aircraft were approaching from the north in a light cross-wind, the information confirmed the assessment made by the deputy Master Bomber that the bombs were well placed around the north Aim Point, but that there had been some overshooting of the south Aim Point.

Crews from the other Australian squadron, No 476, complained that the photo-flashes and flares had both destroyed their bomb aimers' night vision. Plt Off W Mackay collided with another Lancaster over the target at 7000 ft, its tail wheel was badly damaged but it managed to land safely at Swinderby. Plt Off Ainsworth complied with standing instructions and abandoned the mission because of a faulty bombsight.

Another crew which abandoned the sortie over the target was that of No 9 Squadron's Flt Sgt Redfern. They claimed that by the time they had received the information about the wind, the markers could not be seen. However, the other crews of the Squadron claimed that their bombing had been well centred. The Squadron's aircraft 'Y' was damaged by moderate anti-aircraft fire which came from six heavy and two light guns in the target area. The light guns were described as 'hosepiping'[10] to 6000 ft; because the Squadron's average bombing height was more than 8000 ft the damage must have been caused by the heavier 88 mm guns.[11]

Bombsight problems occurred in the Lancaster flown by Plt Off Street of No 61 Squadron and he also abandoned the trip and returned early. The Squadron's Plt Off Auckland was running in, at 6000 ft, to the target when another Lancaster came over him from the starboard side and they collided, damaging both port engines and port wing. In spite of the variation in reported heights, it must be remembered that the speed of events and general tensions during bombing were such that some inaccuracies in reporting were inevitable. Therefore, it seems almost certain that the other aircraft was the No 476 Squadron Lancaster mentioned above. Fg Off Keith of No 50 Squadron could not hear the deputy Master Bomber's instructions and, in accordance with the standing instructions, broke off the attack and jettisoned most of his bombs into the English Channel.

At 0102 hr the deputy Master Bomber was no longer able to assess the accuracy of bombing because of smoke and cloud, and he gave the order to cease bombing. A few only were affected by that order.

From start to finish the attack had lasted twenty-six minutes, during which time 107 aircraft had dropped 477 tons of HE from an average height of 8000 ft. In terms of the number of bombs dropped that was 1300 — approximately one bomb for every second of the attack. Many crews reported have seen a large explosion at approximately 0055 hr.

The weather forecast for the return to bases had warned of visibility problems over Yorkshire, but that better conditions would prevail further south. In the event, low cloud had reached Yorkshire by midnight and patches of mist and fog were settling over Lincolnshire by 0200 hr. Diversions were plentiful, but some of No 106 Squadron's crews got back to their base at Metheringham by courtesy of the newly installed 'Fido',[12] which dispersed the fog enough to allow some landings to take place. Less fortunate was Plt Off Irving, piloting aircraft 'U' of No 50 Squadron. Diverted to Benson, he was approaching the main southwest/northeast runway when he hit the corner of a barn which formed part of Crowmarsh Battle Farm, a mile or so from the end of the runway. Irving, his navigator Sgt Jewell, and his bomb aimer Sgt Drever were all killed; the rest of the crew got away with shock and minor injuries.[13]

As with the raid on Le Mans, most of the German night fighters had been called away, nearly 200 miles northeast of Tours. Consequently, there were no reports of combats on the way home, and most of the aircraft had landed safely 'somewhere in England' at 0500 hr. The official analysis of the raid credited the Force with having been over enemy-held territory for 2 hrs 10 min of their average flight time of six hours.

Tours was cloud-covered until 23 May when Fg Off L S Darling of No 541 Squadron was able to obtain some aerial photographs. In their first phase report the Photographic Interpreters sorted out the new damage from the old enough to say that the bombing on 19/20 May had been heavily concentrated around the west end of the target; that the locomotive depot and workshops had been severely damaged; the rail lines to Saumur and Poitiers had been cut and the embankments broken down; and that a bridge over the canal had partly collapsed.

Two nights later most of the crews involved in the third attack on Tours were despatched to Duisburg, where several losses resulted.

Boulogne — 19/20 May 1944
Bomber Command Target No Z805A

Well within the range of 'Oboe' ground stations, and presenting a good response to those aircraft fitted with H2S radar, the target was identified easily, even though there were in fact two large rail complexes within one-and-a-half miles of each other. The target was the town's marshalling yards, which formed the more northerly of the two complexes, and contained two rail bridges over the River Liane, a locomotive depot, town passenger station and a goods depot. The north end of the target area terminated near the area which was to become well-known to thousands of British tourists travelling by ferry boat from Folkestone, and by yachtsmen using the town's marina.

The plan for the attack was the same as those used at Le Mans and Orléans and involved No 8 Group Lancasters and No 4 Group Halifaxes. The route out took the Halifaxes from their Yorkshire bases over Dungeness then southeast across the thirty miles of the English Channel, straight to Boulogne. The bombers were to attack as they came in from the northwest, then carry on inland for a short distance before turning west to cross the French coast near Le Touquet and heading again for Dungeness. The average number of track miles for the whole trip was 560 and the aircraft were not expected to be over enemy-held territory for much longer than ten minutes.

Zero hour for the attack was set for 0105 hr on 20 May and, acting on instructions, the 'Oboe'-equipped Mosquitos of Nos 105 and 109 Squadrons approached the target at approximately 0100 hr — just when the Lancasters of No 1 Group were leaving Orléans nearly 200 miles to the south. Both No 105 Squadron Mosquitos had problems. One, piloted by Flt Lt J W Jordan, was upset near the point of release by the slipstream of an unidentified aircraft,[14] the other sustained a technical failure. No 109 Squadron had slightly better luck; one of their two aircraft, flown by Fg Off A A Dray, managed to release four red target indicators, using 'Oboe', at 0057 hr.

By the light of flares, dropped by members of his own squadron, the Master Bomber, Sqn Ldr E K Creswell of No 35 (PFF) Squadron, estimated that the target indicators had overshot the Aim Point by 150-200 yd and he instructed his deputy, Wg Cdr L M Wheltham, to put down some white target indicators. Wheltham's markers were better placed and Creswell gave instructions to the Main Force to bomb on those. Meanwhile No 582 Squadron aircraft had been dropping additional flares and the whole area became so well-lit that the Halifaxes were able to see the target as they flew over the English Channel.

The first recorded photograph was that taken from aircraft 'F' of No 76 Squadron. Timed at 0104 hr the centrepoint of the photograph showed ground detail approximately 750 yd northwest of the Aim Point. Given that the aircraft was heading southeast, at about 160 mph and at 15,000 ft, it looked to be a good shot. However, having seen some general undershoot, the Master Bomber gave instructions for a one-second overshoot; bombs were then seen to be well centred around the Aim Point.

Smoke from the bombs, flares and markers soon made it difficult to identify the white target indicators. Sqn Ldr Creswell dropped a yellow marker and, as the white went out, he gave fresh instructions to bomb 100-150 yd east of his yellow marker using a one-second overshoot. Some crews complained that the Master Bomber's instructions were distorted, and, because they could no longer see the outline of the target, one or two aircraft from Nos 76 and 158 Squadrons had to abandon their mission.

At 0107 hr a huge orange and red explosion added to the already dense smoke which by now was covering the target and drifting over the docks and coast. Two minutes later no target markers could be seen at all and, with the lives of friendly civilians at stake, the Master Bomber issued the code word 'Cartwheel' — cease bombing. One crew affected by the order was that of Sqn Ldr McMillan in aircraft 'A' of No 582 Squadron. Having dropped their flares, they had already abandoned one bombing run in response to new directions, then on their third run they received the code word 'Cartwheel'. Frustrated, they jettisoned their remaining bombs over the sea and headed for home, where their aircraft suffered a brake failure and overshot the runway.

In the short time they were over the target 101 Halifaxes and 32 Lancasters had dropped 2000 bombs, three-quarters of which weighed 500 lb, the remainder were mostly 1000-lb bombs and included two 4000-lb 'cookies'.

The attack on the target was close to others which were taking place on the coastal defences, and attracted a few enemy night fighters. There was some moderate anti-aircraft fire both from the port area and from ships off-shore.[15] The fire was mostly in the form of a loose barrage between 7-10,000 ft. Ten miles out from the target Flt Sgt K V Bourne, an Australian piloting aircraft 'T' of No 158 Squadron, was attacked by an enemy fighter, but his mid-upper gunner, Sgt L Rigby, returned the fire and the enemy called off the attack. His troubles were not over, however. On his first bombing run the bomb doors would not open; by the time the trouble was sorted out he had received the codeword 'Cartwheel'. Plt Off Hamilton of No 640 Squadron sustained slight flak damage to his starboard engine and landed at Old Buckingham. Aircraft 'Z' of No 10 Squadron, piloted by Flt Lt Henderson, a Canadian, had small holes in its perspex windscreen and in the port wing.

The weather had cleared shortly after the Halifaxes had left their Yorkshire bases and was not too bad on their return. Excepting the incidents mentioned already, most of the aircraft were back safely on the ground by 0300 hr, having been airborne for about three-and-a-half hours.

Four hours later, Flt Lt Donaghue of No 541 (PR) Squadron was climbing into his Spitfire XI at Benson. He had returned by 1030 hr, having photographed Boulogne. The film from his f52 cameras was rushed through the processing machines and the Photographic Interpreters issued their First Phase Report No K2207. Trying to sort out new damage from old presented some problems. They credited No 4 Group with having destroyed two buildings near the locomotive shed and for scoring many hits on the sorting sidings. There was no further damage to the main station or goods depot, but there were a number of hits on factories adjacent to the target area, and a small amount of damage in the residential area, west of the target area. The railway layout, and even the alignment of the river were both altered greatly after the war. At the time of writing, the map of the area bears little resemblance to wartime aerial photography.

Amiens (Longueau) — 19/20 May 1944
Bomber Command Target No Z446

Two previous attacks by Bomber Command in March had caused severe damage to the marshalling yards at Amiens, but there was more than one reason why another attack had to be made before D-Day.

First, there were still some parts of the complex to be 'finished off'. Second, a further attack would lend credence to the belief held by some German commanders that the invasion would take place in the Pas de Calais area. In fact, the destruction of the railcentre proved to be as important to the battle of Normandy as many of those targets further south and west were. Many units of the German 15th Army, stationed north of the Somme, and the 2nd Panzer Division would eventually attempt to travel by rail to Normandy from their bases east and north of the town.

Situated southeast of Amiens, Longueau Rail Centre comprised not only extensive marshalling yards but also railway workshops, locomotive depots, and important junctions for the lines from Arras, Tergnier and Compiègne, with those from Rouen, Beauvais and the Pas de Calais area. In 1990 the railyards had been separated from Glisy Airfield to the east by a ring road which ran around the east side of the town.

The attack was timed to take place at 0120 hr on 20 May and was the last of the five attacks on the rail targets in northern France that night. Two attacks on the coastal defence batteries near Dunkirk and Caen were to follow shortly.

Aircraft from Nos 5 and 8 (PFF) Groups were involved, illustrating that, in spite of rivalry over marking techniques, these two groups did work together sometimes. Unlike Tours, Amiens was within 'Oboe' range, and Nos 105 and 109 Squadrons used it to mark the target.

The plan called for the Mosquitos of those two squadrons to open the attack by dropping yellow target indicators to be used as proximity markers. The target would be then illuminated by aircraft of No 97 (PFF) Squadron, which together with No 83 (PFF) Squadron had recently been attached to No 5 Group. Mosquitos of No 627 Squadron would then go in low and drop Red Spot Fires (RSF) onto the Aim Point. The Main Force crews of No 5 Group were to aim their bombs using wind details to be broadcast by the Pathfinders. The Master Bomber, from No 97 (PFF) Squadron, was to direct the attack using back-up aircraft which were to drop yellow and green target indicators to highlight the most accurate markers. The first 'Oboe'-equipped aircraft were to drop their markers at H−8 minutes.

The weather on take-off from the Lincolnshire bases was much the same as that for the attacks on other targets that night, but the cloud was thicker over Amiens. In fact, some crews used 'Gee' to get them to the target area. Crews from No 44 (Rhodesian) Squadron were critical of the Met forecast, which had led them to believe that the convection cloud would have cleared away by the time they arrived at the target.

Most of the No 5 Group Squadrons were airborne at 2315 hr on 19 May. Having an average of 550 track miles to cover they expected to be airborne for almost four hours, of which approximately one hour and twenty minutes would be spent over France. The route out was via Hastings, across to the French coast north of Dieppe, then southeast before turning north and swinging round to attack the target from the northeast. The return flight took them close to Dieppe again.

Mosquito navigators Flt Lt H L Plummer and Plt Off B McPherson both of No 105 Squadron, received their release signals, and the first proximity markers went down a little ahead of schedule, at 0110 hr. A third Mosquito, flown by Flt Lt Dixon was not required. Two No 109 Squadron aircraft had technical failures, and a reserve aircraft was also stood down.

The markers were seen by the illuminators of No 97 (PFF) Squadron. In the light of some rather scattered flares, Flt Lt Steere, of No 627 Squadron, dived to drop Red Spot Fires but, confused by the scattered flares and cloud, his markers fell onto another group of sidings which were located some 2000 yd from the Aim Point. He was followed by another Mosquito which made the same mistake. Realising their mistakes, the two pilots informed the Master Bomber and immediately attempted to mark the correct point, which they had just recognised. Unfortunately, both aircraft had trouble with bombs hanging up and were unable to mark the correct point.

Meanwhile the Master Bomber, Wg Cdr J Simpson piloting aircraft 'D' of No 97 (PFF) Squadron, had been experiencing difficulties with his VHF radio, and had handed over to his deputy. A yellow target indicator was dropped to cancel the wrongly placed RSFs. Further attempts were made to drop new RSFs onto the Aim Point, but, as in the previous runs, the bombs hung up. Consequently, there were no correctly placed markers.

The first attack recorded on film was that by Plt Off Baxter of No 44 Squadron, piloting aircraft 'A', whose bomb aimer released his bombs triggering the flash at 0120 hr — on schedule. Those photographs which could be matched with ground details seemed to show that the bombs were fairly well placed, given the direction of attack, altitude and speed of the aircraft concerned. A few Lancasters from most of the squadrons involved did attack, bringing the total to forty of the 123 aircraft despatched.

At 0123 hr, unable to distinguish either the markers or the correct target, the deputy Master Bomber gave the order to cease bombing. In spite of confirmation of the order by WT (Morse), some aircraft continued to bomb the general area covered by the flares and others bombed where some of the original markers had been seen to go down. According to No 97 (PFF) Squadron's Operations Record Book the deputy Master Bomber re-issued the cancellation order at 0128 hr, but there were several discrepancies in the times of receipt of the cancellation order in the records of other squadrons. However, at 0125 hr most of the Main Force were glad to be flying away from what was described by one No 49 Squadron pilot as 'a highly dangerous situation, with thick cloud making target identification almost impossible and the risk of collision very high'.

There was some criticism by experienced pilots of the handling of the attack. Some thought that the Main Force should have been ordered to descend below the cloud base, which at the time was approximately 5000 ft, thus echoing the more successful attack at Le Mans. At his debriefing Wg Cdr Simpson defended his deputy's decision to call off the attack. In retrospect, and bearing in mind the standing instructions regarding the bombing of these targets and the need to preserve the lives of French civilians, it seemed to have been the correct decision.

Anti-aircraft fire over the target was slight. Plt Off Carrington of No 44 Squadron arrived home with a small hole in the mid-upper turret of aircraft 'D'. Sadly, the crew were not so lucky two nights later when they were reported missing during the attack on Duisburg. Fg Off Smart was piloting one of the No 207 Squadron aircraft that did bomb. He had a minor collision while on the bombing run and was fortunate to make Manston airfield. Wg Cdr Grey of No 207 Squadron hit a tree near his base of Dunholme Lodge, and his bomb aimer, Fg Off Casy, was injured. On the previous day the Squadron had received news that a former member, Flt Lt Street, had been shot while attempting to escape from a PoW camp.

There were a few enemy fighters in the target area[15] and Plt Off

Hobbs and his crew in aircraft 'O' of No 44 Squadron were thought to have fallen victims to a night fighter north of Poix. Three crew members, Sgts Fenwick and Garnsey, and a second pilot Flt Sgt Baker, are buried at Abbeville. One of the survivors, Sgt A G Hall, was picked up by a German boat having spent six hours in the water. He became a PoW.

Of the five attacks carried out on rail targets in France on 19/20 May, Amiens was the only failure. Most of the Lancasters aborted the mission out of consideration for the friendly civilians underneath them, but one aim of the attack was still achieved and was to further confuse the German Intelligence Services, who were trying desperately to work out where and when the Allied invasion would take place.

I feel sure that Plt Off Hobbs' crew did not die in vain, and that the French did appreciate the need for the attack. The final blow dealt by Bomber Command in that area came shortly after D-Day, and just in time to make travel very difficult for the 2nd Panzer Division.

Notes

1 PRO Air 24/276.
2 Ibid.
3 Some reports suggested that they were hit by flak, but there was stronger evidence to suggest that a collision had occurred.
4 PRO Air 27/1977.
5 IPIR K 2212 23 May 1944. Pro Air 24/276.
6 The Bomber Command Summary recorded that white and yellow TIs landed about 2-400 yd NNE of the AP. Because the Main Force were attacking from that direction, and against the wind, it was not easy to understand the order to undershoot (as opposed to overshoot) but 'undershoot' was recorded in several squadrons' record books, and it was not thought to be a typing error in No 635 Squadron's report.
7 IPIR K 2209 20 May 1944. PRO Air 24/276.
8 The official figure given in the Transportation Plan was 120 acres, but this has been checked against the Target Illustration Print, and 300 acres seems to be nearer the mark.
9 'Benny' Goodman retired as Gp Capt J R Goodman, DFC, AFC. He gave me much support in the writing of this book and is the owner of the original painting of the Mosquito seen on the front cover.
10 Using tracer ammunition it was possible to follow the line of shot from quick-firing guns and literally aim the 'jet' of shells like a hosepipe.
11 See Chapter 3.
12 'Fido' was a device based on the burning of petrol which created enough heat to disperse some of the fog. I am not sure if the word was an anacronym for 'Fog intense dispersal of', but that would have been a typical service terminology.
13 At a reunion of PRU pilots and Medmenham Club Photographic Interpreters I met several people who remembered that incident.
14 It was not clear if that was the second marking Mosquito.
15 In fact, No 7 Squadron, which had been unlucky at Le Mans, lost aircraft 'G', piloted by Sqn Ldr Oliver, who was attacking the German radar station at Mount Couple at the time of the Boulogne raid.

CHAPTER THIRTEEN

USAAF Eighth Air Force Attacks

USAAF Eighth Air Force Bomber Command did not take part in the Overlord Transportation Plan until 27 April 1944. On that day seventy-two aircraft attacked Chalons, and 117 went to Blainville, an important rail junction southwest of Nancy. No aircraft were lost on these raids which took place at the same time as another 500 American heavy bombers were attacking 'Crossbow' targets.

Between the 27 April and 6 June (D-Day), the USAAF Eighth Air Force despatched more than 3600 heavy bombers, of which 3113 were involved in fifty different attacks on transportation targets in northern France and Belgium. The loss rate from the attacks was less than one per cent, and only twenty-two aircraft failed to return, a tribute to the scale and success of the fighter escorts that were provided. The Eighth Air Force was still heavily engaged in attacks connected with 'Point Blank' on German airfields and on 'Crossbow' targets, and also had begun their attacks on German synthetic oil plants.[1]

Some of the heaviest American attacks were made against Saarbrucken, Brussels and Troyes. Four such attacks which took place in May 1944, at the height of the pre-invasion bombing of Transportation targets, will now be described.

Troyes, which was located on one of the two most important radial lines in the eastern region of France, was attacked twice during May, and the damage caused was largely responsible for much re-routing of German troop trains, which were later to carry reinforcements to Normandy from south Germany.

On the afternoon of 1 May, following a morning of heavy attacks by Eighth Air Force bombers on 'Crossbow' sites in the Pas de Calais, Eighth Air Force Bomber Command sent eight combat groups, totalling 235 B-17 Fortress and 151 B-24 Liberator bombers, to attack six marshalling yards in north France and Belgium. The force was heavily escorted by fifteen fighter groups of the Eighth Air Force. Part of the force was provided by the 1st Bombardment Division, which despatched fifty-two B-17s from its 1st Combat Bombardment Wing to Troyes.

The weather was generally good, with some slight ground haze in the Troyes area, and a little thin cirrus cloud at 18,000 ft. Flying out over Clacton in Essex, the B-17s rendezvoused with five fighter groups over Ostend at 1700 hr. Then they all took the route via the south of Brussels and Liège before flying due south past Troyes, and turning through nearly 180 degrees to approach the target from the south.

At 1705 hr 'Sigint' picked up radio messages which indicated that some German fighters from JD 4 were being moved to airfields in the St Trond/Florennes area.[2] At 1753 hr the fighters were airborne and were directed to the Verdun area; but they seem to have been more interested in another bomber force which was attacking targets in the Metz area.

At approximately 1818 hr all fifty-two of the B-17s, flying in box formation, were approaching Troyes from the south. The first bombs tumbled out of the aircraft at 1820 hr, and within one minute bombers from the 91st and 381st Groups had dropped 316 bombs, all 1000-pounders, from a height of 19-21,000 ft. Flak during the bomb run was described as moderate but accurate, and several aircraft were hit by shell fragments, some badly.

Photographs taken at the time of the attack showed two heavy concentrations of bombs straddling the target area and subsequent Photographic Interpretation Reports noted that the main weight of the attack had fallen on the Preize marshalling yards where many of the 800 wagons present at the time had been set on fire; the nearby locomotive sheds had received three direct hits. Also badly hit were the constricted points where the lines from the sidings joined the main through lines. A large industrial building 600 yd west of the target area had been struck, and several houses in the residential area to the northwest had been demolished.

The route home went by the coast near Ostend. Some heavy flak was encountered at that point, and one B-17, probably from 81st Bomber Group, was seen to go down. The fighter escorts kept the German fighters from JD 4 at bay, and the latter were heard being ordered to land at 1857 hr. The American fighters left the bombers finally over the Thames Estuary at 1945 hr. On landing at Bassing-bourn and Ridgewell the two groups inspected the damage. Fifteen of the fifty-one returning aircraft had received catagory 'A' damage, but were repairable.[3]

The second attack on Troyes took place between 1042 and 1045 hr on 30 May. The weather was excellent and sixty of the sixty-three B-17s dispatched by the 3rd Bombardment Division were able to bomb visually from heights of 19-21000 ft. During the three minutes that it took the formation to pass over the target, 718 bombs were released. All the bombs were of the 500-lb type, giving a total of 180 tons of high explosives dropped, with bombs exploding at a rate of nearly four per second.

The bombers shared a large fighter escort with other B-17s which were to attack Reims. The escort consisted of 145 P-47 Thunderbolts and 139 P-38 Lightnings, 284 fighters in all, which went all the way to and from the target areas without seeing any enemy fighters. It was learned later that the Luftwaffe had sent all their available fighters from the area to counter a much larger force of Eighth Air Force bombers which was attacking 'Point Blank' targets in central Germany.

The flight to and from Troyes on that occasion was so easy that the combat wing commanders were moved to include several enthusiastic personal observations in their reports. Lt William G McDonald, an experienced navigator from New York, said:

> *It was the greatest display of fighter strength I've seen in 30 missions, a regular decoration day parade over Europe, with Thunderbolts, Mustangs and Lightnings massed around us.*

Tail gunner S/Sgt Francis Gardner from Massachusetts declared, 'The sky was full of planes, all ours. There just wasn't room for any Germans'. Even the anti-aircraft fire seemed to have been relatively light, with only a few aircraft reporting any serious flak damage.[4]

With such good conditions it was hardly surprising that the raid was a great success. Again, the Preize sorting sidings received the bulk of the bombs, and the locomotive round houses took several more direct hits.[5] Unfortunately, approximately thirty bombs landed on houses immediately east of the main sidings, a further fifty fell in the suburban area to the north. The main Paris-Troyes road, which ran through both housing areas, was severed in a dozen places, and there were a number of casualties among the French civilians in these areas.

Intelligence reports at the time of the second raid suggested that the number of wagons present was much lower than it had been on 1 May, and, in keeping with the general decline of rail traffic in all SNCF Regions at the time, Troyes was not to handle normal loadings again until well after the war had ended.

In between the two attacks on Troyes there were two other very successful attacks, one on Brussels on 25 May, the other on Saarbrucken on 27 May.

The Brussels attack was made by ninety-six B-17s of the 3rd Bombardment Divisions, and was part of three separate attacks on rail targets in the Brussels area. The Midi junction was attacked by twenty-eight aircraft; eighteen bombers attacked the Melsbroek area, and fifty B-17s attacked the marshalling yard at Schaerbeck. All the aircraft, together with strong forces of bombers from two other Bombardment Divisions were heavily escorted by fourteen Eighth Air Force fighter groups and by five from the Ninth Air Force, making a total of more than 700 fighters. The Brussels force was escorted by eighty-five P-38s. The 20th Fighter Group, led by Lt Col Rau, provided over half the Brussels escort and joined up with the bombers near Amiens at about 0810 hr, an hour after leaving their bases in England.[6]

The Schaerbeck marshalling yards were estimated to be about one third full at the time of the attack and the five bomber groups which had been assigned the area all reported good results.[7] Fifty-two B-17s attacked between 0914 and 0926 hr and dropped 510 bombs, all of the 500-lb type, from a height of 22-24,000 ft. Enemy opposition was so slight that their escorts took it in turn to dive down and add their weight to the attack by shooting up trains and other military targets in the area. The fighters claimed the destruction of a troop train, fifty loaded flat wagons, and six locomotives.

Anti-aircraft fire over the target included two ground-to-air rockets which exploded, leaving long white streamers. The main concentrations of flak were experienced in the Amiens/Poix area, where two B-17s, probably from 388 Bomber Group, were seen to go down, and on the coast near Dieppe and Breskens. The fighter escorts paid quite heavily for their part in the attack. Lts Bench and Watson from the 79th Squadron and Lt Boel from the 55th Squadron all failed to return home, and Lt Saltman was slightly wounded by ground fire. A further eight fighters were damaged quite badly but managed to reach their base at Kings Cliff, near Stanford.

Photographic Interpretation Report SA 1869[8], issued by the ACIU at Medmenham later in the day and based on photography at the time of the attack on Schaerbeck, noted that a large concentration of bombs had fallen south of the target area, with three hits at least on the locomotive depot. The report noted also that four groups of bombs had blanketed the residential area south of the marshalling yards.

On 27 May 282 B-24 Liberators of the 2nd Bombardment Division attacked the rail centres at Saarbrucken, Kons and Neuenkirchen. At the same time another force, consisting of forty-nine B-17s from the 3rd Bombardment Division, bombed the marshalling yards at Strasbourg. All the targets lay on what were expected to be the main border crossing points for reinforcements approaching Normandy from south Germany. The bombers which approached these targets were in fact only part of a massive force totalling approximately 1000 bombers and as many fighters, which the 'Mighty Eighth' had despatched against a variety of targets in northeast France and south Germany.

Enemy fighter opposition was relatively strong that day, particularly against the seven leading Combat Wings of B-17s, which were flying in box formations towards the Ludwigshaven and Mannheim marshalling yards. All 1040 escorting fighters were kept busy during the early part of the day, and one escort group reported that they met 150 enemy fighters between Epinal and Strasbourg. The fighter escort was comprised of twenty-five groups from the USAAF, fifteen of which were provided by the Ninth Air Force,[9] and four RAF squadrons of Mustangs.

The six groups of Liberators sent to attack Saarbrucken was the largest force ever to attack a single target in northeast France during the lead up to D-Day. Assembling over their Norfolk bases at approximately 1100 hr, almost 160 bombers, all from the 2nd and 14th Combat Bombardment wings, joined up with the smaller forces making for Kons and Neuenkirchen, and they all made their way to Brighton where they set course for the enemy coast near Le Havre. Having met up with their fighter escort, the combined force flew southeast then east to the south of Paris and on to Epinal, where the main force turned north towards Saarbrucken. Their escort consisted of 108 P-47s, ninety-two P-51s and forty-seven P-38s — all from the Ninth Air Force.

A few enemy fighters were seen south of Paris and near the turning point at Epinal, but they did not press home their attacks. The weather was good, with some ground haze in northeast France, but not enough to prevent the bombardiers from using their usual bomb sights. Intelligence reports had indicated that Saarbrucken was moderately busy, and that there would be a number of locomotives in the area of the roundhouses.

Approaching from the south, at approximately 1325 hr, 145 of the 159 aircraft dispatched began their bombing runs. In the ensuing twenty-five minutes the bombers dropped 1500 500-lb bombs, giving a total of 382 tons of high explosives dropped. As usual, the Germans waited for the aircraft to steady on their bombing runs before they put up an intense barrage of 88 mm shells which reached the bombers easily because they were flying at heights of 17-22,000 ft. Two B-24s were seen to have gone down.

Photographs taken during the attack showed that almost 200 bombs had burst within the target area, and that direct hits had been made on the two locomotive roundhouses and the repair sheds; also badly hit were the goods transhipment sheds and passenger station. Sixty-two hits were counted on the marshalling sidings, and the through lines were cut in several places.

'Sigint' reports on the movements of German fighters suggested that Jafue 5 was confused by both the scale of the attack and the different directions taken by the bomber forces. In spite of the number of bombers and their escorting fighters over northern France, one Luftwaffe Gruppe failed to make any contact. Signals were also intercepted from 7 Jagddivision, which had not been associated with previous operations in that area.[10] Such was the strength of the American escort force that many of the 'Little

Brothers' were able to divert from their primary duty of escorting and attacked airfields and transportation targets. Claims made by the entire escort force included thirty-seven locomotives and fifteen wagons destroyed, and many others damaged. Nine of the escorting fighters were lost in the attacks.

The route home from Saarbrucken took the bombers via Luxembourg and the Dutch/Belgian border to the Scheldt Estuary. Two B-24s were lost during that part of the trip — probably to flak near the coast. Most of the force returned to England over Clacton, but some of them recrossed the coast a little further north, near Cromer, near to which another B-24 was lost, following a collision with an unknown aircraft.

The bombers landed at approximately 1530 hr, and squadrons and groups both assessed the damage. Men of the 389th Group from Hethel, which had lost the two crews over Saarbrucken, had the unpleasant task of removing one dead and four wounded airmen from other aircraft of the group. Eight of the B-24s which landed at the 445th's base at Tibenham had major damage. The 44th and 492nd Groups based at Shipdham and North Pickenham respectively, both had four aircraft badly damaged by shell splinters. Of the twenty-four Liberators from the 392nd Group which landed at Wendling, one was so badly damaged that it had to be written off.

In spite of the high level of enemy fighter activity and some intense flak over all the target areas, it had been a good day. All the targets had been bombed in weather which was described as 'CAVU' (Clear and Visibility Unlimited), and the results were generally good. The total cost was twenty-two heavy bombers — approximately 2.2 per cent of the 1000 dispatched. The figures for the fighters were very much the same. One B-24 from 492 Bomber Group was damaged over the target and landed in Switzerland.

By D-Day the USAAF Eighth Air Force had dropped a total of 1300 tons of bombs on twenty-three of the targets allocated to it under the Transportation Plan. Fifteen of the targets had been classed as 'Category A' as a result.[11]

Notes

1 See Chapters 14 and 17.
2 PRO Air 40/616.
3 Ibid.
4 Office of Air Force History, microfilm roll A5973, frame 1158.
5 On my visit to the site in 1989 I was told that the roundhouses had been so badly damaged that they were never rebuilt.
6 Office of Air Force History, microfilm roll A5972, frame 1156.
7 The Groups involved were Nos 94, 95, 100, 385 and 447.
8 Office of Air Force History, microfilm A5972, frame 1280.
9 Ibid, frame 1938.
10 PRO Air 40.
11 *Army Air Forces in World War II*, Vol III, p155.

CHAPTER FOURTEEN

'Point Blank' — Spring 1944

Placing the strategic air forces under General Eisenhower's control did not lead to their complete withdrawal from the 'Point Blank' plan. On the contrary, General Spaatz had been given permission to conduct trial attacks in connection with his 'Oil Plan', and the wording of Eisenhower's first directive to Bomber Command (whilst making mention of the task of reducing the strength of the Luftwaffe and disrupting enemy rail communications) still carried much of the wording of the earlier directives, particularly with regard to the task of disorganising German industry. The new directive was also designed to be more palatable to Spaatz and Harris by saying that the rail targets should be attacked when both the weather and the moon made deeper penetration attacks unwise.

A further diversion of effort came when British and American heavy bombers were both called upon to disrupt the build-up of German V-weapon sites, which were appearing in ever increasing numbers in the Pas de Calais and Cherbourg Peninsula, and posing a threat to Allied troops and material which were being concentrated around the ports of southern England.

The American attacks on German oil supplies started early in May,[1] and RAF Bomber Command joined in the new offensive later that month. A significant number of important attacks on 'Point Blank' targets took place during the spring of 1944. Between 1 March and 30 May RAF Bomber Command dispatched 11,000 sorties against German targets, dropped 37,000 tons of bombs on industrial towns, and lost, or had written off, approximately 500 heavy bombers.[2] During the same period the RAF also made over 3000 sorties over Germany, in the form of diversionary sweeps or bombing by small groups of Mosquitos mostly from Nos 5 and 100 Groups.[3]

The USAAF Eighth Air Force, which did not join in Transportation Plan operations until the end of April, carried out more than twice the RAF's number of sorties against Germany during the same period and, whereas the equalising crossover between attacks by the RAF on German and French targets occurred at the end of April, the same point was not reached by the Eighth Air Force until the end of May (see illustration). In the same 90-day period the Eighth Air Force operated against targets in Germany on thirty-nine different days; they lost 870 heavy bombers and had more than 9000 aircrew missing or killed. The percentage of aircraft lost to aircraft despatched was 3.5 per cent, less than the RAF, but they were heavily escorted by the Eighth and Ninth Air Forces' Fighter Command, which lost fighters at a rate of 1.2 per cent.

Early in March, the Director of RAF Bomber Operations had drawn up a list of targets, partly to counter the Transportation Plan, which he considered should be attacked during the eight weeks following 18 March. The targets were proposed under the caption of the Combined Bomber Offensive (CBO), and included thirty aircraft component or ball-bearing factories; fourteen synthetic oil plants in east Germany and the Ruhr; and three refineries in north Germany. The list also included nine Romanian refineries.

During March, the RAF's bombers made seven major attacks on Germany, the largest occurring on the night of 15/16 March when 230 Halifaxes and more than 600 Lancasters made a none-too-successful attack on Stuttgart and its Daimler-Benz Aero-engine plant; thirty-seven bombers failed to return. Two nights later a similar mixture of Halifaxes and Lancasters, totalling 846 aircraft in all, dropped 1367 tons of HE on Frankfurt and the Alfred Teves Aircraft Components Works. A further three attacks, involving more than 800 aircraft, followed in quick succession: one on Frankfurt, where the tonnage of incendiaries dropped exceeded that of the high-explosives dropped earlier; one on Berlin, known to crews as 'The Big City'; and one on Essen. The end of the month saw the disastrous attack on Nuremberg when ninety-five of the 795 aircraft sent failed to return. (For a full

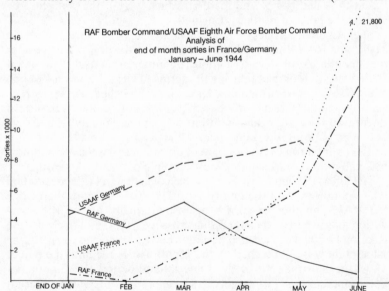

RAF Bomber Command/USAAF Eighth Air Force Bomber Command
Analysis of
end of month sorties in France/Germany
January – June 1944

and interesting account of this affair the reader is advised to read Martin Middlebrook's book on the subject.)[4]

April saw a significant drop in Bomber Command's effort against German targets; the Main Force operated six nights only and with reduced strength. On three of the six nights the Force was split between two different targets: on 22/23 April a total of 596 aircraft from Nos 1, 3, 4 and 6 Groups carried out a major attack on Dusseldorf, while a total of 265 bombers from Nos 1 and 5 Groups flew on to the more distant artillery tractor and rail works at Brunswick. Both attacks were successful, but thirty-three aircraft failed to return — twenty-nine from Dusseldorf and four from Brunswick.

Two nights later, a mixed force of 637 aircraft from all Groups, except No 5, blasted the Gustav and Genshau works at Karlsruhe; while another 260 aircraft from Nos 1 and 5 Groups bombed Munich. Two nights after that a mixed force of almost 500 aircraft went to the Ruhr and dropped bombs on the Krupps Works at Essen. A smaller force from Nos 1 and 5 Groups flew down to the ball-bearing works at Schweinfurt, where they created havoc with their heavier bombs, but lost twenty-one aircraft (9.2 per cent).[5]

RAF Bomber Command attacks on German industry in May dwindled away to two major attacks only.[6] One, against Duisburg, on 21/22 May, involved a total of 532 aircraft from Nos 1, 3 and 5 Groups. The other was carried out the very next night when the force was split again between Dortmund and Brunswick. At Dortmund a combined total of 329 Lancasters and Mosquitos, from Nos 1, 3, 6 and 8 (PFF) Groups, badly damaged the steel and tar distillation plants. At Brunswick, 215 Lancasters from Nos 1 and 5 Groups dropped 613 tons of bombs on the rail and artillery tractor works. Losses over the two nights were high, in comparison with the parallel attacks on the French rail system; sixty aircraft went missing (5.2 per cent of those despatched), proof enough that the Luftwaffe was still capable of taking the rate of attrition of bombers and aircrew beyond acceptable limits.[7]

As shown in the Analysis on page 108, the number of bombers that the Eighth Air Force sent to Germany did not begin to fall until the end of May, but there was an even, albeit slight, drop in the number of actual raids per month. In March, the total aircraft despatched to targets in Germany amounted to almost 8000, with 280 lost.

One of the heaviest raids, which had the second highest casualty rate for any one day, was that of 18 March when all three of the heavy bombardment divisions put up a total of thirteen combat wings involving 550 B-17s and 238 B-24s.[8] On that day the 1st Bombardment Division sent five combat wings to attack Luftwaffe airfields at Memmingen, Lechfield, Oberphaffenhafen and Landsberg. They were accompanied by a small Pathfinder force and were joined later by aircraft from the 3rd Bombardment Division who had found their airfield targets near Munich covered in cloud. The 2nd Bombardment Division fielded four combat wings and its own Pathfinder force and bombed through cloud to hit two separate aircraft component factories at Friedrichshaven. Particularly good results were reported by the photographic interpreters who studied the post-strike photographs of the Manzel Focke-Wulfe 190 components factory. Of the 788 bombers sent to attack, 738 bombed the targets, forty-three failed to return (including three which were shot down by Swiss anti-aircraft gunners), and thirteen landed in Switzerland where their crews were interned. One aircraft was lost when bombs fell on it from another aircraft flying above.

Having operated on fifteen days in March the total fell in April to thirteen days. 11 April saw the biggest effort.[9] No less than 643 B-17s and 241 B-24s from all three bombardment divisions attacked six Focke-Wulfe and Junkers assembly plants from Rostock in the north, to Cottbus in the east. The 3rd Bombardment Division sent 302 aircraft via the north route, across the Danish peninsula to Rostock, Stettin, Politz and Arnimswalde. The 1st and 2nd Bombardment Divisions used the more southerly route across Holland, to approach targets in central and east Germany. Bad weather prevented the 3rd Bombardment Division from attacking the more distant targets, but at approximately 1215 hr 108 B-17s of the 1st Bombardment Division made a particularly successful attack on the aircraft assembly plants at Sorau, dropping a total of 2800 bombs, mostly of a small calibre, from a height of 10-12,000 ft. The 2nd Bombardment Division bombed targets in central Germany, at Bernberg and Oschersleben.

In spite of their escort of thirteen fighter groups from the Eighth and Ninth Air Forces, the bombers faced some very determined enemy fighter opposition. Of the 917 bombers despatched only 345 reached their primary objectives, the greater proportions, including most of the 3rd Bombardment Division's aircraft, attacked secondary targets. Sixty-four bombers were lost which, at ten men per aircraft, meant that the equivalent of nearly a battalion of infantry was lost in one operation, an unusually high percentage rate.[10]

In May the number of days of operations against Germany fell to eleven. Although not the largest attack in terms of aircraft despatched, the operations of 12 May are worth mentioning. On that day, USAAF Eighth Air Force Bomber Command began its major offensive against German synthetic oil production. Five targets were chosen, Merseburg/Leuna, Lutzkendorf, Zeitz and Bohlen in central Germany, and Brux in Czechoslovakia. The aircraft component factory at Zwickau was attacked also during the same operation.

Ten combat wings of the 1st and 2nd Bombardment Divisions attacked the targets in central Germany, and four combat wings of the 3rd Bombardment Division attacked the targets in Zwickau and

Brux. A total of 874 bombers were escorted by 450 fighters, 241 of which were P-51 Mustangs which had a greater operating range.

Picking up their fighter escorts over Clacton, the bombers crossed the Essex coast at 1030 hrs. By the time they reached Frankfurt enemy fighter reaction had become violent. Altogether, it was estimated that 200-250 fighters of Jagddivisions 1 and 2 had flown down from their bases in north Germany to join fighters in Jagddivision 3's area. Flying in formations of almost fifty aircraft each and well coordinated by their ground controllers, the fighters attacked mostly from ahead of the bomber formations (some B-17s actually being rammed). Twin-engined day fighters joined in the fray during the withdrawal phase of the operation and a few single-engined fighters attempted interceptions most of the way home.

Of the forty-six American bombers lost on the mission, thirty-four were seen to go down to the guns of enemy fighters and three only to flak; seven met unknown fates and two crashed on landing in England.[11]

The vigorous defence of German oil installations, which were quite closely grouped, was an indication of the sensitive nature of the targets. Albert Speer, the Minister of Production, had long-feared the attacks, which were to deny the Germans of the very life blood for their tanks and aircraft during the final struggle.

Bad weather prevented the Eighth Air Force from returning to attack the oil targets until 28 May. In the meantime, the Fifteenth Air Force, operating from bases such as Foggia in Italy had been hammering the Romanian refineries around Ploiesti.

Notes

1 General Spaatz was authorised to carry out the attacks in April, but bad weather prevented deep penetration operations until 12 May.
2 That period included the Nuremberg Raid.
3 Combination of PRO Air 22/203 and Air 22/339.
4 See Bibliography.
5 In a survey conducted after the war it was discovered that the smaller American bombs damaged buildings but not machinery.
6 That did not include an attack on 24/25th May against rail facilities in Aachen.
7 During the same month, however, the Luftwaffe lost almost 600 pilots which added weight to Spaatz's theory that the Luftwaffe could be destroyed by forcing them to defend important targets.
8 PRO Air 40/578.
9 PRO Air 40/598.
10 Several escorting fighters were lost also.
11 PRO Air 40/626.

CHAPTER FIFTEEN

Mailly le Camp — 3/4 May 1944

It was probably true to say that had the attack on Mailly le Camp not taken place on 3/4 May, this book might not have been written. It was during that raid that my brother, Nigel, lost his life whilst flying as a navigator in Lancaster 'J' of No 101 Squadron which was based at Ludford Magna. It led me to research not only the circumstances of his death but the activities of Bomber Command and also of the USAAF Eighth Air Force during that critical phase of the Second World War.

On that brilliantly moonlit night, no less than forty-two bombers failed to return to their bases in eastern England (11 per cent of the force despatched). So vivid were the memories of exploding aircraft in the minds of some survivors that they later referred to that night as the worst 'chop night' of the whole campaign. Other survivors said that it was worse than the Nuremberg debacle, which had taken place a month or so before.

Mailly le Camp was. and is again at the time of writing, a French Army artillery training area, which had been taken over by the German Army in 1940. Under German occupation, the depot consisted of an area of permanent barrack accommodation; garaging and workshops for tanks and vehicles; semi-buried ammunition and fuel dumps, which were served by rail; and a large, open training area, used for tank driving and gunnery practice. At the time of the attack, the depot was occupied by a permanent staff of battle-hardened instructors and by various tank units which had been sent there for re-grouping and training. Amongst those units was a battalion of the 21st Panzer Division which was to be one of the first in action in Normandy a month later.

Located just east of the N77 road, almost halfway between Troyes and Châlons sur Marne, the whole complex covered approximately fifty-five square miles, but the barracks, workshops and garages were concentrated into about 400 acres at the northwest corner, forming an extension to the village of Mailly le Camp. Ground defences, known to be within the target area, consisted of two six-gun batteries of radar-controlled, 88 mm, heavy, anti-aircraft guns and approximately twenty light guns of 37 and 20 mm calibres. Expecting trouble, the Germans had dug many trenches, but as we will see later some trenches became death traps.

Bomber Command Operations Instruction No AC515, issued on 3 May 1944, detailed Nos 1 and 5 Groups to provide the main force, and No 8 (PFF) Group to provide two 'Oboe'-equipped Mosquitos. No 100 Group was also requested to provide support in the form of six Mosquitos and three ECM-equipped Halifaxes of No 192 Squadron to carry out Special Duty patrols in the target area.

The attack was planned to take place in two phases: 173 aircraft of No 5 Group were to go in first and aim their bombs at a point near the southeast end of the barracks area; this was to be followed by 173 Lancasters of No 1 Group, most of which were to attack the northwest end of the barracks, but thirty aircraft were to concentrate on a special point near the workshops. The Commanding Officer of No 617 Squadron, Wg Cdr Leonard Cheshire, was to act as marker leader and, with three other Mosquitos from his squadron, was to mark the Aim Points from a low level in the light of flares dropped by Nos 83 and 97 (PFF) Squadrons. The latter Squadrons were attached to No 5 Group, and would be guided to the area by proximity markers dropped by the Mosquitos of Nos 105 and 109 Squadrons. The Master Bomber, or his deputy, both of No 83 Squadron, would control the attack. Zero hour was set at 0005 hr, the marking was to start at 2358 hr, and the whole affair should have ended at 0025 hr. Group instructions were then issued: No 1 Group detailed 10 Lancaster squadrons, and No 5 Group, 14 Lancaster and two Mosquito squadrons, bringing the total of Main Force aircraft attacking the target to 346 Lancasters and 16 Mosquitos.

Most Squadron orders were issued soon after midday on 3 May; No 101 Squadron's Battle Order was signed at 1215 hr. Aircraft were fuelled and loaded with mostly one 4000-lb and sixteen 500-lb bombs; the usual crew briefings were held in the late afternoon. The weather forecast was for mostly clear skies and good visibility in all areas, and there was a nearly full moon.

Both Groups began to get their aircraft away from their bases around Lincoln at approximately 2130 hr, and all were airborne by 2225 hr. The route to the target was via Reading, Beachy Head, the French coast (ten miles north of Dieppe), thence to Châlons, which was to be the assembly point before approaching Mailly from the north.

Arriving a little early, Wg Cdr Cheshire and his three other Mosquitos decided to make their own feint by flying down towards the German Luftwaffe base at St Dizier, some thirty miles away. In his absence, Sqn Ldr Bird of No 105 Squadron and Plt Off Thomas of No 109 Squadron both claimed to have released their green target indicators (certainly some greens were seen to cascade at 2356 hr by Fg Off Benton of No 97 Squadron).[1]

By the time Cheshire got back, he was able to see that Nos 83 and 97 Squadrons had started illuminating the target area. In the distance, he could also see the yellow marker near Châlons which had been dropped by Fg Off Saint-Smith of No 627 Squadron as a datum point for the main force.

When the Aim Points were clearly visible, Cheshire dived down to 1500 ft and released two Red Spot Fires over the southeast Aim Point. His own assessment was that they had fallen a little too far northeast. Ever the perfectionist, he called in Sqn Ldr Dave Shannon, one of the original 'Dam Busters', to try for a more accurate result. Cheshire informed the Master Bomber, Wg Cdr Deanne, flying aircraft 'D' of No 83 Squadron, to hold off the main attack until he, Cheshire, was satisfied with the marking. It was approximately 0003 hr. Three minutes later, and well satisfied with Shannon's marking, Cheshire gave the go-ahead to Deanne.

Although a few minutes late, things had gone according to plan until that moment. When Deanne tried to pass the order to bomb to No 5 Group over his VHF radio, his transmission was distorted and almost blotted out by what appeared to be an American news broadcast. Attempts to get the message across by WT (Morse) were also thwarted because the radio was some 30 Kcs off frequency. (Although I have yet to discover any proof, it is my belief that the so-called American broadcast might well have been the result of some rather clever German jamming.) Whatever the cause, the results were disastrous, the few crews that had heard the garbled order attacked, and were followed by a few more who, mindful of the consequences of such delays over targets, attacked on their own initiative.

At the same time three other events were taking place: Luftwaffe controllers had made up their minds that Mailly seemed to be the main target and were beginning to direct fighters of NJGs 1 and 4 towards the area; the remainder of No 5 Group and all No 1 Group Lancasters were orbiting the yellow marker near Châlons; and Mosquitos of No 627 Squadron were endeavouring to 'take out' the flak batteries around the target. The combination of being able to see that some bombing was taking place and that Lancasters were already being shot out of the sky by German fighters was too much for the increasingly nervous crews. They broke radio discipline and demanded to know what was happening and why they were being kept waiting.[2]

Wg Cdr Deanne's deputy, Sqn Ldr Sparks, piloting aircraft 'R' of No 83 Squadron, had heard his leader's garbled order and could hear also the increasing 'back chat' from the Main Force, but because his orders were to take over only if the Master Bomber was shot down, or when he was asked to do so, he was in a difficult situation. Cheshire, well aware of the dangerous situation which was developing, tried to transmit the message to bomb also. When that failed, he tried to get the attack called off, but he too had radio difficulties, a lot of which was caused by the breakdown in radio discipline, which was becoming acute by then.

Totally frustrated, and in spite of the bombs falling from Lancasters above, Cheshire decided to carry on and mark the second phase. He called in Flt Lts Fawke and Kearns who released RSFs, very accurately, onto the northwest Aim Point. Additional markers were dropped by a Lancaster of No 97 Squadron, flown by Fg Off Skingley. Hearing and seeing the results of the new marking, Sqn Ldr Sparks decided to take charge and ended the confusion by giving a clearly heard order to 'go in and bomb'. The time was approximately 0025 hr; five minutes only after the scheduled time of attack by No 1 Group, but it must have seemed an eternity to the circling crews. The effects of the order were immediate, and were described by one crew as 'like opening the starting gates at the Derby'.[3]

The effects on the ground were devastating. Lulled into believing that the raid was over, a number of German soldiers rose from their trenches to try to recover kit and personal belongings from their already damaged barrack blocks. The suddenness and intensity of the second wave caught some of them in the open; others, who had dived into trenches close by the buildings, were buried alive by the trench walls which collapsed under the enormous overpressures of the 4000-lb bombs, or by rubble from the buildings.[4]

Not all of the No 5 Group crews heard Sparks' first order to bomb, and it was well after 0030 hr when the last aircraft began its run in. The last bomb release recorded by photograph was that of No 619 Squadron's aircraft 'F', flown by Fg Off Dougherty, who bombed at 0037 hr — twelve minutes after the attack should have ended. I believe that some, including Sqn Ldr Sparks, bombed as late as 0044 hrs — at the very moment that Hauptmann Martin Drewes, the commander of 111/NJG/1 from Laon, claimed the third of his five victories that night. His Me 110 was fitted with the deadly 'Schräge Musik' cannon installation.

In spite of the individual triumphs of German night fighter pilots, reaction by the fighter controllers seemed to have been generally confused and poorly coordinated. The success of the Luftwaffe operation seemed to have been largely due to the fact that the pilots, flying in very good visibility, were able to see the markers and act on their own initiative.[5] The first alert was heard by the RAF listening station at Kingsdown at 2253 hr, approximately the time when the Main Force were approaching Dieppe. Half an hour later, fighters from NJG 3 in northwest Germany were ordered from the Elbe to the Osnabruck area (possibly a reaction to the Mosquito attack on Ludwigshaven) but nothing more was heard of the formation. Jagddivision 4, covering northeast France, opened a running commentary at approximately 2320 hr. At 2330 hr they reported that the spearhead of the bomber attack was south of Amiens. Between 2338 and 2345 hr the controllers reported that the British bombers were circling Beauvais.

At 0002 hr, just after the attack had started, fighters from NJGs 1 and 2 in Holland were ordered to an area southwest of Florennes, some eighty miles north of the bombers' outward track, but the units were later ordered back to the Rhineland. As the attack on Mailly developed, Jagddivision 4's controllers began ordering their fighters to the area south of St Quentin (probably in response to an attack which was developing on Montidier airfield, by eighty-four Lancasters of No 8 (PFF) Group). A rather late call at 0040 hr reported that the leading bombers were circling Mailly, but fighters of 11/NJG/4 and 'Wilde Sau', single-engined fighters were already at the scene.

The Bomber Command combat reports partly confirmed the running commentary between the German controllers and their aircraft. According to crew reports the Mailly force was first intercepted on the outward leg south of Compiègne, that concurred with the German order concerning the Beauvais area, but did not explain the report that the bombers were circling the area. It was possible that some 'Window' was released in the area, causing the Germans to think that the aircraft were circling. There were

Extract from navigational log of Flt Lt Castle, No 101 Squadron's Navigational Leader at the time of the Mailly raid. 'Bombs gone' at 0029 hrs and the route to the first turning point took them just to the east of Voué.
(Flt Lt Castle)

'B' section CTU 1944. Photographic interpreters from the British and American services worked together at Danesfield House, Medmenham. Here the section studies the latest air photos of V-1 and V-2 sites. *(Photo by kind permission of the Officers Mess Intelligence Corps).*

No 17 OTU Silverstone 1943. *L to R* Sgt Jack Woods, Wireless Op; Sgt Ted Borton, Air Gunner; Sgt Bryan Bowditch, Pilot; Sgt Bowles, Air Gunner; Sgt Nigel Lacey-Johnson, Navigator; Sgt Billy Bishop, Bomb Aimer. Bowditch was killed over Schweinfurt in February 1944; their new pilot F/O Kenneth Muir, and Special Operator P/O Gorman, joined the crew later. All were killed on the Mailly le Camp raid in May 1944. *(L. Lacey-Johnson).*

Professor Solly Zuckerman. He was brought back from Italy to help Leigh-Mallory with the air plan for 'Overlord' and was the chief architect of the 'Transportation Plan'. *(Lord Zuckerman).*

General Dwight D. Eisenhower, Supreme Allied Commander, in front of a map showing the Transportation Targets. He had the responsibility for the liberation of Europe and President Roosevelt 'would not impose any restrictions on military action by the responsible commanders'. *(IWM).*

The Gnome-Rhone aircraft factory before and after the precision attack lead by Cheshire and Martin. *(Crown Copyright/RAF Photo).*

The threat to both the RAF and USAAF: the 88mm was probably the most successful gun of the war. Against aircraft it was effective up to 26,000 ft, against tanks it was lethal up to 500 yards. *(IWM)*.

The Transportation Plan aimed at delaying the arrival in Normandy of German tanks. The Pz V 'Panther' was the most reliable, with a 75mm gun. *(IWM)*.

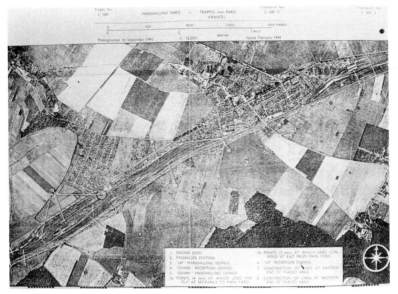

The target illustration print of Trappes used by aircrews for the first experimental attack of the Transportation Plan. The results of the attack confounded Harris who did not believe that such accuracy would have been possible. *(Crown Copyright/RAF Photo)*.

F/O 'Benny' Goodman with his navigator F/O 'Bill' Hickox standing in front of their Mosquito IV 'G' George of 627 Squadron. They helped 'take out' the flak batteries at Mailly. *(Gp Capt Goodman)*.

Tergnier the morning after. Two of the three circular housing areas were virtually obliterated. Fortunately, most of the railway workers' families had been warned of the raid by the BBC and had been evacuated, but they lost their homes. *(Crown Copyright/RAF Photo).*

Chambly Rail Depot after the attack by Lancasters and Stirlings of 3 Group. The attack owed its accuracy to good back-up marking and control by the Master Bomber. *(Crown Copyright/RAF Photo).*

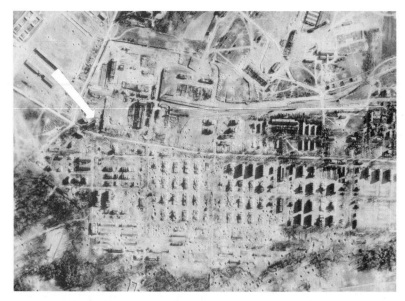

Mailly le Camp. This air photo taken by P/O Mouzon of 541 (PR) Squadron on 4 May shows that a large number of the brick barrack blocks were pulverised. The white arrow indicates the water tower from which the ground photograph (below) was taken. *(Crown Copyright/RAF Photo)*.

A ground photo taken about three days after the attack. *(Flt Lt R. Emeny)*.

numerous sightings of enemy fighters in that area but five combats only were reported, four of which resulted in claims by No 5 Group crews that two single-engined and two twin-engined fighters had been destroyed. Eight attacks on bombers were reported between 0024 and 0037 hr; all the main types of fighters were reported to have been seen, twin-engined types having formed the majority. A formation of six Messerschmitt 410s, apparently with their navigation lights on, were seen west of Châlons.

Reaction by the Luftwaffe's Flak Arm along the outward and homeward legs was slight, except in the area of Poix where the flak belt seemed to have been extended. Over the target, the two heavy

2.5.44	Hptm. Drewes	00.45	Lancaster	23.	269.	Dr
2.5.44	Obl. Prües	00.47	4-mot	2.	270.	D.
3.5.44	Oblt. Then	0.55	4-mot	1..	271	D
4.5.44	Oblt. Schmidt	00.03	4-mot	22.23.272.		D
4.5.44	Oblt. Schmidt	00.14	4-mot	23.24.273.		D
4.5.44	Hptm. Drewes	00.26	Lancaster	24.	274.	Dr
4.5.44	Hptm. Drewes	00.36	Lancaster	25.	275.	Dr
4.5.44	Oblt. Prües	00.37	4-mot	3.	276.	Dr
4.5.44	Hptm. Drewes	00.44	Lancaster	26.	277.	Dr
4.5.44	Lt. Ebhardt	00.44	4-mot(d.l)	2.	278.	Dr
4.5.44	Oblt. Schmitz	00.46	4-mot(d.l)	24.25.	279.	Dr
4.5.44	Hptm. Drewes	00.50	Lancaster	27.	280.	Dr
4.5.44	Hptm. Drewes	01.18	Lancaster	28.	281.	Dr
4.5.44	Oblt. Then	01.15	4-mot	2.	282.	Dr

Copy of the entries in the 'claims' book of III/NJG/I for the night of 3/4 May 1944, showing the five claims of Martin Drewes between 0026 and 0118 hrs on 4 May. (*Bundesarchiv*)

batteries were firing accurately, with shells bursting between 5000 and 9000 ft. The light guns, aided by three searchlights, were 'hosepiping', their shells self-destructing at 10-12,000 ft. There was a fair amount of hot metal flying about but, thanks to the efforts of No 627 Squadron's Mosquitos which were dive-bombing the gun positions, the German gunners did not have it all their own way.

The single-engined fighters of JD 4, operating as 'Wilde Sau' in both the moonlight and the light from flares and fires, together with the twin-engined fighters of NJGs 1 and 4 claimed nearly half their total of forty-two victims between the assembly point at Châlons and the village of Voué thirty miles further south. Martin Drewes, a pilot of III/NJG/I, claimed five aircraft alone.

There is not room in this account for a full analysis of the fate of each individual aircraft and crew. I can describe two or three incidents which have come to light during my general research.

Louis Clement, one-time mayor of Voué who helped me reconstruct the circumstances surrounding the death of my brother, Nigel, described the air battles over the countryside surrounding his village as terrible; aircraft were on fire, exploding in the air and falling in pieces over a wide area. He said that Nigel's aircraft was on fire when it exploded at about 1500 ft, the engines and parts of the mainplane and fuselage fell more or less together in a field, close to the northeast edge of Voué, but there were pieces of aircraft scattered along a mile-long path which ran generally in an east-west direction. The remains of the crew were collected by a few local inhabitants and buried quickly by the Catholic priest of Voué, together with the body of Flt Sgt Bodsworth, an air gunner who had been seen to drop with his parachute on fire, having jumped from a No 166 Squadron Lancaster which was also on fire and crashed only a mile away, on the east side of the N77. The graves were marked with wooden crosses and remained that way until they were taken over by the Imperial War Graves Commission in March 1949. Four headstones were erected in 1952, and the graves were tended carefully for many years by Madame Charpentier who lived in Voué.

During the time of the Mailly raid most of No 101 Squadron's aircraft were fitted with 'Airborne Cigar', an electronic jamming device designed to interfere with German fighter control frequencies. Consequently those aircraft carried an extra crew member, known as the special operator. During my initial enquiries I was presented with two silk escape maps which had been taken from the wreckage of Nigel's aircraft by André Thouard who had been one of the helpers that night in May 1944, and who has since died. One of the maps was placed in No 101 Squadron's museum cabinet at Brize Norton.

Most of Nigel's crew had been together since their OTU days at Silverstone. Their first pilot had been killed and they were on their first operational trip with their new pilot, Fg Off Kenneth Muir. From the position of the line of wreckage I had every reason to believe that they had bombed the target and had been caught by a fighter as they turned westwards towards home. The crew were formally identified in 1952 from a photograph of the mid-upper gunner, Sgt Ted Borton, which had been found near the crash site.[6]

In another incident involving a No 101 Squadron aircraft, Sgt Jack Worsfold, the rear gunner of SR-'Z', had a remarkable escape when his aircraft blew apart over the village of Aubeterre, a mile or two south of Voué. His aircraft was alight and having received orders to bale out, Worsfold made to get his parachute but, on discovering flames all down the fuselage, quickly shut his turret doors. The next thing he remembered was waking up in the tail section of the aircraft, which was resting at an angle in some woods. Apparently, that section had come down onto some overhead power cables and had trampolined into the trees.

Worsfold was found and given first aid by Monsieur Noel and his eighteen-year-old daughter, Nellie. He was taken to the village Mairie and laid on the conference table, but having sustained both a broken thigh and a bullet wound in the neck, the Germans soon discovered him and he was taken to a hospital in Troyes. Later the Germans put him on the back seat of a car and took him to a hospital in Paris, where he remained until he was well enough to be interrogated. He was moved finally to Stalag Luft 3 at Heydrekruge in East Prussia. The news that he had survived reached England via the French Resistance network. He still visists Nellie Noel who lives with her mother in Aubeterre. The rest of the crew were killed and are now buried in the Canadian cemetery at Dieppe.[7]

Part of the Bomber Command support for the raid involved three ECM-equipped Halifaxes of No 192 Squadron. Their task had been to monitor and acquire the frequencies used by the Germans. One of the aircraft, flown by Flt Lt H R Gibson, had been circling the area and it too was caught by a fighter and shot down near the village of Brienne. All the crew, except one of the gunners, baled out.

In the course of writing this book, I was invited to attend a ceremony in the village of Villeret during which the Flight Engineer of the aircraft, John Ackroyd, and Jim Carpenter, the Chairman of the Air Gunners' Association, were presented with a parachute harness bearing the name of one of the air gunners who had baled out and had been killed on landing, thus providing some evidence that the gunner who had gone down with the aircraft had been Sgt Cottrell. Both gunners are buried in Ville au Bois.

Sgt Ackroyd evaded capture for over a week, having been given civilian clothes by members of the French Resistance. Because he was wearing these clothes he was handed over to the Gestapo and ill-treated to such an extent that he was asked to make a formal statement in connection with the Nuremberg War Trials.

Altogether, more than 300 aircrew lost their lives during that attack on Mailly le Camp. The names of 176 of them are contained in the War Graves Commission's registers, covering three districts, Marne, Aube and Yonne. Those who were not named therein were buried in cemeteries scattered along the routes to and from the target. In addition to the missing aircraft, a further twenty-four Lancasters were damaged by enemy action, and another three were damaged when other Lancasters exploded in their immediate vicinity.

In spite of the communications failure which led to such tragic and unexpectedly high losses of aircrew that night,[8] the raid was perhaps the most concentrated and therefore the most successful of all those described in this book. Two days later a No 541 Squadron Spitfire, flown by a Belgian, Plt Off L Mouzon, brought back irrefutable evidence of the devastation in the accommodation and workshop areas. Local Resistance sources spoke of German survivors walking around in a dazed condition more than twenty-four hours after the attack. Such was the loss of life amongst the highly trained NCO staff that the camp commandant was ordered to provide a report explaining why the loss of life had been so great.

I feel sure he would have been greatly assisted, when compiling his report, by a copy of the Photographic Interpreters report, had he been able to obtain one, which described the destruction as:

114 Barrack blocks hit and mostly destroyed.

47 Transport sheds hit.

102 vehicles, including 37 tanks, destroyed.

218 German soldiers killed and 156 seriously injured.

Mouzon's aerial photographs showed that the troops had taken to the woods and were housed in tents. They remained so accommodated until the depot was overrun by the Allied Armies in August 1944. For the Germans that attack on Mailly le Camp was a warning of the damage that could be inflicted by heavy bombers, not only on materials and equipment, but also on the morale of the most seasoned troops.

I do not think my brother and the other members of Bomber Command aircrews all died in vain that night.

Notes

1 Wg Cdr Deanne gave the time as 2359 hr. PRO Air 27/688 and 768.
2 The Squadron records contained several reports of 'Scarecrow' shells. See Chapter 3 for my own assessment of this phenomena.
3 See Appendix 5. The orders for the Master Bombers were altered as a result of the experience of Mailly le Camp.
4 BAMA Letter to the 21st Panzer Division dated 15 May 1944.
5 PRO Air 24/273-276, Interceptions and Tactics Report.
6 Personal letter from my father to the mother of Fg Off Muir, 3 March 1953. The photograph was probably from Sgt Borton's escape kit.
7 Commonwealth War Graves Register Fr 587. Apparently they were buried initially at Aubeterre, but their remains were removed by some Americans who were collecting the remains of their own aircrew in this area. I have yet to discover how or why the remains were re-interred at Dieppe.
8 I believe that things could have been worse. With so many fighter bases nearby it was not easy to pick a good route, but poor fighter control and other bomber attacks on the same night must have resulted in less concentration of German fighters than might otherwise have been achieved.

CHAPTER SIXTEEN

Bourg Leopold — 11 and 27 May 1944

Following the successful raid on Mailly le Camp on 3/4 May, Bomber Command decided that another German military depot should be attacked. The target was to be the permanent camp and training area near Bourg Leopold in northeast Belgium, which was being used by the German 15th Army for re-grouping and for training units resting from the Eastern Front. Like Mailly le Camp, the camp was also used as a tank training area. The 1st SS Panzer Division was stationed in that general area, and it was estimated that some 10,000 German servicemen were housed within the camp's boundaries.

Located in sandy heathland forty miles northeast of Brussels, and quite close to the border with Holland, the depot was captured by the Germans in 1940. After the war, it reverted to its original role as the main training area for the Belgian Army. The camp formed a military extension to the small Belgian town of Leopoldsburg (Bourg Leopold was the French version of the name, introduced during French Occupation in 1794), but due to the proximity of the small village of Beverlo on its western side, it was generally referred to by the Belgians as 'Camp Beverlo'. The differences in nomenclature gave rise to some false speculation about the first Bomber Command attack.

There were two attacks carried out by Bomber Command in May 1944: the first was a disaster; the second was much more successful and, although not as concentrated as the one on Mailly le Camp, it caused a lot of damage and casualties amongst the German forces stationed there.

Bomber Command Instruction AC546 issued on the morning of 11 May detailed No 5 Group to provide 190 Lancasters and eight Mosquitos, and No 8 (PFF) Group to furnish three 'Oboe'-equipped Mosquitos. The planned night attack followed a day in which over 200 aircraft of the USAAF Eighth Air Force attacked rail centres in Brussels and Liège. The plan was that the No 8 Group Mosquitos would drop yellow target indicators eight minutes before Zero hour, to be followed by target illuminating aircraft from No 83 (PFF) Squadron, attached to No 5 Group. The Mosquitos of No 5 Group would then go in and mark the northeast Aim Point with RSFs, and the southwest Aim Point with green markers. The Master Bomber, from No 83 (PFF) Squadron, would then assess the marking and direct the attack accordingly. Zero hour was set at 0010 hr on 12 May.

The route to and from the target was via the Norfolk coast, across the southern part of the North Sea to attack the target from the north before turning north to recross the Dutch coast, and heading for East Anglia. It was a round trip of 550-600 miles for the No 5 Group Lancasters and, with the usual allowances, only 1000 gallons of fuel would be required, leaving plenty of payload weight for bombs. In fact, most of the Lancasters carried between 12-14,000 lb of bombs, mostly weighing 500 lb, but there were some 4000-lb 'cookies'.

Most of No 5 Group's squadrons started to get their aircraft airborne at approximately 2230 hr. There were a few early returns, one of which was Wg Cdr Jeudwine of No 619 Squadron whose starboard outer engine caught fire shortly after taking off from Dunholme Lodge. The Mosquitos of Nos 109 and 627 Squadrons took off a little later. The weather forecast was cloudless skies from bases to the target, but the wind details given at the briefing and in subsequent broadcasts were badly out, both in direction and strength. The result was that Flt Lt Curtis, the navigator in the leading 'Oboe'-equipped Mosquito of No 109 Squadron, probably became aware of the problem as soon as he tried to join the 'Oboe' track. Realising that he was behind schedule he probably advised his skipper, Flt Lt Burt, who would have pushed on until they could achieve the full 'Oboe' control.

The net result was that they were only two minutes late in releasing their yellow TIs.[1] By the time the No 83 Squadron illuminators and No 627 Squadron's Mosquitos arrived, some five minutes later, the yellow TIs were beginning to go out. The flares became scattered and the Mosquitos were unable to see the Aim Points. One only of the No 627 Squadron Mosquito crews had a brief glimpse of the proximity markers and they and the four other crews started searching at low level for some signs of the target. As the flares became even more scattered and drifted even further west, the deputy controller, from No 83 Squadron, asked if he could drop a RSF as a marker for the illuminators. The Master Bomber acceeded to this request and his deputy released a marker at 0024 hrs.[2]

By that time the Main Force had arrived on the scene and, being grateful for some indication of the target, but not realising the true purpose of the marker, went in to bomb. Desperate efforts by the Master Bomber to stop the bombing were to no avail, and No 627 Squadron's Mosquitos, finding themselves under a hail of bombs, had to abandon their efforts to find and mark the target properly. Sqn Ldr Mitchell tried for nine minutes to stop the bombing, but once again his VHF radio proved unreliable and it was not until 0034 hr that a WT message got through. By that time, ninety aircraft had dropped nearly 200 tons of bombs onto an area well south and west of the target. Even after the message came through a few more aircraft continued to attack.

A brief CIU report, issued after a PRU sortie in the area, recorded that there was no damage to the barracks or the immediate surroundings. Of the seventy-four photographs taken during the bombing, only thirty were able to be plotted in the general area and they mostly contained ground detail of an area approximately three miles west or southwest of the target. Twenty-four of the photographs taken that night by No 5 Group were plotted eventually in the Louvain area, thirty miles southwest of the target. The remaining twenty photographs were never plotted.

A few of the crews who had responded to the call to stop bombing claimed to have bombed Hasselt rail yards, fourteen miles south of Bourg Leopold, which had been designated as a secondary target. Bearing in mind that most of the crews had been well west of their intended position, it seemed very likely that they bombed Louvain by mistake.

The Luftwaffe's reaction was mixed. Medium-range single- and twin-engined fighters were in action against the bomber force. Units of NJG 1 were in action and a victory call was heard at 0030 hr. The controllers seemed a little hesitant about committing the fighters in case an attack developed in Germany, but those fighters that were committed followed the bombers back over the North Sea. Ground defences near the target consisted of slight, heavy and light flak, the shells exploding between 2000-17,000 ft. There were no searchlights.

Most of the crews were back at their bases at 0215 hr. One notable exception was Flt Sgt Waugh of No 467 Squadron who, having received the signal to return to base, was attacked by a fighter and jettisoned his 4000-lb bomb in order to gain height quickly, but hung on to the rest of his bomb load, intending to drop it in the sea. When he came to release the other bombs he found that he could not get the bomb doors open. After flying around for a while, Waugh gave orders for all the crew, except the Flight Engineer, to bale out over Coleby. Eventually, he landed safely at his base at 0353 hr.[3]

Five aircraft failed to return to their bases that night. Plt Off Bunnager of No 9 Squadron crashed at Wilsele, a few miles north of Louvain. He died with his crew and all are buried in the village churchyard. No 61 Squadron's Lancaster, LM454, piloted by Plt Off Eastwood, crashed and exploded near the village of Milsele, four miles west of Antwerp. Eastwood and his navigator, Fg Off Kayser, are buried at Schoonselhof near Antwerp. Sgt R O Ellis became a PoW. No records are immediately available concerning the fate of the rest of the crew. Flt Sgt A R Barber and Plt Off L T Watson, the Wireless Operator and the Flight Engineer respectively, of No 467 Squadron's Lancaster LL792 are buried at Leopoldsburg. The remaining crew members, including the pilot, Plt Off Ward, and the second pilot, Wg Cdr Balmer, are buried at Heverlee. Their aircraft was seen to blow up in mid-air and the greater part of the wreckage fell near Beverlo.

No 630 Squadron lost two aircraft. One, Lancaster ME737, crashed in flames three kilometers south of Herenthout. The pilot, Plt Off Watt, is buried at Heverlee; five crew members are buried at Schoonselhof, and two others, Flt Sgt Stuart and Sgt Witham, escaped from the burning aircraft before it hit the ground. The fate of the second No 630 Squadron Lancaster, flown by Plt Off Jackson, was not known, but it may have come down in the sea. A further three aircraft were damaged by flak or fighters, one was damaged by machine-gun fire from another Lancaster, and one was damaged as it overshot the runway.

As serious as the loss of life was amongst the aircrews, an even greater tragedy was to unfold in the Belgian countryside, south and west of the target. The village of Beverlo was particularly badly hit; eighty-four people were killed and many more were seriously injured. One survivor, George Vantilt, who was fifteen years old at the time, described how he and his family had taken refuge in a friend's air-raid shelter, and how the terrific overpressures from the big bombs hurt their ears. One street in the village was totally destroyed, and the smell of burning and dead animals in the fields was sickening. In spite of that George Vantilt bore no ill-feeling towards the RAF. At the time of writing, he is the Chairman of a local society known as The Limburgian Friends of the Allied Air Forces whose aims are to foster friendship between ex-aircrew members and the Belgian people.

For some time it was thought by the local inhabitants that the target planners had made a mistake and, because the name of Beverlo was often used to describe the camp, Bomber Command had actually intended to bomb the village. Peter Loncke, a First Sergeant in the Belgian Air Force and a member of the Limburgian Society, has taken great pains to disprove that erroneous local theory, and has produced a valuable booklet concerning the two raids. I was pleased to have been able to assist him in its production, thereby establishing the facts and clearing the name of Bomber Command in connection with that unfortunate incident which could have led to intense and permanent ill-feeling.

The second and more successful attack took place two weeks later on the night of 27/28 May. More than 1100 aircraft of Bomber Command were operating over the near Continent that night, including a force of 170 heavy bombers which attacked the Rothe Erderail yards at Aachen, forty-five miles southeast of Bourg Leopold.

The Main Force sent to attack Bourg Leopold consisted of 150

Halifaxes of No 4 Group and thirty-two Lancasters and 117 Halifaxes of No 6 (Canadian) Group. No 1 Group was to provide ten 'ABC'-equipped Lancasters from No 101 Squadron, and No 8 (PFF) Group dispatched fourteen Lancasters and eight Mosquitos.

The plan was that the marking would be done using the controlled 'Oboe' or 'Musical Parramatta' technique by four Mosquitos and four reserve aircraft. Pathfinder Lancasters would then follow and, using either their H2S radar, or hopefully the 'Oboe'-placed markers as reference points, would release their flares. Back-up markers were to drop white TIs, when ordered by the Master Bomber. Zero hour was set at 0205 hr, and marking was to commence at 0155 hr. The main attack was to be in two waves, each of five minutes duration, with a five minute interval between waves.

The weather forecast was for a little cloud and moderate visibility at the bases, and fine weather over the Continent, with only a little cloud and good visibility. There would be very little moonlight. Different routes were arranged for the two waves. The first wave, consisting of seventy-five Halifaxes from each of Nos 4 and 6 Groups, was to fly via Orfordness to a point north of Brussels, then on to the target from whence it would break away, turning starboard and return, via a more southerly route, to Orfordness. The second wave, having a similar mixture of 150 aircraft, was to follow the same outward route as that of the first wave, flying 2000 ft lower at an altitude of 8-10,000 ft; having bombed, the aircraft would turn to port, take a more northerly route home, making a landfall near Southwold.

Both main groups began to get their squadrons airborne at approximately 2330 hr on 27 May, and all were away soon after midnight for what was to be, on average, a five-hour trip. The weather forecast proved to be reasonably accurate, with the outward run clear, except for some fog off the Dutch and Belgian coasts; the wind, blowing on their starboard side, was approximately 20 kt.

The first TIs were released by five aircraft of No 105 Squadron at 0154 hr. The more accurate ones fell approximately 320 yd west of the Aim Point. The first wave of Halifaxes responded well, flying in from the west and dropping their bombs from heights of 9-11,000 ft and the Master Bomber, Wg Cdr S P Daniels of No 35 Squadron, observed some very accurate bombing. Later, when smoke began to obscure the TIs, the bombing began to drift northeast; Daniels ordered the bombers to bomb closer to the white TIs with a one-second overshoot. The bombing became concentrated once again and a very large explosion occurred at 0207 hr.

German fighters were scrambled from their bases nearby, at St Trond, Deelen, Venlo and Florennes, when the bombers approached the Dutch coast, and at 0155 hr German fighter controllers were heard to direct their aircraft towards the area. Seven combats were reported on the approach to the target, and it was probable that of the ten aircraft lost, four fell to night fighters during their run in to bomb.

One of the aircraft attacked at 0210 hr was 'G' George of No 420 (Snowy Owl) Squadron RCAF, piloted by Plt Off Kalle. The aircraft was five miles west of the target, at 7000 ft, when the rear gunner, Sgt Metcalfe, gave a warning and ordered a 'corkscrew port'. The Flight Engineer, Sgt George Burton, finding the fuselage on fire, calmly put it out and returned to his crew position, from where he saw that the port mainplane and inner engine were on fire also. Attempts to put out the fire, using the Graviner fire system, failed and Burton advised the pilot to try to blow out the fire by diving steeply.

Meanwhile, Metcalfe had hit the enemy fighter and had watched as it burst into flames and crashed. Plt Off Kalle gave the order to prepare to bale out, but the dive did blow out the fire and at an altitude of 350 ft Kalle pulled the Halifax into level flight on three engines. Taking a roll-call, Kalle discovered that the mid-upper gunner, Sgt Elsinger, had mistaken the 'prepare to bale out' order and had departed via the rear emergency exit. Elsinger survived and evaded capture for a while with the help of some Belgians, but eventually he became a PoW and was released later by the Russians.

After a further two attacks and flying on three engines only, Burton discovered that the aircraft was still carrying seven 500-lb bombs which were almost rolling around in the bomb bay. Unable to jettison them because the bomb doors would not open, the skipper gave the remaining crew the option to bale out, but they declined; they all landed safely at the American base of North Peckenham. So great was the damage to 'G' George that the aircraft was written off.[4]

As well as some heavy and light flak between eight and twelve thousand feet, German fighters were active over the target and all the way to the Dutch and Belgian coasts and beyond. A further two bombers went down near the target and another four went down on the homeward leg. One of the luckier crews on the way home was that of Sgt Bowner of No 10 Squadron, who was approached by an Me 210 which started its attack by releasing red, green and white flares, but was driven off by long bursts from the two gunners, Sgts Grundy and Campbell.

Of the ten crews lost all but one were from the Halifax squadrons of Nos 4 and 6 Groups. The exception was Lancaster 'K' from No 101 Squadron, piloted by Plt Off T A Allen, which was providing 'ABC' support. Of the seventy-four aircrew reported missing from that raid, fifty-one were killed and the majority of them were buried in Heverlee cemetery in Belgium; fourteen became PoWs; and nine escaped with the aid of Belgian helpers.

On returning to Yorkshire, many crews found their bases shrouded in fog, and had to make diversions to East Anglia. Some of the aircraft did not touch down until after 0500 hr when it was discovered that a further twelve aircraft had been damaged as a result of enemy action. A further seven aircraft had been damaged as the result of accidents, including two which had been hit by machine-gun fire from 'friendly' aircraft. Dawn having broken well and truly, the tired crews attended their normal debriefings. At the same time crews of the Eighth USAAF were making their final preparations for a major effort against German oil targets.

Of the 100 flash photos taken at the time of the bombing, sixty-nine showed detail of the target area. When the aerial photographs, taken later by Sqn Ldr Ball of No 542 (PR) Squadron, were run through the processors the Photographic Interpreters' first phase reports listed 150 personnel huts and all the main barrack blocks as having been destroyed or badly damaged, and mentioned that there was great activity around some of the shelter trenches, which had been partly obliterated by bomb craters.

The German war cemetery at Lommel, a few miles away, contains the graves of more than 200 German servicemen who were killed in the raid. One such victim was Eugen Mannus, a sailor, who had just survived the sinking of his U-boat and was 'recuperating' at Bourg Leopold. The Belgian Resistance reported, at the time, much higher casualty figures amongst the Germans, and, like Mailly le Camp, mentioned soldiers wandering around in a daze and hiding in the woods. Although not as serious as the 'Tragedy of Beverlo', a considerable amount of damage was caused to the town of Leopoldsburg, including a school and twenty houses; civilian casualties were listed as twenty-two killed and a few wounded.

Notes

1 Sqn Ldr Mitchell, the Master Bomber, put the time at 0004 hr, the marker was scheduled to be dropped at 0002 hr.
2 Air 27/6883 and Air 24/274.
3 Air 14/3411.
4 In a different aircraft named 'G' George the crew made an emergency landing at White Waltham in July 1944. A 500-lb bomb exploded. All but one of the crew were seriously wounded; the wireless operator, Sgt Charles Cusack, died later of his injuries.

CHAPTER SEVENTEEN

Pre Invasion Attacks on V-1 and V-2 Sites

Work on German liquid-fuelled rockets began in the early 1930s[1] and the German Army began test-firing the A4 (known to the Allies as the V-2) at the experimental establishment at Peenemünde, on the Baltic island of Usedon, in June 1942. Development of the FZG 76 (which became known as the V-1 or Flying Bomb) was carried out by the Luftwaffe's Flak Arm, thus adding credence to the cover story that it was a pilotless aircraft used for target practice by anti-aircraft gunners.[2] Test firing the V-1 commenced with that of the Army's V-2. The story of the PRU observations and RAF Bomber Command's attack on Peenemünde in August 1943, can be read in Volume 3 of the official history of British Intelligence in the Second World War, or in Constance Babington-Smith's *Evidence in Camera*.

By June 1943, SIS reports and intelligence estimates of the performances of both V weapons pointed to the fact that the Germans intended to use them against London and targets in south and west England. Estimated ranges suggested that the weapons would be launched from sites in the Pas de Calais and Cherbourg Peninsula. Apart from the actual launch sites, which were quite different in nature, both weapons required extensive back-up facilities in the form of storage and check-out bunkers. Early in June 1943 PRUs were asked to carry out an intensive air survey of the likely areas in northwest France.

The early sorties produced evidence of unidentified constructions in several areas, but it was not until July that intelligence analysts, using a model produced by the model section at Medmenham, concluded that there was probably some connection between a large concrete bunker situated at Watten in the Pas de Calais and German V weapons. On 23 August the Vice Chiefs of Staff accepted a recommendation that Watten should be attacked by heavy bombers, and on 27 August[3] USAAF Eighth Air Force Bomber Command carried out the first attack on what were to become known as 'Crossbow' targets. Photographs taken at the time of the raid showed that two heavy concentrations of bombs fell on the target, but a subsequent photographic sortie by No 542 Squadron on 30 August revealed that, although a few of the 2000-lb bombs had penetrated the foundations, a further attack would be necessary.[4]

The attack was carried out on 7 September and the CIU was able then to confirm that construction at Watten had ceased, at least for the time being. However, the CIU reported that several similar constructions had been located elsewhere; moreover, in conjunction with the SIS, they had discovered some smaller sites which consisted of concrete strips and ramps, aligned roughly with London. By the end of November, seventy-five of what were termed 'Ski' sites had been found in the Calais area and a further seven on the Cherbourg Peninsula.

Discussions in December 1943 ended with the decision to employ medium bombers and fighters of the USAAF Ninth Air Force and 2nd Tactical Air Force against the new sites; but the results were disappointing and RAF Bomber Command was called in. On 16 December, an 'Oboe'-equipped Mosquito from No 105 Squadron marked two 'Ski' sites for a small force of heavy bombers from Nos 3 and 5 Groups. RAF Mosquitos and Stirlings between them made twenty-four attacks on 'Ski' sites in January 1944, and by the middle of the month the CIU reported that of the fifty sites attacked, thirteen had been put out of action.

Meanwhile General Arnold, Commanding General of the USAAF, had become interested in the problem and was keen to find the best method of attacking the sites. He ordered that concrete bunkers and ramps be set up in the proving grounds at Elgin Field in Florida. They were identical in every way to those found on the sites in France, and were attacked, using a variety of aircraft and weapons. The outcome of the Elgin Field experiment indicated that low-level attacks by fighters or medium bombers produced the best results.

There then followed some arguments, similar to those concerning the Transportation Plan, opinions concerning the best use of the heavy bombers being divided. However, a Combined Chiefs of Staff Directive of 13 February 1944 listed 'Crossbow' targets as the second principal task of the heavy bombers. As a result a combined offensive, in the spring, involved heavy bombers of the USAAF Eighth Air Force, RAF Bomber Command Mosquitos, and medium bombers of the AEAF. The main force of RAF Bomber Command was withdrawn from the campaign at the end of January, partly so that the Stirlings could step up their support for the French Resistance in the Haute Savoie area, and they did not bomb the sites again until after D-Day.

By mid-March photo-reconnaissance showed that of the ninety-six 'Ski' sites then identified, fifty-four had received major damage as a result of the bombing, but that most of them were under repair. Fearful of the consequences of a major flying bomb attack on the troops gathering in the south of England, and conscious of the fact that the heavy bombers would soon be involved with the Transportation Plan and later would be supporting the ground forces, the Chiefs of Staff agreed to intensify the offensive against the launch sites, using the heavy bombers of Eighth Air Force Bomber Command.[5]

For a while, it seemed that the increased level of bombing was having the desired effect, but in late April the CIU discovered the first of a series of new sites. What had happened was that General Heinemann, Commander of the German LXV Army Corps which controlled V-1 and V-2 operations, had decided that existing 'Ski' sites were too elaborate and vulnerable, and he ordered that they should be replaced by sites which could be concealed and constructed rapidly from pre-fabricated parts.

As soon as the new sites were identified, PRUs, aided by Tactical Reconnaissance squadrons of both the 2nd Tactical and Ninth Air Forces, set out to search the whole of northern France. By D-Day they had identified sixty-one new sites and reported that twelve of the original ninety-six sites were fit for use.

Preoccupation with the V-1 sites had diverted the Allied Staffs from the V-2 problem, which was further behind in development, but it had been generally accepted that some of the large sites were probably connected with the operational use of the V-2. There were seven of those large sites: Watten, Wizernes, Sottevaast, Martinvaast, Siracout, Lottinghem and Mimoyecques, and the Chiefs of Staff agreed to bomb all of them.

In the first three months of 1944, there were thirty attacks on those sites, sixteen by the Eighth Air Force, and fourteen by the AEAF. The CIU then produced a report which estimated that Martinvaast would take three months to repair, Lottinghem needed between six to twelve weeks' work, and Siracourt and Sottevaast could both be repaired in two to six weeks probably; little damage had been done to the other three sites. It was noted also that Mimoyecques was substantially different from the others.[6] After considering the report, the Chiefs of Staff again asked for more help from the Eighth Air Force. In April and May the Eighth Air Force, with rather less help from the RAF's 'Oboe'-equipped Mosquitos, carried out further attacks on Mimoyecques, Watten, Wizernes and Siracourt.

The following is a brief summary of the distribution of effort in the offensives against V-1 and V-2 sites in the first five months of 1944.[7]

RAF Bomber Command	448 sorties
Eighth Bomber Command	8940 sorties
AEAF	23,500 sorties

Notes

1 W Domberger, *V2* 1954.
2 FZG stood for Flakzillgerat, meaning Anti-aircraft Target Apparatus.
3 Hinsley, *British Intelligence in the Second World War*. Craven and Cate date these attacks at 30 August and 7 September.
4 PRO Air 40/436. Mission No 87. The bombs were fused to 1/10th of a second. One hundred and eighty-seven B-17s attacked. In spite of a heavy fighter escort, flak was intense and four bombers were shot down, all from the 1st Combat Wing.
5 Although it was agreed by all concerned, there was no direct order given to that effect.
6 Of the seven, Watten, Wizernes, Sottevaast and Martinvaast were intended V-2 launch sites, but the latter was converted into a V-1 site. Siracourt and Lottinghem were both designed as V-1 launch sites. Mimoyecques proved to be the site of a multi-barrelled, long-range gun known as the Hochdruckpumpe.
7 Leigh-Mallory Despatch, PRO Air 40/530-614 and Air 22/335.

CHAPTER EIGHTEEN

'Spoof' Raids

It was impossible to conceal the fact that the Allied invasion of Europe was imminent, or that air attacks would continue against Germany and the Occupied countries. The whole business of deception therefore revolved around attempts to mislead the Germans into thinking that the landings or air attacks were to take place at points other than those intended. Hoax, or 'spoof' raids, as they were called, fell into two categories: long-term deception plans conceived by Counter-Intelligence Staffs, and short-term measures, which were written into battle orders by operations staffs or commanders, designed to draw the enemy's attention away from the main attack.

The short-term measures included many feint attacks by No 8 (PFF) Group's Mosquitos which became known as the Light Night Striking Force (LNSF), but heavy bombers of both the RAF and the Eighth Air Force often provided their own diversions. They were greatly assisted by aircraft from OTUs and HCUs; by regular 'Gardening' sorties, and by aircraft on training or 'Bullseye' flights. Most of the diversions were in support of regular bombing raids on targets in Germany and Occupied Europe but the heavy bombers also played a significant part in the overall deception plan used when the Allied Forces crossed the English Channel (Operation Neptune).

'Spoof' raids began in earnest when the strength of RAF Bomber Command began to build-up in 1943. In April, eleven Mosquitos of No 2 Group accompanied more than 400 heavy bombers to Stettin and Rostock. Before reaching the main targets the Mosquitos peeled off towards Berlin, dropping 'Window' as they went. The Peenemünde raid in August owed some of its success to eight Mosquitos of No 139 Squadron which, after accompanying the Main Force to Peenemünde, flew south towards Berlin where they managed to draw out most of the German night fighters. By the time German fighter controllers realised their mistake, most of the Main Force had bombed the experimental rocket establishment and the Germans caught up with the last wave only as it returned to England.

In Autumn 1943, AVM Bennett began to expand the scale of the diversionary attacks by using his heavy bombers. On the night of 22/23 September twenty-nine Lancasters of No 8 (PFF) Group, backed up by Mosquitos of No 139 Squadron, carried out a 'spoof' raid on Oldenburg, at the same time as almost 650 aircraft bombed Hannover successfully with a much reduced loss rate. A very successful 'spoof' raid occurred on the night of 3/4 December when, at the height of the Battle of Berlin, Harris chose to attack Leipzig. More than 500 heavy bombers and ten Mosquitos used one of the 'usual' routes to Berlin, but at a point northeast of Magdeburg the bombers turned through ninety degrees towards Leipzig. The ten Mosquitos, six from No 139 and four from N 627 Squadron, flew east to Berlin, dropping 'Window' as they went. Arriving over the capital, they began to drop target indicators, which drew most of the 'Wild Boars' aircraft to the area. A contemporary ORS report illustrates the fact that the number of attacks by German fighters was increasing as the bombers flew along the outward route to the point where the 'spoof' began. At that point, the number of attacks dropped off sharply until the Germans realised, rather late in the proceedings, what was happening and caught up with Main Force only after they had bombed. Of the 527 bombers twenty-three only were missing (4.3 per cent), but a third of Leipzig lay in ruins, including much of the site of the World Fair which had been converted to factories and included a Junkers aircraft assembly plant.[1]

By the spring of 1944 diversionary attacks were often coordinated with mining ('Gardening' sorties); short, sharp intruder patrols by Mosquitos against German airfields; and training ('Bullseye') sorties over the North Sea. The nightly dilemmas of the confused and often overwhelmed German fighter controllers were compounded by orders to conserve aviation fuel, and by radar screens clouded by 'Window' and electronic jamming. Sorting the real attacks from the false was guaranteed to produce new ulcers upon those which already existed!

Feints and diversions became a regular feature of operations by both RAF and Eighth Air Force Bomber Commands, not only over Germany but over Belgium and France also. Sometimes, multiple attacks in one night on Transportation Plan targets had much the same confusing effect on German defences. During the earlier attacks, however, German Fighter Controllers were more concerned with the threat to the homeland, and very small forces of Mosquitos attacking targets in Germany were able to draw attention away from bombers which were attacking the railways in France; but it did not always work. By mid-April the Germans began to appreciate the significance of the attacks in France and Belgium, and even multiple attacks, coupled with 'Nickel' raids on France, and Mosquito attacks on Germany, did not prevent a 6.3 per cent loss rate at Tergnier on the night of 10/11 April 1944.

When it finally came on the night of 5/6 June, the Allied invasion of Normandy was supported by six different 'spoof' raids and two major electronic jamming operations which were all carried out by RAF Bomber Command.

The two most complicated deception plans, devised by Wg Cdr E J Dickie, the senior navigator in the Bomber Command Radar Department,[2] involved Lancasters from No 617 Squadron, led by Leonard Cheshire, and from No 218 Squadron, led by Wg Cdr Fenwick-Wilson. The No 617 Squadron ruse, codenamed 'Taxable', was a joint Naval/Air Force operation, designed to make the Germans believe that an attack was being made against the coast between Dieppe and Cap d'Antifer. The Royal Navy employed eighteen small craft as tugs to tow balloons which produced the signatures of larger ships on the screens of what was left of the German coastal radar. The 'convoy' extended for fourteen miles and was fifteen miles wide, the timing and speed of movement was such that it was made to appear that a landing would take place just before dawn.

The aerial part of the plan involved sixteen Lancaster crews who had been training since the attack on Mailly le Camp in May.[3] Flying in two lines, four aircraft abreast, they formed a 'box' twelve miles wide by four miles deep over the naval convoy. A series of thirty elongated orbits were flown with the longer axes of the orbits at right angles to the coastline. Each orbit began precisely 0.82 miles nearer the coast than the preceding one; accuracy was achieved with the aid of signals from the southern 'Gee' chain. The additional use of 'Window' helped to create the impression on German radar of a convoy moving at seven knots towards the coast.

From its start at 0030 hr the 'convoy' covered twenty-four miles and ended just over three and a half hours later at nautical twilight.[4] The operation was a masterpiece of accurate flying and it was no fault of the people concerned that it did not provoke much reaction from the Germans.[5] Although care had been taken to leave one or two German radar stations serviceable in order that they might take the bait, it seemed that Allied bombing and radar jamming in the area had been too good.

Another combined air/sea operation was codenamed 'Glimmer'.[6] The destination of its 'convoy' was the beaches near Boulogne. The Operation was very similar in concept to 'Taxable', but involved fewer boats and only six aircraft of No 218 Squadron. The distance covered by the 'convoy', although much the same as 'Taxable's', involved crossing a narrow part of the English Channel, making it appear that the Force was taking one of the expected routes.[6] The Operation was an instant success. Searchlights and guns opened up on the 'convoy', and the nearby 'ABC' operation was mistaken for air cover and many German fighters were put up against it. German E-boats were also sent to the area.

Other attempts at deception, as opposed to jamming, were codenamed 'Titanic', and were aimed at simulating airborne landings behind the 'Taxable' beaches and on the Cotentin Peninsula, south of the area chosen for the American airborne landings. 'Titanic 1' involved fifteen aircraft from No 3 Group's Nos 138, 149 and 161 Squadrons. With the aid of 'Window' the aircraft created the impression initially of a much larger force, then dropped dummy parachutists accompanied by noises of battle in the area of Yvetot, on the road between Rouen and Le Havre. The first reaction of the ruse was timed at 0100 hr on 6 June when an unknown German Army station reported parachute drops near Le Havre.

'Titanic 2' was cancelled and was to have taken place in much the same area as 'Titanic 3 and 4' which involved sixteen aircraft from Nos 90, 138 and 149 Squadrons. Approaching from the west they flew north of Coutance on a track parallel to and approximately fifteen miles south of that taken by the invasion force. Two of the false formations simulated landings in the Maligny area while the third ('Titanic 3') flew on to Villers Bocage which lay south of the British invasion beaches. The Maligny feint drew 915 Infantry Regiment of 352 Infantry Division away from the American 82nd and 101st Airborne Divisions' landings; they were having a hard time coping with an inaccurate drop and the swamp land between Ste Mère-Eglise and Carentan. 'Titanic 3' seems to have produced little enemy reaction; two Stirlings of No 149 Squadron were lost in that operation.

The Airborne Cigar (ABC) operation by No 101 Squadron Lancasters and the 214 Squadron's B-17s has already been mentioned, but it is worth noting that between them the twenty-nine aircraft carried no less than eighty-two radio sets which were used to jam German night fighter frequencies. They spent four and a half hours on patrol at a height of 24-27,000 ft.

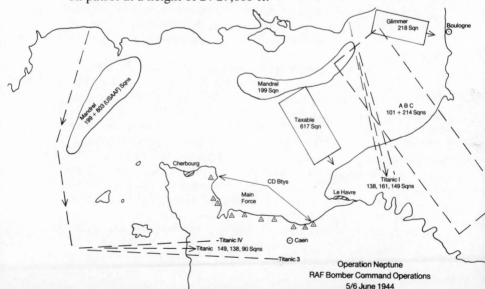

Operation Neptune
RAF Bomber Command Operations
5/6 June 1944

A further electronic operation was carried out by Stirlings of No 199 Squadron and B-17s of the 803rd USAAF Squadron. For five and a half hours they flew at 1800 ft around twelve different points in mid-Channel, six off Portland and six off Littlehampton. Using 'Mandrel' they effectively jammed all but about five per cent of the German coast-watching Freya radars between Cherbourg and Le Havre which had not been bombed out of action previously.

That night, RAF Bomber Command provided 111 diversionary sorties in the 'Neptune' area, despatched thirty-one aircraft on a diversionary operation to Osnabruck, and provided a further twenty-five intruder Mosquitos and twenty-seven bomber support aircraft. From all these operations only five aircraft were lost.

The long-term deception plan for Operation Neptune was helped considerably by the fact that Sigint sources had expanded greatly in the previous months. The original Anglo/US deception plan was drawn up at the end of 1943. Known as 'Bodyguard'[7], it was designed to draw attention away from France altogether, and hoped to persuade the Germans that an attack was to be made in Norway, in conjunction with the Russians, and that Germany would be brought to its knees by strategic bombing. However, German signals indicated that the bait was not being taken, and that the Germans were preparing to meet a cross-Channel invasion.[8]

In January 1944 SHAEF's Intelligence Staffs began work on 'Fortitude', a new deception plan which, while accepting that the Germans knew that the invasion was to take place 'somewhere between Belgium and Biscay', set about trying to convince the Germans that Normandy was the least likely area for the invasion, and that the Pas de Calais was more likely.

It was not an easy task for the architects of the Transportation Plan because the original requirement was to create a railway desert within 150 miles of Caen. The map on page 50 shows that of the fifty-nine rail centres chosen for attack by the heavy bombers prior to D-Day, only twenty fell within the prescribed radius, the remainder lay east and northeast of Paris with connecting rail links to the Calais area. While that conformed with the requirements of 'Fortitude', anything but a railway desert existed in the Brest and Cotentin Peninsulas, and led to the German 7th Army's Transport Officer recommending quick routes to Normandy from Rennes to Coutance, Laval to Flers and Le Mans to Argentan.[9]

Another result of strict adherence to 'Fortitude' manifested itself in a temporary lull in the bombing of bridges over the Seine by the AEAF. Luftflotte 3 signals indicated that attacks on those bridges on 7 May had led the Germans to conclude that Normandy had been chosen by the Allies for the landing. A ban was immediately imposed, but was lifted later when it was realised that bombing the Seine bridges would disrupt the flow of traffic to and from Normandy.

A ban on the bombing of bridges over the Loire remained in force until after D-Day.

The second requirement of 'Fortitude' was that, for every radar or coastal defence site bombed within the 'Neptune' area, two would be bombed outside the area. The general concept of heavy bombers being used against such targets was never popular with Harris and Spaatz, and the idea of wasting bombs on targets that would have no influence over the battle was an even greater thorn in their sides. However, they realised that it was in a good cause. There can be no doubt that in Operation Fortitude, the Allied bombers helped to persuade the Germans that the Pas de Calais was the most likely area for the invasion. Soon, there would be little need for further 'spoof' raids.

Notes

1 Gordon Musgrove, *Pathfinder Force* p32.
2 Dudley Saward, *Victory Denied* p337.
3 See Chapter 15.
4 Nautical twilight is a little earlier than civil twilight which begins when the sun's centre is six degrees below the horizon and when the horizon becomes clear.
5 The German OKW discounted reports of 'major enemy forces heading for Cap d'Antifer' which were sent in by Naval Group West. David Eisenhower, *Eisenhower at War* p261.
6 AHB narratives.
7 *British Intelligence in the Second World War*, Vol III Pt 2 p45.
8 Ibid.
9 See map on page 196.

CHAPTER NINETEEN

'Neptune' and 'Overlord'

Operations Neptune and Overlord were the greatest combined operations the world has ever seen. 'Neptune' was the code name for the crossing of the English Channel and the Normandy landings. 'Overlord' related to establishing a foothold in Normandy and liberating those countries in Europe which had been occupied by Nazi forces since the dark days of Dunkirk in June 1940.

Our concern now centres on the part played by Allied heavy bombers in the six weeks before the breakout from the Normandy beach-head. The Main Force of RAF Bomber Command began preparing for 'Neptune' during the afternoon of 5 June 1944. Orders were issued to Groups by HQ Bomber Command at 1230 hr,[1] and referred to Operation Order No 188 which had been sent out under special cover on 2 June. By the time squadron briefings were taking place, at approximately 1830 hr,[2] rumours were circulating to the effect that 'this was the big one'. Operation 'Flashlamp' called for a total of 1136 heavy bombers to neutralise ten heavy gun batteries between Le Havre and Cherbourg.[3] The plan required each of the batteries to be attacked at different times, the general concept being that the attacks should finish at first light, when Eighth Air Force heavy bombers and AEAF medium bombers began their attacks. There were three main exceptions to the timing: two batteries in the American sector and one in the British had to be attacked before airborne forces landed. Other minor differences in timing were planned to meet variations in the landing times of assault craft, which, because of the time differences in low tides, were earlier on the American-invaded beaches than on those in the British sector. All the attacks were to be preceded by No 8 (PFF) Group Mosquitos using 'Oboe', and the route to the most easterly targets was via Hastings; the more westerly targets were to be approached via Bridport. All aircraft except those of No 3 Group would come back over Hastings.

The attacks opened at 2331 hr when on 5 June ninety-two Lancasters from No 1 Group, led by two 'Oboe'-equipped Mosquitos began dropping bombs on the guns at Crisbecq Fontenay, which covered the American Utah beach on the east side of the Cherbourg Peninsula. Transport aircraft carrying the 82nd 101st US Airborne

Divisions were due over the area an hour later, so it was essential that No 8 (PFF) Group aircraft marked on time (using 'Musical Parramatta'). In the ensuing ten minutes No 1 Group Lancasters, bombing through cloud, dropped 534 tons of high explosives, mainly in the form of 1000-pounders.

Ten minutes later, a further ninety-four Lancasters from the same Group were bombing the St Martin de Varreville battery, which lay a few miles further south between the beaches and the 101st US Airborne Division's dropping zone. In a slightly longer attack, which took place between 2343 and 0100 hr, the bombers dropped 547 tons of bombs onto the casemates, which had been well marked by five Mosquitos. American paratroopers who captured the battery positions soon afterwards reported that, although the bombing had been accurate, the guns had seemingly been moved prior to the raid.[4]

The last of the initial attacks was against the Merville battery, which lay very close to the area chosen for landing the British 6th Airborne Division. Low cloud obscured the target when seventy Halifaxes and ten Lancasters from No 6 Group attacked at 0025 hr. Three only of the five Mosquitos sent had been able to release their markers, which were rather scattered and appeared as indistinct glows beneath the cloud. Fifteen minutes later the bombers were withdrawing, eighty-three aircraft out of a total force of 104 having attacked. Nearly all their bombs had missed the target, and had given the 6th Airborne Division's advanced party some nasty moments.[5]

Then followed a lull in Main Force operations until 0314 hr on 6 June when the first of the remaining seven batteries were attacked by 100 Halifaxes of No 4 Group. The positions at Maissy, close to the American Omaha beach, were bombed between 0314 and 0339 hr. The battery had been bombed already on the night of 4/5 June. Although silenced during the actual seaborne assault, the photo plot of the raid indicated that most of the bombs fell east of the target, and the gun crews recovered to fire, and be fired on by the US Navy, until 10 June. When finally overrun, two days later, it was discovered that one gun had been knocked from its mounting, but it was not possible to tell if this had been done by bombing or naval gunfire.

Le Pernelle, on the Pointe de Barfleur, was a six-gun battery which commanded the approaches to the American beaches. Using 1000-lb bombs, 108 aircraft of No 5 Group dropped 600 tons between 0331 and 0444 hr. The attack opened with marking by four 'Oboe'-equipped Mosquitos from No 8 (PFF) Group followed by four of No 5 Group's Mosquitos dropping ground markers. The battery was silenced during the initial assault, but opened up again later and continued to fire until overrun by the Americans in the last week of June. When it was captured it was discovered that only one casemate had been damaged, probably by naval gunfire.

For Houlgate the bombs carried by the 102 Halifaxes of No 6

(Canadian) Group were mostly of the 500-lb type, and although the gun crews seemed to have been put off for a while, the guns were not silenced permanently and, in fact, became a source of worry until temporarily put out of action again by naval gunfire on 19 June. The guns were in a position to bring down enfilade fire on the British beaches, and were still intact when captured in August. Although none of the aircraft were lost during the raid, one from No 426 Squadron crashed near Bircham Newton killing all the crew.

During the next hour and a quarter the remaining four batteries, Longues, Mt Fleury, Pointe de Hoe and Ouistreham, each received over 500 tons of bombs. Pointe de Hoe, which was considered to be the most dangerous, had 637 tons dropped on it by 108 Lancasters of No 5 Group. It was the heaviest and best concentrated attack of the night, but it incurred the greatest losses also: one Lancaster from each from Nos 50 and 582 Squadrons and two from 97 Squadron. An attack by Marauders of the USAAF Ninth Air Force followed at first light but unfortunately, when the American Rangers reached the casemates they found that the guns had been removed and replaced by telegraph poles, probably because of attacks before D-Day; the guns had been re-located approximately 1000 yd inland. The attacks on Longues and Fleury by Lancasters and Halifaxes of Nos 4 and 6 (Canadian) Groups both resulted in losses. Nos 76 and 578 Squadrons each lost one Halifax on Mt Fleury, and No 582 Squadron lost a Lancaster at Longues. The No 578 Squadron Lancaster crashed into the sea near the Cherbourg Peninsula and three of the crew were rescued.[6]

Ouistreham was the last target to be attacked, between 0502 and 0515 hr. All but one of 106 Lancasters of No 3 Group dropped their 1000-lb bombs onto the No 8 (PFF) Group markers. Although they destroyed service buildings, the casemates remained intact, and, in spite of reports in the German 7th Army Telephone log of partial damage by air attacks, the guns appeared intact when captured late on D-Day.[7]

In the first few hours of the 'Longest Day' RAF Bomber Command had dropped more than 5000 tons of bombs onto the ten most feared coastal batteries in the Bay of the Seine. They had encountered little opposition from flak or enemy fighters, but the weather deteriorated and patches of low cloud obscured half the number of targets. The cloudy conditions persisted into the daylight hours to such an extent that it was not possible to obtain any photographs for post-strike analysis. The cloud conditions interfered also with the daylight bombing which was to follow. As the last of the RAF Lancasters and Halifaxes pulled away into the lightening sky,[8] aircraft of the AEAF and USAAF Eighth Air Force Bomber Command began to lend their support to the great armada of boats which was approaching the Normandy beaches.

Eighth Air Force heavy bombers started to assemble over the skies of East Anglia just after 0200 hr; because the attack was planned to take place in waves, the last B-17 did not become airborne until after 0500 hr. Flying six squadrons abreast with H2X Pathfinders leading, their aim was to saturate the beaches ahead of the landing craft. Each attack was planned to end ten minutes before the first landing craft touched the target beach. A total of 1361 B-17s and B-24s from three Bombardment Divisions were briefed to take part in the first of the daylight missions. 1083 aircraft attacked forty-five targets, dropping nearly 3000 tons of bombs, most of which were fitted with instantaneous fuses so as not to crater the beach and hinterland and so impede the movement of the invaders' vehicles. The attacks began shortly after 0600 hr when the first of twelve waves of B-24s from the 2nd Bombardment Division flew to the east side of the Cherbourg Peninsula. Each wave contained thirty-six aircraft and they made for Omaha beach. Less than an hour later 650 B-17s and sixty-three B-24s of the 1st and 3rd Bombardment Divisions bombed the British beaches of Juno and Sword. One aircraft only was lost on that mission, a B-24 of the 3rd Bombardment Division.

The first, and probably most successful, daylight mission by USAAF Ninth Air Force was undertaken by Marauders of the 98th and 99th Combat Bombardment Wings. Their mission had almost been cancelled because of low cloud, but their commander, Brig Samuel E Anderson, sought permission to go in under the cloud at approximately 3500 ft and 278 aircraft found and successfully bombed the defences behind Utah beach. The heavy guns of two battleships and two cruisers fired into that area also, and one hour later, when the landing craft of the US 4th Infantry Division were on their final run ashore, the bombing switched to the beaches which were being fired on with rockets and light calibre shells from smaller support craft.

For the troops huddled behind the bow ramps of their landing craft it was the moment of truth. 'Neptune' was 'on', and they were all hoping that the Air Forces had done a good job on the beaches ahead of them. At Utah beach the plan seemed to have worked well, but fear of 'shorts' had led to the bomb aimers being briefed to delay bomb release for up to thirty seconds past the release points. This precaution, agreed by Eisenhower, resulted in some of the defences in the immediate vicinity of the beaches receiving less than their allocation of bombs, and to problems for the invaders when they waded ashore in the face of machine guns which should have been silenced.

Throughout the day, AEAF medium bombers and heavy bombers of the Eighth Air Force all continued to operate in a tactical role. For the second mission of the day 500 heavy bombers of the Eighth Air Force were despatched at 0900 hr to bomb the so-called choke points in nearby towns such as Caen, Thury-Harcourt, Vire and St Lo. However, persistent low cloud and a lack of blind bombing aids caused all but three of the bomber groups to abort the mission.[9] A later attack by fifty-six Liberators was more successful and, coupled with the earlier attacks by the AEAF, left only one bridge over the River Orne intact, thus helping to delay the arrival of the 21st Panzer Division.

In the last mission of the day 550 heavy bombers of the Eighth Air Force bombed Transportation Plan targets from Coutances in the west to Lisieux.[10] The attacks were at the request of HQ AEAF and marked the change from planned to tactical operations. A total of 736 aircraft were briefed to take part, but weather conditions for assembly over England were so bad that most groups flew higher than intended and some aircraft joined up with the wrong group. Good results were recorded, however, by a small group of B-24s which bombed Coutances on the west side of the Cherbourg Peninsula. The combined total of sorties flown on D-Day by the Eighth and Ninth Air Forces was 8722. Some of the crews had flown two missions, and seventy-one aircraft had been lost, many of them from the Fighter Commands — less than one per cent.

During the first night (6/7 June) 1160 aircraft of RAF Bomber Command attacked nine choke points which the Eighth Air Force had been forced to abandon during the day. The points included bridges and road and rail junctions at Coutances, Achères, St Lô, Caen, Argentan, Vire, Châteaudun, and Lisieux. Cloud again affected most of the targets and at Achères near Paris it was so bad that the Master Bomber called off the attack for fear of killing too many French civilians. More than 1060 aircraft attacked and dropped 11,500 tons of bombs, most of which were of the 500-lb type. The attacks commenced at 0017 hr when five squadrons of Halifaxes from No 6 (Canadian) Group bombed visually onto red and green TIs, dropped by three Mosquitos and two Lancasters of No 8 (PFF) Group. The target was a rail and road junction at Coutances, and the attack was accurate and well concentrated. Flt Lt Pullar, flying aircraft 'O' of No 408 Squadron, had the first recorded bomb release, timed at 0017.30 hr. There were no losses during the attack, but one Halifax of No 426 Squadron crashed near Torquay and two of the crew were missing.

As the Canadians were heading out to sea for home, four squadrons of No 1 Group started their attack on Vire. W/O Clough, of No 625 Squadron, was one of the first to bomb at 0035 hr (exactly Zero hour). The whole affair was over in about five minutes, during whch time the bombers had managed to hit all the choke points, and had partly destroyed the railway station. The centre of the town was a shambles, with rubble blocking the roads. Three aircraft were missing: Nos 103, 460 and 576 Squadrons each lost one Lancaster.

Two of the aircraft were lost to enemy fighters, the other to flak.

The last of the initial attacks that night was on the rail centre at St Lô, and was carried out by 103 Halifaxes of No 4 Group. The Master Bomber, Wg Cdr S P Daniels of 35 (PFF) Squadron, controlled the attack well. Having dropped his markers from 4000 ft, just below the cloud, he was able to observe some good, concentrated bombing on the town and railway yards; the locomotive depot was partly destroyed.

The central group of targets, Argentan, Conde and Lisieux, were next on the schedule. Approximately 100 aircraft from each of Nos 3 and 6 Groups attacked Conde and Lisieux, while No 5 Group sent two separate forces each of more than 100 aircraft to Argentan and Caen. One Lancaster of No 115 Squadron, piloted by Fg Off McBride, failed to return from the Lisieux raid, but the Canadians did not suffer any losses at Conde; both attacks produced satisfactory results. No 5 Group was less fortunate, losing one Lancaster to flak at Argentan (which incidentally had three Aim Points), and six at Caen, most of them to fighters which they met on the way home. In addition to the sudden and unexpectedly high loss of aircraft, one Lancaster of No 92 Squadron crashed at Grantham on returning from Argentan, and all but one of the crew were killed.

Both the No 5 Group attacks followed the pattern of pre D-Day attacks on rail centres, the Group's Mosquitos dropped ground markers onto the markers dropped by No 8 (PFF) Group 'Oboe'-equipped aircraft. The centre of Caen was left in flames, the river barrage over the Orne was destroyed, four other bridges were destroyed or had their approaches blocked, and the main roads from the town to Falaise and Bayeux were badly cratered.

The penultimate attacks of the night were against the rail junctions at Châteaudun and Achères. At the former 100 Halifaxes of No 4 Group were directed by Sqn Ldr E L Chidgey, flying in Lancaster 'F' of No 35 (PFF) Squadron. After four failures to mark the target using 'Oboe', it was finally marked at 0204 hr. Seeing that his back-up markers had landed some way from the Aim Point, Chidgey ordered the Main Force to bomb on those dropped by his deputy, Flt Lt Lambert. The Halifaxes did a good job in what were perhaps the clearest conditions of the night. One Halifax of No 578 Squadron was lost to flak.

To the east the No 1 Group attack on Achères was in trouble. Thick cloud obscured the target and the markers that had been dropped could not be seen. A few of the crews took it upon themselves to drop below the cloud and start bombing. The Master Bomber, Sqn Ldr G W Godfrey of No 156 Squadron, decided that the risk to life amongst the French civilians was too great and called off the attack. Approximately half of the ninety-seven Lancasters sent did not bomb. Aircraft 'F' of No 550 Squadron, piloted by Plt

Off Sherrington, did not return to its base at North Killingholme.

Apart from the chance incident at Caen there was little or no enemy fighter activity during the first night of 'Overlord' operations, and it was thought at the time that the Luftwaffe were holding back its fighters against the possibility of a second and major airborne landing in the Pas de Calais area.

The next five days and nights followed a similar pattern regarding operations by the heavy bombers, and included the well-known attack on the Saumur rail tunnel, which No 617 Squadron blocked using 12,000-lb 'Tallboy' bombs on 8/9 June. Enemy reaction became more noticeable after the first forty-eight hours. RAF Bomber Command lost twenty-nine aircraft on the night of 7/8 June, thirteen of them at the rail centre of Massy-Palaiseau, near Paris; but it seemed that the losses were more often the result of flak rather than encounters with fighters. In a night attack of 7/8 June, 212 aircraft from Nos 1, 5 and 8 Groups were sent to bomb a German fuel dump in the Forêt de Cerisy, near St Lô. The attack, which was made at the request of the US 1st Army, was not a success because the Main Force bombed on a stray marker which had been dropped inadvertently six miles from the target.

On 8 June better weather tempted Eighth Air Force Bomber Command to attack the bridges over the River Loire for the first time since the landings.[11] A small force of B-24s of the 3rd Bombardment Division carried radio-controlled bombs to the bridges at Vannes, Porcaro and Redon, but the weather turned sour on them and that part of the plan had to be abandoned. Other Bomber Groups did attack bridges and airfields on the Cherbourg Peninsula, but of the combined total of B-17s and B-24s sent 735 only attacked their targets. They were escorted by over 1000 fighters, twenty-two of which were shot down. Three heavy bombers were lost also.

During the same period AEAF medium and fighter bombers provided constant ground attack support for the armies as they struggled to enlarge the beach-head and make room for the mass of equipment and troops which were following the initial assault. Fighter aircraft covered shipping, from the beaches to fifteen miles offshore, and formed a protective screen inland. Almost 2000 fighter sorties were flown on D-Day alone, while the medium bombers flew approximately 700 sorties against coastal defences, bridges, radar stations and other targets, at the request of the armies. The need for airfields in the lodgement area, realised during the planning stages, became even greater as the weather deteriorated because many of the UK airfields were closed down. One transport strip was useable on 8 June, but the first fighter bomber strips were not available until 19 June.

At 0418 hr on 13 June the first V-1 flying bomb dropped near Gravesend, and, following much talk in Whitehall, RAF Bomber

Command was ordered to divert part of its force to attack launch sites in the Pas de Calais area. The new campaign opened on the night of 16/17 June when 315 RAF heavy bombers made the first attack on a 'Crossbow' target since January. They were joined on 19 June by aircraft of Eighth Air Force Bomber Command, and on 23 June by Ninth Air Force medium bombers, which had been concentrating mostly on the bridges over the Seine and the Loire. The V-1 threat was considered to be so great that in the next ten days V-1 launch and supply sites utilised approximately thirty per cent of the Allied bombing effort.[12] That diversion from tactical targets connected with 'Overlord' became a source of intense debate between Allied Air Commanders.[13]

In the midst of the new turmoil, Harris and Spaatz both managed to assemble considerable forces of heavy bombers to attack, what was to them, the more important targets in Germany. In the last two weeks of June, RAF Bomber Command attacked the synthetic oil plants at Gelsenkirchen, Scholven/Bauer (twice), Sterkrade and Hombe, losing fifty-six aircraft in all. The heavily escorted Americans attacked Bremen and a further five plants, losing eleven B-17s, one of which landed in Russia, having bombed the synthetic oil plant at Ruhland Schwarzheide. Both Bomber Commands were involved also in attacks on German fuel dumps in France, one of the most important being an attack on Châtellerault on the night of 15/16 June when 119 aircraft from RAF Bomber Command destroyed approximately one quarter of the dump's total capacity.

Naval targets, particularly the heavily protected U- and E-boat pens, also came under attack by heavy bombers during the first week of the Normandy Landings. With the exception of No 6 Group, all the other operational groups of RAF Bomber Command carried out successful attacks on Le Havre and Boulogne on 14 and 15 June. At the same time 'Gardening' sorties were intensified greatly. Meanwhile, the AEAF and the Eighth Air Force both made heavy attacks against German airfields within 150 miles of Caen.

The calls upon the stategic air forces in the latter part of June and in July 1944 were frequent and infinitely varied. To produce a balanced account of the events leading up to the Normandy Landings, mention should be made at this point of the part played by the AEAF.

When the USAAF Ninth Air Force became available for pre-invasion bombing duties in March, it was allocated twenty-five targets in northwest France and Belgium. During the period March to May groups of up to 100 medium bombers, mostly B-26 Marauders, returned generally good results. They were escorted and backed-up by P-47 Thunderbolts, and RAF Typhoons and Mosquitos of the 2nd Tactical Air Force, which formed the RAF element of the AEAF. To supplement the attacks, the targets of which were part of the Transportation Plan, Leigh-Mallory authorised large-scale fighter sweeps against moving trains. The 'Chattanooga Choo-Choo' missions, as they were called, caused great disruption of the French railways, damaging 500 locomotives and cutting lines in 150 places. Perhaps the most decisive part played by the Ninth was the bombing of bridges over the rivers Seine and Loire.[14]

When the ban on bombing Seine bridges was lifted on 24 May, Ninth Air Force Marauders and Thunderbolts began a series of low-level attacks on the bridges at Le Manoir, Poissy, Maisons Laffitte, Le Mesnil Ande, Orival, Rouen, Conflans, Juvissy, Athis and Meulan. The B-26 proved itself to be ideal for this type of attack, which was particularly successful when the targets were finished off by P-47s dive-bombing with 500-lb bombs and by rocket-firing Typhoons. Occasionally, however, it was necessary to employ heavy bombers to drop larger bombers onto the more solid piers and abutments.

By the time of the Normandy Landings, all the bridges over the Seine below Paris had been destroyed. By way of comparison, it was interesting to note that 4500 tons of bombs were used to achieve that result whereas, during the same period, approximately 71,000 tons had been dropped on the rail centres by heavy and medium bombers. The early destruction of the Seine bridges was far from the end of the story. Enormous efforts were made by the Germans to repair or replace the bridges, and air reconnaissance, photographic and tactical, became an important factor in the battle to keep the bridges closed. Bad weather during June created a problem for the Allies in that respect but, generally speaking, the AEAF kept up with any repair work on the bridges, especially during the initial weeks of the invasion.

The weather, which had forestalled attempts to bomb the Loire bridges on 8 June, deteriorated further and there were virtually no air operations on 9 June. By 17 June all of the nineteen road bridges between Tours and Nantes had been subjected to heavy attacks by the Ninth Air Force, as had the nine rail bridges over the same stretch of river, and a further three between Tours and Orléans. Strong reaction by Luftwaffe Fighter and Flak Arms was an indication of the great importance attached to keeping those crossing points open. Desperate measures were employed by the Germans to get some traffic moving from the south to the Normandy area. After nine days' hard work at Tours La Riche they were able to use the bridge by pushing one carriage at a time over a dangerously weakened structure. In the Paris-Orléans gap nine points were selected for attack, one of them, Chartres, being attacked six times between the middle of June and the first week in August. Nor were the bridges in Brittany neglected. On 18 July the Ninth Air Force destroyed five spans of the high-level viaduct at Laval, returning on 21 July to destroy the repairs which had not even been completed.

By way of rounding off this brief summary of the work of the AEAF the following quote from Craven and Cate's *History of the Army Air Forces in the Second World War* provides a useful comparison between the rail centre offensives and those against the bridges:

> *With RAF and the Eighth and Ninth Air Forces cooperating, attacks on freight yards alone involved over 15,000 Allied sorties and using nearly 35,000 tons of bombs dropped in the period of 6 June-31 July. In the same period Allied planes flew over 16,000 sorties and directed more than 24,500 tons of bombs against bridge targets.*[15]

The Normandy city of Caen was regarded as the key to the British lodgement area. Montgomery had hoped and planned to capture it by the evening of D-Day. (The reasons for failing to do so have been the subject of many studies. I do not believe that the lack or misuse of air support, or poor intelligence, were among the factors which contributed to that failure.)

After 7 June, Montgomery decided 'not to butt up against the place', and two attempts at encirclement followed.[16] The first, on 13 June, involved a drive towards Villers Bocage, but the heavy bombers were to become involved in the V-1 campaign and were not used.

Consequently, the ground attack failed. A second attempt began on 25 June, having been delayed by the great storm over the Channel between 19 and 23 June. However, the heavy bombers were grounded by residual bad weather in England, cancelling again the preliminary aerial bombardment. The British troops came up against units of the 1st SS Panzer Corps and very little progress was made. However, early on 30 June, 266 aircraft of RAF Bomber Command bombed German tanks which had been concentrating for a counter-attack; two aircraft were lost and the German attack failed.

The first direct assault on Caen, involving a preliminary air bombardment by RAF Bomber Command, took place on 8 July. At dusk on 7 July, 467 Lancasters and Halifaxes of Nos 1, 4 and 6 Groups, led by fourteen Mosquitos of No 8 (PFF) Group, attacked the German lines in front of the city. Watched by cheering troops of the 3rd and 59th Infantry Divisions and those of the Canadian 3rd Infantry Division, the aircraft dropped 2500 tons of bombs onto well laid markers, in clear weather conditions. Caution had dictated that the bomb line should be well ahead of the British forward positions, thus the Aim Points were situated more in the city centre rather than on the German positions on the northern outskirts. Smoke and dust soon obscured the markers but the Master Bomber, Wg Cdr S P Daniels of No 35 (PFF) Squadron, did a good job in returning the bombing to the target area.

As it turned out, there was little German defence in the city itself;

The crew of Halifax 'G' George from 420 (Snowy Owl) Squadron. Shot up as they were making their bomb run on Bourg Leopold, pilot P/O Kalle, standing centre, got them all home safely except for Sgt Elsinger (on Kalle's left). He baled out after a warning order, thinking the aircraft was out of control. The aircraft was a write off. Later, in a new aircraft, all the crew except Elsinger's replacement were badly injured when a 500lb bomb exploded as they were making an emergency landing. Sgt Cusack (second left, back row) died of his injuries. Photo courtesy of Mr G Burton. the Flight Engineer, seen sitting left.

The tragedy of Beverlo. The mass funeral of the 84 victims of the attack on Bourg Leopold on the 10/11th May. *(Peter Loncke)*.

A Halifax over Siracourt, one of the most bombed of the heavy 'Crossbow' sites, 6 July 1944. *(RAF Museum).*

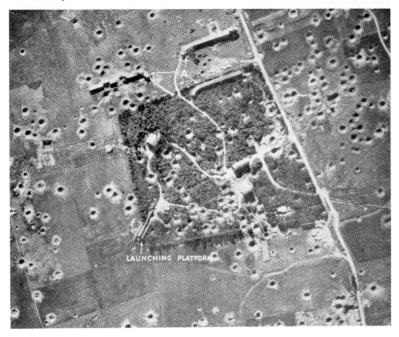

'Ski' launching site for V-Is. The name 'Ski' was taken from the shape of the support buildings, marked 'A' on the photo. *(RAF Museum).*

The destruction of the city of Caen. The photo was taken after the city was captured on 19 July. *(RAF Museum)*.

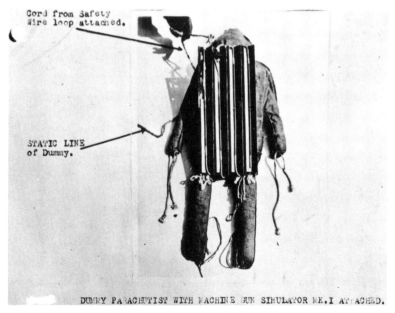

Cord from Safety
Wire loop attached.

STATIC LINE
of Dummy.

DUMMY PARACHUTIST WITH MACHINE GUN SIMULATOR MK.I ATTACHED.

'Spoof gear': a dummy parachutist with cracker devices strapped to its back, dropped as part of Operation 'Titanic'. *(PRO)*.

The rail bridge at Port de Graviere, south of Rouen, after an attack by
AEAF medium bombers. As the damaged Seine bridges were repaired, so
they were attacked again. *(RAF Museum)*.

A rare photo of the Maquis in June 1944. Yvon, the leader of 'Commandos
M' (seated centre, wearing a beret) welcomes new members from Soulaines
near Brienne, who later operated against German troop trains and road
convoys in the area to the east of Troyes. *(M. Bertin)*.

Trappes the morning after the first trial attack in March 1944.
(Mme Renée Guillerm).

Saarbrucken marshalling yards after the VIIIth USAAF attacks in May.
(IWM).

Albert Speer, Hitler's Minister of Production. He feared the attacks on oil, but said later that industry was brought to a halt by the inability to move raw materials over the rail networks. *(IWM)*.

Aunay-sur-Odon after an attack by Bomber Command on 14/15 June. The effect of such a concentration of bombs on troops and their equipment was described by General Bayerlein, commander of the Panzer Lehr Division: 'Nothing was visible except smoke and dust, my front lines looked like the face of the moon, 70 per cent of my troops were dead, wounded, crazed or numbed, all my forward tanks were knocked out.' *(RAF Museum)*.

A tank of the 21st SS Panzer Division caught in an orchard at Guillerville, northwest of Caen, during the attack by RAF Bomber Command on 18 July. The diagram on p.150 illustrates the concentration of bombing that was achieved. *(PRO)*.

A B24 Liberator of the VIIIth USAAF is hit by flak and breaks up. One disadvantage of daylight operations was the fact that crews could see their friends going down. *(USAAF Photo)*.

Most of the crews lost in the Tergnier attacks were eventually buried in the churchyard at Poix which now contains the graves of 149 aircrew from Britain and the Dominions. *(L. Lacey-Johnson).*

Part of the wreckage of Lancaster LM 467 from 101 Squadron — the author's brother's aircraft which blew up over Voué. *(M. André Thouard)*

and, because there had been a six-hour delay between the end of the bombing and the ground attack,[17] only newly arrived troops of the 16th Luftwaffe Field Division were affected by the bombing (the more hardened men of the 12th SS Panzer Division had recovered before the British troops attacked). After some fierce fighting, the British troops finally gained the centre of the city, only to be delayed by rubble.

The city was in ruins; some of the French inhabitants who had ignored the warnings to evacuate stayed in their cellars or wandered around in a dazed condition amongst the piles of rubble that had been their homes. By the time the British troops had gained the River Orne, they found that all the bridges had been blown up and that there was some very stiff opposition on the far bank. During the air attack, the RAF had encountered intensive flak from the south of the city. One Lancaster of No 166 Squadron was missing, two had crash-landed behind British lines and a further two, one from No 460 and one from No 626 Squadron, together with a No 8 (PFF) Group Mosquito, crashed into the sea off Beachy Head.

The operations to break out from the beach-head were planned to take place in the latter half of July. The British attack in the Caen sector, known as Operation Goodwood, was designed to draw German armour away from the American sector so that their Operation Cobra could strike swiftly south from the north of the Cherbourg Peninsula, which was by then in Allied hands. In view of the enemy strength in the 'Goodwood' area, the plan called for a great deal of air support from RAF Bomber Command. Initially, Harris resisted the call for help on the grounds that the Army appeared never to take advantage of such bombing,[18] but it was agreed eventually that aircraft from his command would join those of the Eighth and Ninth Air Forces. Operation Cobra also included massive air strikes which were to pave the way for General Bradley's infantry divisions, making a gap through which his armour could pass on its way to Coutances and beyond.

At dawn on 18 July, 1032 heavy bombers of RAF Bomber Command attacked five target areas south and east of Caen, each target was marked by No 8 (PFF) Group Mosquitos and Lancasters. At Colombelles, 126 Lancasters from No 5 Group, and sixty-four Halifaxes and thirty-three Lancasters, all from No 6 Group, flew in at altitudes of 6-9000 ft, dropping mostly 1000-lb bombs onto prepared positions belonging to the 16th Luftwaffe Field Division. Almost simultaneously, between 0540 and 0557 hr, Nos 1 and 4 Groups, each using more than 100 aircraft, attacked the area around Sannerville. The three remaining targets were attacked between 0600 and 0625 hr. Nos 3, 5 and 6 Groups' aircraft attacked Mondeville; Nos 1, 3 and 4 Groups' aircraft attacked Mannerville; and Nos 3 and 8 Groups' aircraft attacked Cagny. Marauders of the Ninth Air Force attacked five gun positions, while 570 B-24s of the Eighth Air Force dropped fragmentation bombs onto three other concentrations of German troops, one each of the villages of Troarn, Solier and Frenville.

In all, it was one of the greatest air bombardments of troops ever seen. In one orchard, near the village of Guillerville, fifteen tanks and nearly all the motor vehicles belonging to a company from 21st Panzer Division were completely destroyed, some of them being thrown into the air to land on their backs like struggling beetles. In spite of heavy flak, the RAF lost only seven aircraft. However, on returning from the attack on Emieville, Lancaster 'J' of No 115 Squadron crashed on to a farm at Great Offley, killing all the crew and Mrs Alice Handley and her two daughters, one of whom was on leave from the ATS. Another Halifax crashed at White Waltham, killing all but the rear gunner who had baled out.

GUILLERVILLE

PLOT OF CRATERS & VEHICLES IN MAIN ORCHARD AREA

NOTES

1 The circles showing positions of craters are not drawn to scale but are shown as 30 ft diameter.

2 The silhouettes of vehicles do not necessarily point in the correct direction but they are in the correct positions.

LEGEND

⊕ H.E. Crater
⊖ Direct hit on vehicle
▲ Target indicator
⊷ Tank
⊶ Armoured vehicle
⊶ Supply vehicle
⚏ Unexploded bomb
▧ Badly damaged buildings

CHURCH INDICATED DIAGRAMMATICALLY

50   0   50   100   150   200   250
Feet

B A U REPORT No. 22

There has been much discussion and criticism of the 'Goodwood' plan and its apparent failure, but none of the criticism was levelled at the Air Forces concerned. Most of the German prisoners taken in the early stages of the battle remained completely deaf and ineffective for twenty-four hours after the bombing. The defensive belt had been thicker than forecast and with the onset of heavy rain on 20 July the ground attack became literally bogged down. In the corridors of power there was talk of sacking Montgomery.

On the western side of the beach-head, General Bradley had been planning to start Operation Cobra on 20 July.[19] But bad weather forced a postponement until 24 July. Even then the weather closed in again causing great problems for the commanders of the heavy and medium bombers which were to provide air support. The air armada, led by six groups of Ninth USAAF Marauders, took off according to plan, but three groups were recalled because of deteriorating weather conditions, and the remainder were unable to provide any observed results of their action. They were followed by approximately 1600 heavy bombers from all three Bombardment Divisions of the Eighth Air Force.

Efforts to cancel the mission were only partly successful; but fortunately, the cloud was so bad that most groups made their own decisions not to bomb. Approximately 350 heavy bombers, mostly from the third wave who had a brief glimpse of the ground, did bomb and several cases of 'shorts' occurred.[20].

Approximately sixteen American troops were killed and seventy wounded. Efforts to cancel later attacks by medium and fighter bombers were more successful, but great damage had been done, not only to the troops on the ground, but also to the cover of the whole operation, which had then been blown. The Germans knew the place and almost the time of the ground attack which was to follow. There was no question of postponing 'Cobra' any longer, and the order went out for the attack to begin at 1100 Bhrs on 25 July.[21]

The revised air plan was for 560 fighter bombers of the Ninth Air Force to open the attack at 0938 hr by bombing and strafing the area south of the St Lô-Perriers road which was south of the American forward positions. Some of the aircraft were to carry napalm bombs. They were to be followed, at 1000 hr, by 1500 heavy bombers of the Eighth Air Force whose task was to saturate an area of approximately one mile wide and five miles long on the general axis of the American advance. B-17s and B-24s were to fly across, rather than along, the axis. Precautions taken to avoid bombing their own troops included marking the forward area with cerise and yellow panels. The B-17s and B-24s were to be followed by 380 medium bombers of the Ninth Air Force which were to bomb the roads leading to St Gilles and Maligny.

The bombing by the medium and fighter bombers went according to plan, but the B-24s and B-17s were forced to amend their pre-planned bombing heights because of a difference between the actual and forecast cloudbases. Bomb aimers hurriedly reset their bomb-sights and release mechanisms, and formations became loose and bombed from altitudes of 12-15,000 ft. Panel and smoke markers proved to be of little value as they soon became obscured by smoke and dust caused by the bombing. Most of the bombing errors ran in an east-west direction, but small errors were compounded to such an extent that a considerable number of bombs fell onto the American lines. A lot of the bombs fell onto the 30th US Infantry Division which had taken the brunt of misplaced bombing the day before. Early reports reaching England spoke of bombs falling as far north as the American gun lines. In all, the cost in Amercan lives was reported to be 102 killed, including Lt-Gen Lesley J McNair, and nearly 400 wounded.[22]

The results of that air bombardment (in which more than 600 tons of bombs were dropped) were not all that had been hoped for by some of the Allied planners, but the effect on the German troops seems to have been considerable. Maj Gen Fritz Bayerlein, a veteran tank soldier, lost all communication with his advanced command posts, and was forced to take to a motorcycle to find out what was going on. From a very solid stone tower, he was able to watch the final stages of the bombing which threw tanks about like toys and created what he could only describe later as 'a lunar landscape' out of his well prepared positions. Opposition from the Luftwaffe was negligible; a few small units attacked the heavy bombers without success. The five heavy and one medium bombers that were lost all fell to flak.

Much was learned from an analysis of the successes and short-comings of the 'carpet bombing' which preceded the 'Goodwood' and 'Cobra' Operations, and the lessons learned were well applied during the remaining two months that the heavy bombers were under Eisenhower's command. In terms of the numbers of heavy bombers involved in any one operation, the two events marked the peak of close air support by the Strategic Air Forces.

Notes

1 PRO Air 24/277.
2 The Operations Order forbade crew brieflngs before 1815 hr. It gave instructions also that bombs were not to be jettisoned in the Channel, and that all aircraft were to be refuelled and bombed immediately upon return. There were eleven special instructions of that nature in the order.
3 The guns were mostly 155 mm calibre. Batteries comprised between two and six guns, but see text for notes on individual batteries which disclose some interesting lapses in otherwise good intelligence.
4 *British Intelligence in the Second World War* Vol III, p130. Probably the result of a previous attack on 28/29 May.
5 Ibid.
6 PRO Air 24/280. That was a very experienced crew, all on their second tour of operations. They were hit by flak and caught fire. The pilot, Sqn Ldr Watson, gave his life for his crew, four of whom managed to bale out. The flight engineer, air bomber and wireless operator were picked up by an invasion craft; the navigator, Fg Off Hall, was not found.
   It was one of several incidents in which I came across the same description of fire in a wing 'eating its way through like a blow torch'.
7 AHB Translation VII/70.
8 Civil twilight was at approximately 0530 hr but at 10,000 ft the aircraft would have been in a much lighter sky.
9 That was a direct vindication of the argument put forward by AEAF against the Tactical concept of the Transportation Plan.
10 Craven and Cate, *Allied Air Forces in the Second World War* Vol III, p193.
11 See note 9 above.
12 Interpolation of figures from *British Intelligence in the Second World War* Vol III, and David Eisenhower's *Eisenhower at War*.
13 Wilmot, *The Struggle for Europe* p347. The diversion helped to sustain the German's belief that a second landing was about to take place in the Pas de Calais area.
14 See Chapter 18 for reasons why the attacks on the Loire bridges were delayed.
15 Craven and Cate, *Allied Air Forces in the Second World War* Vol III, p214.
16 Letter from Montgomery to the War Offlce, 7 June 1944.
17 The air attack had been planned for the 8th but was brought forward because of bad weather forecast for that morning.
18 See 17 above. Harris seems to have been misinformed.
19 'Cobra' was planned to take place in conjunction with Goodwood which, according to some accounts, was designed to keep German armour away from the American sector.
20 In one mishap the bomber aimer pressed the release switch in a reflex action when his aircraft was hit by a bundle of 'Window' dropped from another aircraft. The bombs fell onto a newly constructed Ninth Air Force airfield at Cheppelle.
21 Bhrs = two hours ahead of Greenwich Mean Time.
22 Craven and Cate, *Allied Air Forces in the Second World War* Vol III, p234.

CHAPTER TWENTY

Attacks by the French Resistance
and Special Forces

It would be unwise for anyone other than a trained historian to try and unravel the extraordinary political intrigues that dominated so much of the thinking and allegiances of the various organisations in France which resisted German occupation during the greater part of the Second World War. The full story of the part played by the Special Operations Executive (SOE) in France has been recorded in some detail in M R D Foot's official history on the subject.[1]

The SOE's role was to coordinate and, if necessary, initiate subversive and sabotage activities in every German-occupied country. Although the Belgian and Dutch Resistance movements were very much involved in helping to defeat the Nazis in northwest Europe, much of their planned sabotage was overtaken by events because of the rapid advance of Allied ground forces after the breakout from the Normandy beach-head. Most, if not all, of the French Resistance were actively involved in plans to prevent German reinforcements reaching Normandy both before and after the Allied landings.

Of the six SOE sections which operated in France, two were not directly involved with the Transportation Plan, and a further two did not become involved until after the Allied landings. Of the two sections not directly involved, one was the EU/P Section which worked amongst the Polish speaking refugees in France, and the other was the DF Section which ran the escape routes for Allied airmen and others wishing to get out of the country. Of the two sections which did not become involved until after the Allied landings, one was the AMF Section which operated from Algiers into southern France and was closely connected with the American Office of Strategic Services (OSS). The other section was known as the Jedburg Teams, who wore uniform and were also connected with the OSS; they were parachuted into France as part of 'Overlord', specifically to help organise armed resistance groups behind enemy lines.

Of the two remaining sections, Section 'F' consisted mostly of those agents who were not involved in the political struggle between Generals de Gaulle and Giraud, and were in fact referred to as the 'independents'. Most F Section agents were not French citizens, and were sent to France to perform specific tasks laid down by the SOE's Higher Command to meet outline directives issued by British Chiefs of Staff. 'RF' Section consisted of agents who were nearly all French and who were lined up solidly behind de Gaulle. Their orders were prepared jointly by de Gaulle's staff and the SOE. Although RF agents did carry out some distinguished acts of sabotage, their main aim was to persuade the French to help get rid of both the Vichy Government and the Germans from their country. F and RF sections both sent approximately 400 agents into France between 1941 and 1944, of which approximately one quarter were lost.

Plans to use SOE agents in support of the Allied invasion were considered as early as August 1943, and included an increasing number of sabotage attacks on German HQs and aircraft, the removal of German explosives from mined bridges likely to be used by the Allies, and, as D-Day approached, an all-out attack on roads, railways and telephone lines. As with the Transportation Plan the problem of security for the invasion plans was paramount, and initial SOE attacks were spread evenly over all the possible areas where a landing might take place. Plans to carry out attacks in the Pas de Calais area, and so encourage the German belief that the attack would come in this area, were abandoned when it was realised that most of the local inhabitants had been evacuated and their places had been taken by German troops and the Gestapo to guard the V-weapon sites. An SOE agent could not have survived long in such an area.

One of the main problems facing the agents of F and RF sections was a general lack of arms and supplies with which to encourage and equip resistance teams. One reason for that was bad weather, particularly during the winter of 1943/44 when many sorties by Special Duties squadrons were delayed or cancelled; but the main reason was competition for and a general shortage of aircraft, coupled with a reluctance on the part of the C-in-C Bomber Command, ACM Harris, to part with any aircraft that could be used to bomb Germany. In January 1944 there were twenty-three Halifaxes, four Hudsons, nine Lysanders and two Wellingtons available for all clandestine operations — dropping and picking up agents, and landing supplies. Some additional help was given by Harris when, occasionally, he released some of his least effective four-engined bombers, namely Stirlings. In January 1944 Liberators and Dakotas of the 801st Bomber Group of the USAAF Eighth Air Force commenced 'Carpet Bagger' operations also. Arguments concerning priorities for aircraft continued between the various factions until March 1944 when, after several formal but unsuccessful appeals by the Chiefs of Staff for more aircraft for supply drops, the Chief Executive of SOE, Gen Sir Colin Gubbins, introduced Michael Brault to Churchill. Brault, who had field experience of the Maquis, told Churchill of the large army of friendly Frenchmen which could be raised, provided they could be armed. A flurry of activity followed at the end of which, in spite of efforts by the SIS and others to prevent it, the SOE's share of aircraft was increased dramatically. Bomber Command and the Eighth Air Force 801st Group combined to raise the number of containers[2] dropped from 8619 in the first quarter of 1944 to 21,526 in the second, with a corresponding increase in sorties from 600 to 1250. Later, after the invasion, the Eighth Air Force used B-17 Fortresses to drop supplies to the Maquis. In Operation Cadillac on 14 July no less than 359 B-17s dropped almost 4000 containers into the Vecors and Correze areas.

At this point some readers might benefit from a brief explanation of the relationship between the SOE controlled networks of agents ('circuits' as they were called) and the more widely known Maquis which was larger. The Maquis (the word described the thick under-growth in parts of Corsica) originated as bodies of young men who had taken to the woods to avoid slave labour in Germany, and as such they were originally no more than unarmed and hungry outlaws. The task of SOE agents sent to France was to enlist the help of local sympathisers, make contact with the Maquis groups, arrange the supply of arms, food and clothing, and train them in the art of guerilla warfare and sabotage. It has been estimated that by late spring 1944 there were almost 100,000 men in Maquis units in southeast France who tied down some 10,000 German troops. By the same time, 80,000 Sten guns, 30,000 pistols, 17,000 rifles and large quantities of explosives had been dropped into France. By August, most of southwest France was under the control of its own inhabitants, armed and encouraged by SOE circuits.

SOE circuits varied enormously in size and capability. F Section alone was running approximately forty circuits in April 1944 and 'Scientist', 'Ventriloquist', 'Donkeyman', 'Historian', and 'Head-master' were all active within 150 miles of Caen before D-Day. To the south 'Digger', 'Wheelright', and 'Pimmento' initiated the delays imposed on the 2nd SS Panzer Division. Just outside the Caen 150-mile radius 'Farmer', 'Silversmith', 'Tinker', and 'Diplomat' all helped to sabotage railways and roads, and slowed down the movement of German reinforcements and supplies.

Not all of the sabotage carried out resulted in spectacular explosions. 'Pimmento', under the leadership of one of the SOE's most experienced agents, A M Brooks, replaced axle oil with carborundum in rail transporters which had been set aside for transporting tanks of the 2nd SS Panzer Division. Later, the replacement transporters were ambushed by a party from the 'Wheelright' team, which included two sisters in their early teens. A more subtle form of sabotage occurred at the Peugeot factory at Sochaux, which was making tank turrets and aero-engines for the Germans. Here, a member of the Peugeot family was persuaded to arrange for his factory to be put out of action by sabotage rather than having it attacked by Bomber Command.

The Jedburg Teams consisted of two officers and one sergeant, all of mixed nationality (usually British, French and American). They wore uniform and approximately ninety teams were parachuted into France on, or soon after D-Day. Their purpose was to provide HQ Staff for local Resistance groups and to coordinate their activities in accordance with Allied plans. They were joined by American Operational Groups, SAS parties and seven SOE Inter-Allied Missions, which ranged in strength from two to twenty-five members and which were sent in to France between D-Day and the end of August 1944.

The International SAS Brigade consisted of the Belgian Independent Parachute Squadron (5 SAS), two Free French battalions (3 and 4 SAS) and 1 and 2 SAS which had been brought back from the Mediterranean. By the early summer of 1944 the Brigade had a strength of more than 2000 men, working from five main areas behind German lines where the SOE had already established contact with the local forces. All five main areas were well placed for cutting road and rail communications to the Normandy area. Unlike the other uniformed parties behind the lines, the SAS did not come under the control of the Etat-Major des Forces Francaises de l'Interieur (EMFFI) which General de Gaulle had set up in March 1944. However, it did work closely with the SOE, and its primary role was much the same in that it provided valuable training for Resistance forces and often formed the hard core of attacks on the Germans. Its other roles included the acquisition and passing of useful tactical intelligence for use by Allied aircraft, and highly mobile operations such as 'Wallace' when Roy Farran's heavily armed jeeps swept across northern France, wreaking havoc and damage on German supply lines. On D-Day, two small SAS teams were landed as part of Operation Titanic with the object of diverting some German attention away from American landings, which were taking place six miles further west.[3]

Apart from the supply of arms, etc, a problem shared by all the clandestine forces was radio communication. German radio direction finding teams were both numerous and efficient; radio sets were broken on being landed; the business of encoding and enciphering radio traffic was complicated; and there was always the possibility that operators had been captured and that their sets were being manned by the Germans. How was the SOE to get its messages safely to its agents. The answer came as early as 1941, when powerful BBC transmitters began to be used nightly to broadcast scores of messages which overtly sounded like family greetings but covertly they contained instructions to agents on special operations. Many of the messages were sent in two parts, the first part warned a particular agent, and the second imparted the action the agent should take. Although public, it was, with one exception, quite secure. The exception was a message passed to sabotage groups on the eve of D-Day. Fortunately, the Germans appear to have been unconvinced of their earlier luck in discovering the code.

The foregoing may have given the reader the impression that the very formidable forces already in France were poised and capable of bringing the railways to a halt. There were, however, many uncertainties associated with the clandestine forces; many pick ups or drops went wrong, and a considerable number of weapons intended for the Maquis fell into German hands. Suspicion and jealousy abounded and political intrigue was rife within the French Resistance. Also, without wishing in any way to decry their efforts, there was a natural concern among the commanders of the more conventional forces, who questioned the reliability of those forces and their ability to achieve and maintain the complete dislocation of the railways.

In January 1944, during one of the many meetings connected with the Transportation Plan, promises by the SOE that it could destroy 1000 locomotives in the ensuing four months were treated with some scepticism by the commanders, who preferred to know exactly when an attack had taken place, and liked to see photographic evidence of the results. Much of the concern voiced by the commanders was removed during May when, in the same way that the strategic bombers had been brought under Eisenhower's control, a set of priorities was drawn up for sabotage attacks on the railways.[4] In the south of France, where the Germans had employed many German rail workers to keep the lines open, the priority lines for sabotage were:

1 Montauban-Limoges-Vierson
2 Bordeaux-Poitiers-Tours
3 Nîmes-Tarascon-Avignon-Lyons-Dijon
4 Modane-Chambery-Amberien

By way of another example: a road map, dated 21 May 1944, showed the road from Miramount to Poitiers as being a 'Priority 1' target from D+1 to D+3.

The French Resistance could not be the sole judge of where its attacks were most needed; it was essential that its operations be coordinated with those of other units against German lines of communication.

As the Allied invasion of Normandy approached, more and more men and women of the French Resistance[5] huddled, nightly, around clandestine radios, waiting for 'personal' messages via the BBC which told them where and when to expect parachute drops, and which plan should be put into operation. One such group was formed in the area between Charmont-s/Barbuise and Fontaines-Leuyeres, north of Troyes, in 1942. Led by Pierre Mulsant[6] and assisted by Major Cowburn of the SOE, the group of approximately 350 people became known as the 'Commandos M', or the Abelard Buckmaster

Network. The group operated in sections of twenty to twenty-five people, one of which narrowly escaped capture after being denounced by a collaborator. It participated in a number of arms drops and received a number of SOE agents to whom they gave initial shelter and directions. Between 1 June and 22 August it watched and attacked the railway and telephone lines between Châlons and Troyes which were in constant use by the Germans. It also removed explosive charges placed by the Germans on many of the bridges and culverts in the Aube district and, as a result, aided the advance of the American Army in that area. At a memorial service held in July 1945 the group met on Hill 192 (one of their wartime bases) to commemorate fifty comrades who had been killed in the war.[7]

A similar, but smaller, group, led by Hippolyte Perrot, operated in an area a few miles east of the 'Commandos M' area, at a place called Piney. Although a company of SS troops was based in its village the group cared for wounded aircrew and, when the time came, turned against the German troops, capturing or shooting 130 of them before the American Army arrived. (It was that group which helped Sgt John Ackroyd.)[8]

As the Americans advanced, the two groups were responsible for nineteen attacks on a short stretch of railway between Troyes and Arcis sur Aube, fifteen miles to the north. They also ambushed seven German troop convoys between Troyes and Arcis and on the road between Troyes and Lesmont eighteen miles to the northeast. Additional attacks were carried out in the area by the Maquis Montcalm and the Communist FTP. The map on page 160 summarises the attacks made by the French Resistance on railways in the Aube Region. The sabotage at Troyes is also shown on the map.[9]

According to M R D Foot's official history of the SOE in France the French Resistance made 950 attacks on railways during the night 5/6 June, and in the first three weeks of 'Overlord' almost 2000 line-cutting operations were carried out. Attacks by the Resistance in Belgium and Holland reached a peak as Allied armies broke away from the beach-head, but many of their planned operations were overtaken by the rapid advance of the 21st Army Group. When the battle for Normandy developed, there was scarcely a road or rail link in France which the Germans did not need to watch over; nor were their telephone lines safe. The Resistance, helped by the French PTT, cut all but a few lines in the area, on D-Day or very soon after. Cutting those telephone lines forced the Germans to use their radios which, of course, were closely monitored by Allied listening stations and thus provided much valuable tactical intelligence for the Allied land and air forces.

All those pinprick attacks led the Germans to divert approximately eight divisions[10] to the task of securing both their lines of communication and their supply dumps. Students of the British Army's post-war operations against terrorist organisations and peace-keeping efforts will appreciate that the effort required to deal with such situations is out of all proportion to the small number of so-called terrorists actually involved. It is possible that the number of men and women actively engaged in sabotage in France during that period of the War did not exceed 3000.

Notes

1 See Bibliography.
2 Container loads varied, but a standard drop of twelve containers could have contained six light machine guns (Brens), thirty-six rifles, twenty-seven Sten guns, forty grenades, twelve HE charges with fuses etc, 6600 rounds of 9 mm ammunition and 3168 rounds of .303 ammunition.
3 See Chaper 19.
4 PRO Air 37/504.
5 I use the term in its broadest sense to cover Maquis, SOE and other groups.
6 He was later arrested and shot by the Gestapo. He was replaced in October 1943 by Capt Maurice Dupont, alias Yvan.
7 Notes on 'Commandos M' by Hubert Jeanny, one-time leader of the Fontaines-Luyeres group.
8 See Chapter Fifteen, Mailly le Camp.
9 According to M R D Foot, the F Section circuit in that area at the time was code-named 'Diplomat'. Monsieur Bernard, archivist in Aube district, said that the attack on the locomotive roundhouse at Troyes was carried out under the leadership of Ben Cowburn of the 'Tinker' circuit. Foot showed that circuit to be inactive at that time.
10 Mostly low-grade divisions; nevertheless they did contain troops which were badly needed at the front.

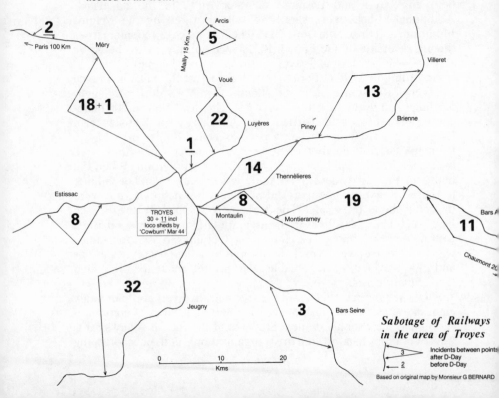

Sabotage of Railways in the area of Troyes

Based on original map by Monsieur G BERNARD

Part Three

CHAPTER TWENTY-ONE

Cumulative Effects of the Transportation Plan on the French Railway System

Before proceeding to study the results of bombing the French railways prior to 'Overlord',[1] it might be useful to take stock of the effort expended against both the French and the Belgian railways and to summarise the post-strike reports recorded in Part 3 of this book.

From 9 February to 6 June (D-Day) 1944, Allied Air Forces flew almost 22,000 sorties and dropped 60,000 tons of bombs onto Transportation Plan targets. The following table gives a breakdown of those offensives:

Air Force	No of targets	Total sorties	Tonnage dropped
AEAF	19	8736	10,486
USAAF Eighth Air Force	24	4462	7886
RAF Bomber Command	37	8751	44,494[2]

By D-Day all of the eighty targets under the Transportation Plan had been attacked at least once, and had been categorised as follows:

	AEAF	Eighth Air Force Bomber Command	RAF Bomber Command
Category A (no further attack needed)	14	15	22
Category B (requires further attacks)	3	8	13
Category C (little or no damage)	2	1	2

In addition, the USAAF Fifteenth Air Force dropped 3074 tons of bombs onto rail targets in southeast France. A table showing the division of effort between the two main heavy bomber commands is shown in Chapter Fourteen.

Between 6 March and 6 June 1944 RAF Bomber Command lost 224 heavy bombers during those attacks[3]. Eighth Air Force Bomber

Command, which did not start bombing French and Belgian railways until 27 April, lost sixty-five four-engined bombers and a number of escorting fighters during attacks on rail targets. However, it was engaged already in bombing oil targets in Germany, and was providing valuable support to the AEAF in its offensive against V-1 and V-2 sites in northwest France.

It has been said that statistics can prove almost anything; I certainly believe that they can be manipulated and become misleading. As time passes, the human memory becomes subject to fond beliefs and inaccuracies, and there comes a time when facts can only be established by careful comparison of diaries and contemporary reports. I tried to resolve that dilemma by drawing information from a variety of sources and striking mean values. I resisted the temptation to select information only from those documents which appeared to be the most authoritive,[4] because I was conscious of the fact that some of those documents were composed by those with an interest in proving a certain point.[5] However, I had no reason to doubt the accuracy of the figures or the observations made at the time. I dealt with some of the conclusions with an open mind, until I received confirmation from other sources.

Throughout my examinations of the results of bombing railway centres in France and Belgium, I became increasingly aware of the enormous pressures which must have been put on the planners of those operations. Almost daily, they calculated bomb loads, in the knowledge that a great number of the bombs dropped would cause loss of life and great destruction to the property of friendly civilians living in the immediate vicinity of the target areas. I would hasten to add that, as part of the liberation process from Nazi tyranny, many civilians were killed elsewhere in north France and the Low Countries.

However, I did query if the planning figures were ever fully explained, or appreciated, by those concerned with the adverse effects on the civilian population of those countries. With a few notable exceptions[6] the French and Belgians seem to have accepted the situation with great stoicism, which, in my mind, has never been appreciated fully on the English side of the Channel. One of the narratives in Part 3 told how bombs fell at the rate of 850 in three minutes (or four per second), and of an expected rate of ten per cent of those bombs falling within the target area. At the height of the London Blitz, Clapham Junction, equivalent to the smallest of the five rail targets in the Paris area, was hit on several occasions, but Home Office bomb plots for the area showed that approximately twenty high-explosive bombs landed in the vicinity.[7]

I was unable to discover positively reliable figures for the number of French and Belgians killed and wounded in the attacks; as with Hamburg or Dresden the exact number may never be known.

Estimates contained in files at the Public Records Office varied enormously. French sources probably exaggerated a little, but in one report a figure of 1276 killed was given for the attack on Tergnier on 18/19 April 1944, and in the same report an even greater number was given for the casualties at Rouen. In a note to the Chief of the Air Staff, the Deputy Director of Bomber Operations quoted a number of 840 killed at Tergnier during the two attacks described in part 2.

In the same file, Zuckerman was quoted as having provided an 'ideal' figure for the whole of the Transportation Plan of 12,000 killed, 6,000 badly wounded and 30,000 slightly wounded. The figure of 10,000 killed was used as a guideline by the British War Cabinet, and was referred to in the signal sent by Churchill to Roosevelt.[8] Together with that now famous signal, was a copy of a telegram Churchill had received from the British Ambassador in Algiers. It referred to a note passed to the Ambassador by Mr Massigli, a member of the French Committee for the Liberation, which contained a warning of the adverse effects that the bombing was having on French Resistance workers and the population as a whole. Being a trained aerial photographic interpreter, who has instructed in the art of bomb damage assessment and has studied some of the post-strike photographs, my own view is that an estimated number of 12,000 killed is probably nearer the mark, more than half that number being killed in the six weeks between 10 April and 15 May 1944.

There was no doubt that the loss of life amongst French and Belgian civilians would have been far greater had they not received some warning of the attacks via the BBC.[9] It was my belief also that without the improvements in target-marking techniques, particularly the use of a Master Bomber, it would have been impossible to carry on with the planned attacks. However, the Transportation Plan was carried out to its full extent, and an examination of its effects on the railway system in northwest Europe, more particularly on the French railways, the Société Nationale Chemins de Fer (SNCF), now follows.

Indications of a falling off in the amount of traffic on the French railways was first noticed immediately after the first attacks in March, and it was natural that the Northern Region, which took the brunt of the earlier attacks, led the others in that decline. By the time of the Allied breakout from the beaches in July 1944, traffic on the whole of the SNCF network was down to ten per cent of its January levels. Some parts of the system showed a marked decline immediately after specific attacks, and the effects of the two attacks on Tergnier, is shown by the illustration on page 166.

After the war, several teams of analysts examined SNCF records and produced very detailed reports,[10] in which the analysts drew a useful comparison between ordinary and military traffic. They showed that although all traffic was very quickly affected in the three northerly regions, military traffic was proportionally less affected, indicating that priority had been given already to German troop movements as early as April 1944. Later, as the campaign began to bite harder, military and civilian traffic fell in parallel.

Therefore, there was adequate proof that the levels of activity on the French railways did fall dramatically during the period that the Transportation Plan was in operation. However, the Plan consisted of several phases; was any particular phase more responsible than others for bringing about the decline?

In their examinations of the disorganisation of the SNCF the Bombing Analysis Unit (BAU) and No 1 Operational Research Group (ORG) both analyzed the effects of all types of attack on the three main components of the railway system: the permanent way (lines), bridges, and the haulage facilities. (The reader will have noticed that I have stated 'all types of attack'. In order to obtain a clearer picture of the relative importance of the heavy bombers the analysts of the day found it necessary, as I did, to examine the parts played by both the French Resistance and the AEAF also).

Attacks on the permanent way included those on lines in the open country, near stations, on bridges and at the rail centres or nodal points listed in Appendix 10). Although a few attacks were made in February 1944, the strategic phase of the Transportation Plan began on the night of 6/7 March with the attack on Trappes.[11] The second stage of the Plan commenced on 7 May when attacks began on the

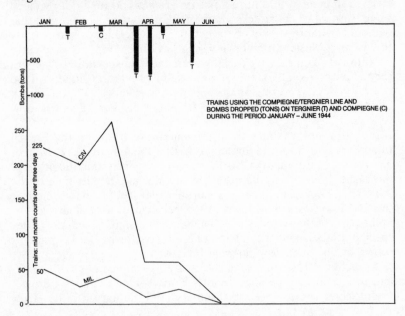

TRAINS USING THE COMPIEGNE/TERGNIER LINE AND
BOMBS DROPPED (TONS) ON TERGNIER (T) AND COMPIEGNE (C)
DURING THE PERIOD JANUARY – JUNE 1944

rail bridges over the lower part of the Seine. The third phase started two weeks later with the 'Chattanooga Choo-Choo' operation (described in Chapter 19). The sabotage of lines occurred during all three phases and, in accordance with the 'Fortitude' plan, most of the attacks prior to D-Day were centred in northwest France and Belgium. After D-Day the emphasis shifted to the Western Region, and incidents of sabotage became much more frequent, the majority occurring on lines in the open country.

When evaluating the distribution and effects of the attacks, No 1 ORG and BAU both used detailed SNCF records of rail operations in the areas most affected by the bombing, namely the Northern, Eastern and Western Regions. The teams found it necessary to classify the cutting of lines according to the phase of the operation: were they caused by bombing or sabotage; did they cause a complete or partial stoppage of traffic; what was the type of the target (open lines, rail centre, etc); and what was the weight of each attack (100 tons being the dividing line between heavy and light attacks)? In practice, the latter criterion generally formed the distinction between attacks by AEAF medium bombers and those by RAF and Eighth Air Force heavy bombers.

A division was drawn also between the various classes of traffic interruptions; for example, those affecting single- and double-tracked lines. The results of that part of the study were based on incomplete and unreliable statistics.

The strategic phase of the operations (the attacks on rail centres) peaked in May 1944. (It should be noted that the decline in rail traffic was well under way before the start of the attacks on the Seine bridges and the open lines.)

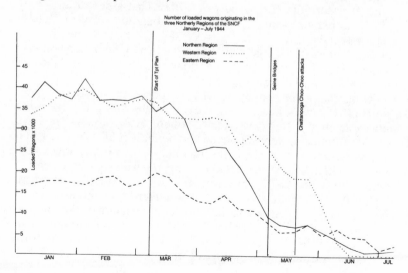

Number of loaded wagons originating in the three Northerly Regions of the SNCF
January – July 1944

Northern Region ———
Western Region ··········
Eastern Region — — —

The total number of cuts recorded in the three most northerly Regions between February and July 1944 was 3328, broken down as:

	Rail Centres	Bridges	Stations	Open Country Lines
Air bombing	367	212	1034	621
Sabotage	—	53	151	890

When translated into percentages, the cuts leading to the complete interruption of traffic were broken down as:

	% Rail Centres	% Bridges	% Stations	% Open Country Lines
Air bombing	95.6	85.1	78	83.4
Sabotage	—	74.4	63.3	54

Two main points emerge from these tables. First, the weight of attacks on rail centres was such that it almost guaranteed complete disruption. Second, bombing was more effective than sabotage for producing total line closure. One explanation for the latter was that sabotage efforts were generally directed towards the derailment of a particular train, and one track only of a multi-tracked line could have been affected.

An important part of the analysts' investigations was the time taken to restore the normal flow of traffic. That aspect of the study led the author to examine several interesting and relevant factors, such as the threat of further attacks; delayed fuses in bombs; the varying degrees of damage inflicted on the bed of the permanent way by different sizes and fusing of bombs; and the availability of manpower, materials and machinery.

The threat of further air attacks, particularly by AEAF fighter bombers, and the effects of the larger bombs dropped were more noticeable in the Northern Region where heavy attacks by RAF Bomber Command were supplemented by the AEAF. On average, it took 127 hours to re-establish through-lines after a heavy attack on a rail centre in the Northern Region, compared with sixty hours after a similar attack in the Eastern Region. However, for the Northern Region the 127 hours' repair time was reduced to eighty-four hours if the attack had been by medium bombers. Sometimes the greatest damage caused by the heavy bombers was due not only to the use of bigger bombs, but also to clever fusing, which was designed to form craters of adequate dimensions at the same time as the bomb produced powerful blast effects on wagons and locomotives, which then had to be cleared by lifting machinery.

For lines in the open country and those at stations the mean time taken to restore a double-tracked line after bombing was fifty-eight and fifty-six hours, respectively. By contrast, the times taken to make good similar lines following sabotage were twenty-three hours and thirteen hours, respectively.

For considering which part of the permanent way system was most affected by the interruptions, and which absorbed the most time and effort in repairs, the table below, drawn up by No 1 ORG after studying the SNCF's detailed records of both the Northern and Eastern Regions, is reproduced.

Contribution of different targets to the destruction of the whole system (in hours and %).

Northern Region

Month	Open track	Stations	Centres	Totals
Mar	922 15%	212 4%	4230 79%	5364
Apr	518 11%	721 15%	3480 74%	4719
May	747 5%	4106 29%	9009 65%	13,862
June	4400 24%	8130 44%	6075 33%	18,605
July	4508 48%	4370 46%	540 6%	9418

Eastern Region

Month	Open track	Stations	Centres	Totals
Mar	321 94%	22 6%	— —	343
Apr	230 22%	33 3%	780 75%	1043
May	195 10%	60 3%	1740 87%	1995
June	1845 48%	1272 32%	720 19%	3837
July	1825 32%	2978 53%	840 15%	5643

The table shows that the rail centres, which were the primary targets for RAF Bomber Command, absorbed by far the greatest repair effort until late-May, when priority was transferred to the stations, which were mostly attacked by the Eighth Air Force and the AEAF. However, the table does no more than echo the shift of emphasis during the second phase of the overall plan, and it should be noted that the heavy bombing of rail centres produced traffic interruptions of the longest duration (possibly because of the need to clear a greater volume of smashed locomotives and rolling stock). It should be noted also, that the attacks on rail centres were made not so much to cut lines, but to destroy the means of repair to haulage facilities over the whole system.

All the data on cuts in the permanent way collected by the analysts after the war, and partly reproduced here, led to the observation that, in spite of the number of cuts and the increasing amount of time needed for their repair, the percentage time during which lines in the Northern and Eastern Regions were closed was actually quite small (12 per cent was the maximum recorded in the Northern Region). The conclusion drawn was that line-cutting alone could not have brought about the degree of paralysis to the whole system which was evident at the time of the Allied invasion. However, there was evidence elsewhere that some well-timed and well-placed attacks on lines, did prove to be a decisive factor in preventing, or at least retarding, some tactical movement of German troops and supplies.

The results of the attacks on bridges were analyzed more easily. One of the more important aspects of that part of the study was discovering which type of air attack was the most cost effective in terms of aircraft and bomb lift.

Experimental attacks on 7 May by P-47 and B-26 aircraft of the USAAF Ninth Air Force led to the destruction of the rail bridge over the Seine at Vernon, and severe damage to others at Oissel, Orival and Mantes-Gassincourt. It was largely due to the success of those experimental attacks, which seem to have been conducted on the initiative of General Brereton,[12] that Leigh-Mallory decided that bridges should become primarily the responsibility of the AEAF. The advantages of using medium and fighter bombers for attacks on bridges was confirmed after the war by an analysis of a number of attacks by all types of aircraft, and the ORG produced the following table:

Aircraft type	Average altitude of attack	% bombs falling within target range of	
		160m	700m
Fighter bombers	700–2000 ft	75	—
Medium bombers	3500–4000 ft	29	64
Heavy bombers	8000 ft	17	45

During the campaign it was calculated that 600 tons[13] of bombs were needed to ensure that a bridge was destoyed by heavy bombers, whereas 100–120 tons were needed when delivered by medium or fighter bombers.

The opening of the attacks on the bridges in Belgium did not suffer the same delays imposed on those on the bridges over the Seine.[14] In early May USAAF Ninth Air Force and other AEAF aircraft cut the bridges at Liège, Herenthals and Hasselt.

The following table is part of one devised by analysts after the war, and is based on operational and intelligence estimates made during the battle. The table describes the condition of the Seine rail bridges

Bridge	MAY	JUNE	JULY	AUGUST
Rouen	×————	————	————	————
Oissel (2)	× ———	— —	————	—
Orival	×	————		
Le Manoir	×————	———	— —	———
Vernon	×————			
Mantes	×	———		
Gassincourt				
Conflans	×————	————		
Maisons Laffitte	×——— - - -	— ——	- -	
Carrières	×————	— - - -		
Athis/Mons	×	— - - - -		
Melun	×			
Tours (2)		× - - ——- -	- - -	————
Cinq Mars		× ——— - --	——— -	—
Saumur		×——— - -		
Chalonnes		× ————	————	
Nantes (2)		×————	— - - -	—

Prior to the bombing it was estimated that 230 trains a week passed over each of the Seine bridges.

KEY

First bombs ×

Closed————

during the time of the Normandy campaign. It should be noted, however, that the same analysts discovered some discrepancies between intelligence estimates and data found in SNCF records for the Western and Northern Regions. Apparently, Photographic Interpreters were more cautious about the effects of attacks, particularly those on masonry bridges which they sometimes classed as serviceable when, in fact, they had been closed.

The table shows that all the main railway bridges over the lower Seine were cut by approximately 28 May 1944 and, apart from some short periods, they remained out of commission for most of the campaign in Normandy. The Germans made enormous efforts to restore the bridges at Oissel and Le Manoir, indicating their great concern of the lack of mobility between their two armies. Steel bridges were the most difficult to repair and, naturally enough, the bigger bridges were the most vulnerable.

When dealing with the effects that the Transportation Plan had on the haulage potential of the French railways, it was necessary to divide the repercussions into two categories: direct — the number of locomotives put out of action by bombing, sabotage or rocket/machine-gun fire; and indirect — the damage done to locomotive repair and maintenance faciltities, which affected the time taken to put into service again all those locomotives out of action either as a result of attacks or because they were being serviced. Although post-War analysts obtained much useful data on the subject from the records of the Northern and Western Regions, the information for the other regions was less complete, and the conclusions regarding those regions were barely admissable.

One point of dissention between the opposing camps in the dispute over the Transportation Plan was: how many locomotives could be made available for use on the SNCF network. Those opposed to the plan argued that there were so many locomotives available that there was not enough time available in which to reduce the numbers to a level that would have any real affect on German troops movements. According to SNCF returns, the complement of locomotives in service[15] increased between January and July 1944; that was because the Germans returned to service approximately 1500 locomotives which they had commandeered in 1940 and had added a further 175 engines, primarily for hauling and distributing coal within the network. In spite of that increase, the number of serviceable locomotives dropped sharply when the heavy bombing began. In the Northern Region, for example, the number of serviceable locomotives fell from 1532 in January to 660 in June, or 43 per cent of the original figure. As could be expected, analysts found a definite association between that decline and the number of attacks and bombs dropped on rail centres.

The fact that the Germans appeared to have been forced to return locomotives to France at that time does indicate that they were aware already of the threat to their reinforcement plans, and that the SNCF was not as overprovided with locomotives as critics of the Transportation Plan had suggested.[16] However, figures for the actual employment of engines in pulling trains showed that they were not used to their full capacity. At first glance that fact could be seen to justify the critics, but the analysts put the under-utilization down to the general disorganization of the entire railway system, which included the cuts in permanent way and signalling systems, sabotage, and 'go-slow' tactics by French railway workers. That seemed, to me, to be the more likely explanation, particularly with regard to the Southeast Region, which was extensively electrified, and where frequent and easy acts of sabotage were carried out against power lines. Without electricity, the locomotives could not have been used, thereby increasing the number of engines unemployed.

Concerning the efficiency of the serviceable locomotives, the analysts approached the problem by taking into account the total weight of and the distance travelled by each train. It was a complicated calculation which involved discovering the distances covered by the locomotives when 'running light'; and other factors, such as German prohibition on daylight travel in certain areas after 26 May 1944,[17] and time lost by the necessity to take cover during air attacks. There does not appear to have been a close relationship between rail cuts and drops in distances covered in most regions; neither was there much of an increase in mileage due to detours around cut lines. Nevertheless, there was an overall reduction in both the number of tons hauled and miles travelled per engine. Those facts could confirm that the locomotives did not receive their normal levels of service when the heavy attacks on the rail centres began (indirect effects). Later in the campaign, the poor condition of the permanent way and the temporary repairs to bridges probably both played a part in reducing the weight pulled by the trains and the distances they travelled. By June, the performance levels of the locomotives had fallen to approximately seventy-five per cent of the January figures.

Another important aspect of the study was the effect of different types of attack on locomotives. Machine-gun and rocket attacks on trains began on 20 May 1944, and the AEAF claimed that, in the first week of that campaign, 230 locomotives were put out of action in the Western Region alone, and that, although claims were less in the other regions, the effects of the attacks were quickly felt throughout the entire network.

The sabotage of locomotives was far more prevalent in the two southern regions, particularly after D-Day when the Maquis virtually controlled large areas of their own country. Estimates of the number of locomotives put out of action by sabotage ranged from 109 in the Western Region to 828 in the Southwest Region.

The indirect effects on locomotives of RAF Bomber Command's attacks on rail centres have been discussed earlier in this book, but it should be noted that approximately 950 engines out of a total of 2100 in the Northern Region were damaged severely during attacks on the locomotive sheds and the repair shops of those rail centres. Although it was less serious in the other regions, it was estimated that approximately twenty-five per cent of the engines in both the Western and Eastern Regions were damaged in that way.

The times taken to repair locomotives damaged in bombing attacks were difficult to assess, not only because of incomplete data but also because there were many variable factors, such as lightly damaged engines being repaired quicker than heavily damaged ones, which often led to the latter being sent to the back of the queue and clocking up many hours out of service before any repairs were carried out. Nevertheless, the analysts did suggest mean values for periods of immobilisation following the different types of attack:

After bombing   104 days
After machine-gun/rocket attacks   82 days[18]
After sabotage   58 days

The number of locomotives repaired after receiving war damage dropped in parallel with the number of those undergoing normal repairs and servicing. In the first half of 1944 the average number of locomotives turned out monthly from French workshops was eighty; by July, that figure had dropped to twenty-six — one-third of the pre-bombing capacity.

Before leaving the effects of the Transportation Plan on the haulage potential of the French railways, mention should be made of the additional number of locomotive engineers drafted into the Northern Region to help cope with the problems. In 1943 there were approximately 6300 skilled men employed in the repair and mainten-ance of locomotives. By May 1944, that number had increased to 7100. At the same time the loss in man hours, due to air raid warnings, attacks, the salvage and transfer of machines between depots, and building of concrete shelters for locomotives and personnel, had risen from 500 man months to 2800 man months.[19] The result was a net loss in skilled manpower.

Having already noted that the amount of traffic using the SNCF network began to decline after the first attack on Trappes, the standards used to make that judgement should be examined. Two criteria were used by the post-war analysts: first, the number of wagons loaded in France and the number entering the country already loaded, both of which provided information about goods traffic only; second, the ton/kilometres affected in the various regions, which gave a more general picture of goods, passenger and German military traffic.

At the beginning of April 1944, approximately 200,000 wagons were loaded within the SNCF network each week. By June, that number had fallen to 50,000. In contrast, the percentage number of wagons already loaded entering the network from Germany and elsewhere, rose from eleven per cent in April to twenty-five per cent in June. The decline in the number of wagons loaded was first noticed in the Northern Region. Traffic in the Western Region was the next to be affected; the numbers for the Eastern Region, after declining steadily from the end of April, recovered to and remained at approximately fifty-five per cent of its March levels during June and July. The two southern regions were not affected until late May. When analysts compared those declines with the weight of bombs dropped, they found a close relationship between the figures in the Northern and Western Regions, but only a very vague pattern emerged for the other regions, indicating that factors other than air bombing had played some part in reducing rail traffic. When studying the ton/kilometres figures for military traffic, the analysts were confronted with difficulties because, in the interests of security, the Germans interspersed some of their military wagons with civilian trains.

The exact causes of the decrease in traffic were very difficult to ascertain, mainly because the factors involved all had some reciprocal effect on each other. The best the analysts could do was to classify the factors into some order of importance. For the first of those, rolling stock, it was concluded that the SNCF was never short of wagons; consequently, that was not a contributory factor in the decrease of traffic.

Troubles with the permanent way, marshalling yards and signalling systems were considered carefully. Cuts in lines were considered to have contributed only slightly to the decreases. Marshalling yards, while showing a marked decline in the numbers of wagons sorted, related only to goods traffic, and the effects on military traffic caused by damage to the yards was considered to have been quite small. Cutting communications and related signalling equipment did result in a number of trains being 'held for acceptance' and being either unable to complete their journeys, or late in reaching their destinations. The main cause for the drop in traffic appeared to have been the shortage of locomotives; either they could not get to the right place at the right time, or servicing and repair facilities had fallen below a practical level.

It seemed, therefore, that the main reason for the decline in SNCF traffic was the heavy attacks on those rail centres which contained locomotive workshops; attacks in which heavy bombers of both the RAF and the USAAF Eighth Air Force played a major role.

Notes

1 Although the Transportation Plan covered French and Belgian rail targets, detailed records of the effects of the bombing were more readily available in respect of the French railways. Therefore, I concentrated on the analyses of those records.

2 My own figures based on Appendix 10 in PRO Air 41/56. Other figures are from PRO Air 40/1669.

3 That did not include thirty-three aircraft lost during attacks on Cologne (4) and Dusseldorf (29) which, although aimed at rail centres, were not in the Transportation Plan list (See Appendix 6).

4 Notably AHB Narratives and BAU reports, PRO Air 41/56, Air 40/1669 and Air 40/317.

5 The point will be discussed in 'Conclusions' section of this book.

6 PRO PREM 3/334/1. For example, Cardinal Lienarts, Bishop of Soissons, made a speech condemning the bombing of Lille in April, and Cardinal Van Roey made an appeal in Belgian churches in which he asked the British to stop the night attacks.

7 Clapham Junction bomb plot. PRO HO 193/1.

8 See Chapter 6.

9 PRO PREM 3/334/1. However, in a German-controlled broadcast, the commentator said that complete evacuation was impossible owing to the density of population in those areas under attack.

10 See Note 4.

11 See Chapter 7.

12 Craven and Cate, *Army Forces in the Second World War* Vol III, p158. This confirmed Zuckerman's earlier advice; see Chapter 6.

13 Ibid page 157. E D Brant of the Railways Executive had been more pessimistic, saying that 1200 tons would be required.

14 See Chapter 19.

15 All locomotives held, including those under repair.

16 See Chapter 6.

17 A result of the 'Chattanooga Choo-Choo' attacks.

18 BAU Report No 20 gave a lower figure of forty-six days for the same form of attack, but it related to the Northern Region only. The heaviest attacks fell in the Western Region.

19 PRO Air 37/1262. BAU Report No 17.

CHAPTER TWENTY-TWO

German Fuel Shortages

Before the Second World War, Germany was importing almost sixty per cent of its supplies of crude oil from countries outside Europe. When the blockade of its ports and seaways cut off that supply, the Germans resorted to political pressure and military victories to obtain crude oil from East European countries, mainly Romania. Aware that the source could dry up, the Germans started to produce synthetic fuels from coal of which it had a good supply if its own. Two methods were used to derive the synthetic fuels: the Berguis Hydrogenation process of combining coal with hydrogen under great pressure, and the Fisher-Tropsch method which relied on producing a mixture of hydrogen and carbon monoxide from the coal and passing it through condensers in order to convert it to a liquid.

The production of fuel from crude oil, which remained fairly constant throughout the war, was carried out in refineries near to the ports of north Germany and near to the oil fields in the Balkans. Ploiesti in Romania contained eight such refineries, all within a few miles of each other, and was to become one of the best-known targets of the USAAF Fifteenth Air Force. The synthetic fuel plants, whose combined production doubled between 1940 and 1943, were well scattered around central Germany, but with two important concentrations, one in the Ruhr, the other in the area around Leuna, approximately 100 miles south-southwest of Berlin.

In September 1942, German reserves of aviation fuel had fallen below two weeks requirements, but at that time flying restrictions were confined to training, transport and communication flights. In the spring and summer of 1943, better weather led to an increase in operational flights and a greater fuel consumption by Luftwaffe aircraft operating on the Eastern and Mediterranean Fronts. In spite of an increase in the production of synthetic fuels, the stock situation remained much the same as it had been during the previous year (approximately 350,000 tons). Increased activity by the German Army and longer lines of communication had both brought about a similar situation to that concerning petrol and diesel fuel for motor transport and tanks.

During the winter of 1943/44, the output of synthetic fuels increased so much that the Germans were able to create large reserves, to be used only with the permission of an appropriate commander. Stocks of aviation fuel were placed into Luftflotten, Command and Führer reserve categories and totalled 440,000 tons.

Reserves of petrol and diesel were similarly categorised and amounted to 680,000 tons. In the first few months of 1944 overall reserves of fuel for the German Army and the Luftwaffe were as high as they had been at any time since 1940.

Allied strategic planners had always classed oil as a primary target for the heavy bombers, but early attacks had been so inaccurate and ineffective that the matter was more or less put to one side until better navigational and bombing aids became available. By the time that new aids came into service 'Point Blank' had been introduced, and the Luftwaffe had become the priority target. However, a special committee, the Hartley Committee,[1] had been formed in 1942 for the purpose of advising the JIC on the production, stocks and quantity of oil consumed by the Germans. In November 1943 the committee began to draw attention to the improving fuel situation in Germany.

Again, the planners had a different priority — Operation Overlord. The arguments concerning the Transportation Plan and General Spaatz's efforts to introduce oil targets as an alternative, have been discussed in Chapter 6 of this book. However, it should be noted that Spaatz was given verbal permission to carry out some experimental attacks on oil installations.

Spaatz had resorted to a considerable amount of subterfuge in order to obtain that permission. He had argued that the attacks on oil supplies would cause the Luftwaffe to fight in their defence, therefore such attacks could be regarded as an extension to 'Point Blank' offensives. He also made his proposed attacks by the USAAF Fifteenth Air Force on the Ploiesti refineries seem to be attacks against the transportation system, which was taking the oil from the Balkans to Germany. In those circumstances, the Fifteenth Air Force restarted its attacks in April 1944 on Ploiesti[2] and the Eighth Air Force began its attacks in May on the synthetic oil plants in the Leuna area.

By the end of July the Fifteenth Air Force had made more than eighty attacks on Balkan refineries, mainly from its bases around Foggia in Italy. Of great importance at that time was the part played by the RAF's No 205 Group, which was part of the Mediterranean Air Force and also operated from bases in Italy. Using Halifaxes, Liberators and twin-engined Wellingtons, the Group carried out many very successful mining sorties over the River Danube against barges which were carrying oil from Balkan oil fields and refineries to Germany. During July and August, fifty barges had been sunk. Albert Speer was later to testify, in his post-war interrogation, that the problems caused by the Danube mining operations had been as serious as those caused by the bombing of Ploiesti.[3]

One of the problems encountered by the Fifteenth Air Force was that early warning radars would give the Germans approximately forty minutes' warning of the attack on Ploiesti, so that, in addition to directing fighters to the area, the enemy would be able to put up very effective smoke screens, thereby preventing the use of normal daylight bombing methods. On 10 June, in an attempt to overcome the problem, thirty-six twin-boomed Lightning fighters, of Fifteenth Air Force Fighter Command, were each equipped with 1000-lb bombs and sent to Ploiesti with orders to dive-bomb the installations. The attack was not successful and, in spite of being escorted by a further thirty-nine Lightnings, twenty-three aircraft were lost as a result of the raid (30 per cent). Whether or not the experiment was repeated is uncertain. What is certain was that Ploiesti was regarded to be the most heavily defended of all the oil targets as a result of that attack. Apparently, the Fifteenth Air Force suffered a higher loss rate in its attacks against the Balkan refineries than their counterparts operating from bases in England.[4]

In spite of the comparatively healthy oil reserves which the Germans had managed to build up in 1943, there was an increasing awareness amongst their more realistically minded industrialists that the Romanian oil fields could be captured by the Russians during the coming year. That fear, coupled with the fact that synthetic fuel production had many useful by-products, led to the conclusion that an increase in that production was the only way ahead. The same conclusion seems to have been arrived at, almost simultaneously, by Allied planners, who put the synthetic fuel plants high on their list of priority targets.

Chapter 14 recorded the attacks made on 12 May against five synthetic fuel plants. The attacks made by RAF and Eighth Air Force heavy bombers on oil targets during the period 12 May to the end of July will now be summarised. I chose to examine that particular period because, during those eleven weeks, Bomber Command aircraft from both the RAF and Eighth Air Force were heavily engaged in 'Overlord' and 'Crossbow' operations.

The table below is based on the records of those operations, and is contained in Air Historical Branch Narrative.[5] The fact that some of the figures do not agree entirely with those in illustration 16 may be due to the fact that the graph relates to attacks on synthetic plants only.

Month	Unit	No of attacks*	No aircraft sent	No aircraft that bombed	Tonnage of bombs dropped	No of aircraft missing
May	Eighth Air Force	10	1716	1270	2786	63
June	Eighth Air Force	15	2337	1873	4595	62
	RAF	11	1156	1091	4495	96
July	Eighth Air Force	15	2843?	2204	5326	36
	RAF	19	987	915	3408	37

* RAF attacks included those made by small forces of Mosquitos.

Information concerning the indirect effects of the 12 May attacks soon filtered through to London via Bletchley Park. On 16 May it became known that five heavy and four light flak batteries, which had been destined for the Luftflotte 3 area, were being diverted to protect the synthetic fuel plant at Troglitz.[6] The plant had not been attacked, but the information reflected a feeling of apprehension in Germany, particularly that of Speer, who later concluded that the 12 May attacks had heralded the end of armament production in Germany.[7] Following his inspection of Leuna after the first attack, Speer wrote that he had groped his way 'through a tangle of broken and twisted pipes' and that a pre-bombing daily production of 5850 metric tonnes had been cut to 4850 metric tonnes. In a personal report to Hitler, Speer said 'the enemy has struck at one of our weakest points'.[8] In spite of more optimistic utterings both by Hitler's Chief of Staff, Keitel, and by Goering, Hitler appeared to have been sufficiently worried by Speer's remarks, and set up a Corps of 350,000 men, under Edmund Geilenburg, for the purposes of building, repairing and, if necessary, moving synthetic oil plants.

Information obtained from early deciphered messages encouraged the JIC, who daily became more convinced that oil was the vital factor in the German ability to counter 'Overlord'. The Eighth Air Force was to continue with its attacks on oil targets in central Germany, and RAF Bomber Command was asked to consider attacking ten oil targets in the Ruhr 'just as soon as their commitments to Overlord allowed'.

An Ultra message of 7 June noted 'Allied interference in the production of aviation fuel, and cuts in supplies for training the 1st Parachute Army', which was based near Nancy. The signal further noted that it had already become necessary to break into OKW (Command) reserves. Any doubts that still existed amongst Allied planners concerning the value of attacking Germany's oil supplies seemed to have been dispelled. In spite of protestations by Harris, plans were made for RAF Bomber Command to join forces with the Eighth Air Force in its attacks on oil plants. On the night of 12/13th June Nos 1, 3 and 8 (PFF) Groups between them despatched a total force of almost 300 aircraft (Lancasters and 'Oboe'-equipped Mosquitos) to the Gelsenkirchen (Nordstern) plant, in the Ruhr. They dropped more than 1400 tons of bombs and seventeen aircraft were lost (more than five per cent).

Being within 'Oboe' range, and no doubt because RAF crews knew the area well, the oil targets in the Ruhr were allocated, almost exclusively, to RAF Bomber Command. The USAAF Fifteenth Air Force attacked targets from the Balkans to Silesia, and the Eighth Air Force continued its attacks on targets in north Germany. As the campaign developed, RAF Bomber Command and the Eighth Air Force together attacked the more central targets, such as Bohlen and Leuna.

Evidence soon came to light that Spaatz was right in his belief that the attacks on oil supplies would cause the Luftwaffe to fight. Together with the heavy loss of fighter aircraft, the attacks led to arguments between Speer and Goering for and against creating a special fighter force, which Speer insisted was vital to the survival of the entire oil industry. Although Hitler agreed that such a force should be created, it never really came into being,[9] thus highlighting the dilemma confronting the German High Command. Army commanders were almost begging for air support for their troops in Normandy, but Speer was telling them that, unless he had fighter protection for his oil installations, there would soon be no fuel for either the aircraft or the tanks. In the West the German Army was suffering not only from the lack of fighter cover, but also from an earlier decision to divert dual-purpose 88mm guns to defend oil targets.[10]

During one of the meetings or arguments concerning the Transportation Plan, the MEW suggested that, because the Germans had such good stocks of fuel, attacks on oil production would not affect the Germans' ability to react to Allied landings. It seems to me that the MEW had underestimated the cumulative effects of bombing forward fuel dumps and the increase in fuel consumption during periods of intensive operations, because it was not long before Ultra was producing evidence of fuel shortages, particularly of aviation fuel. Admittedly the early fuel shortages experienced by the German Army were mainly the result of transportation problems. The rail system was nearly paralysed and roads were becoming unusable except at night[11]. However, on 16 June attacks on forward fuel dumps north of Poitiers destroyed 600 tons of Army reserve fuel and the 21st Panzer Division was deprived of half of its stocks on 21 June.

By 23 June the 1st SS Panzer Corps reported that fuel and ammunition expenditures were outstripping supplies. On 7 July the Quartermaster's department of the German 7th Army was advising units to try and get fuel from OB West reserve dumps. In fact, several of these dumps were empty already, or were claimed to be so by Quartermasters jealously guarding their own reserves.[12] As early as 9 June the Chief Quartermaster of the German 7th Army said that he had no fuel for the 130th Panzer Battalion, which had been ordered to move to Vire.[13]

In his meeting with Hitler in May, Speer predicted that the real crisis would come in September. A SHAEF Staff Intelligence paper of 1 June estimated the total German military fuel requirement to be approximately 900,000 metric tonnes per month, and that industries would require a further 500,000 tonnes per month, making a total monthly requirement of 1,400,000 tonnes. In the same paper, Intelligence Staffs estimated total fuel production to be approximately 900,000–1,000,000 tonnes per month, thus creating a shortfall, or the

necessity to draw on reserves at the rate of 400,000 tonnes a month.[14]
Slightly lower figures were put forward by the Hartley Committee,
who forecast a monthly deficit of between 310,000 and 370,000
tonnes. When compared with the stocks of fuel given above (which
are corroborated elsewhere)[15], Speer's prediction of a fuel crisis
occurring in September made sense. Further evidence confirmed
September as the critical month, especially for the Luftwaffe.
September was the first month after the loss of the Romanian
refineries, which not only denied the Germans of one of its sources of
oil, but also freed the USAAF Fifteenth Air Force to attack
alternative targets, mostly in Silesia. Large stocks of Romanian oil,
however, enabled the Germans to manufacture petrol and diesel for
motor transport for a further few months.

Figures for the production and consumption of fuels in Germany
are inconsistent among the various publications on the subject, and
readers are advised to check carefully whether such figures refer to
totals produced by all methods or totals produced by synthetic
methods.[16] In spite of those anomalies, all of the documents I
examined confirmed that production fell by approximately fifty
per cent in the first two months of the attacks on oil targets, and was
brought to a complete standstill, for at least a week, in September.
The figure of fifty per cent relates to production from *all* sources;
production of synthetic fuels, which included by far the largest
proportion of aviation fuel, was affected more severely and a
situation developed whereby the Luftwaffe was the first to be affected
by the shortage.

The general effects of the air attacks on the production of all
synthetic and aviation fuels is illustrated by the graph on page
183. Figures, interpolated from the line relating to aviation fuel,
corresponded well to figures given in the Air Historical Branch's
narrative on the subject, although it is not made clear in the narrative
that the figures relate to synthetic fuels only.[17] Air Intelligence
estimated the percentage totals for fuel produced as:[18]

Synthetic	35.7%
Refined	51.9%
Benzol/Alcohol	12.4%

An important result of the aviation fuel shortage in September was
that the Luftwaffe was unable to derive any benefit from the fact
that, in spite of 'Point Blank', aircraft production had risen sharply
during the previous three months. More than 3000 aircraft, mostly
fighters, were sitting on airfields, still in factory markings, waiting
for fuel and pilots. Most of those aircraft stayed that way until
bombed, shelled, or captured intact by the Allies. After September
the Luftwaffe's allocation of fuel for aircraft operating on the

GERMAN SYNTHETIC OIL PRODUCTION

AND BOMBS DROPPED 1944-1945

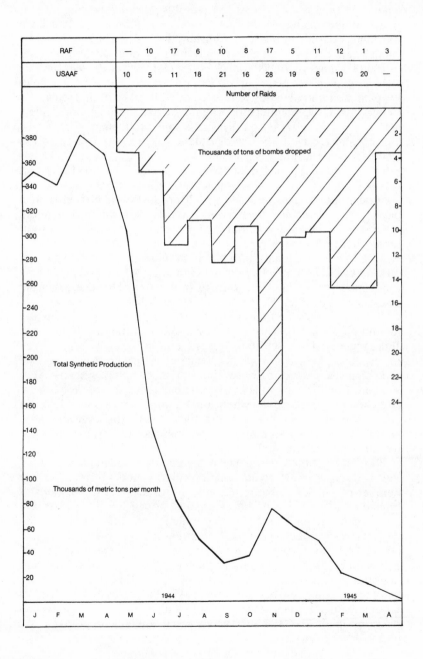

| RAF | — | 10 | 17 | 6 | 10 | 8 | 17 | 5 | 11 | 12 | 1 | 3 |
| USAAF | 10 | 5 | 11 | 18 | 21 | 16 | 28 | 19 | 6 | 10 | 20 | — |

Number of Raids

Thousands of tons of bombs dropped

Total Synthetic Production

Thousands of metric tons per month

1944 · 1945

J F M A M J J A S O N D J F M A

Western Front was cut to 30,000 tonnes per month, one-sixth of its May consumption, and approximately one-tenth of its monthly requirement estimated by Intelligence Staffs at the beginning of the year.

Economies in the use of fuel for non-operational use had been introduced earlier in the war. Consumption of petrol and diesel by civilian cars and lorries had dwindled from the pre-war monthly total of 200,00 tonnes to 70,000 tonnes in the first year of the war, and by 1944 less than 10 per cent of the pre-war figure was available. Propane and butane gases were used as substitutes until Treibgas, a by-product of the manufacture of synthetic fuel, became more widely available. The attacks on synthetic oil production forced the Germans to return to the use of Butane gas and, eventually, to use wood- or coal-burning gas generators.

The building, repair and dispersal of the German oil industry met with varied success. Leuna, which was badly damaged in the first American attack, had returned to full production almost in sixteen days (just in time for the second attack!), but when Geilenburg obtained the necessary labour and materials, he managed to cut repair times substantially.

Allied photo-reconnaissance had to monitor the state of repairs of oil plants, and new attacks were made on them when it seemed likely that a plant was about to return to production. However, damage assessment was often hampered by bad weather or smoke screens, and the bombers sometimes were diverted to other targets. Aviation fuel output, which had been reduced to a daily total of 600 tonnes in June, recovered to reach 2000 tonnes again, in July.[19] The time taken to repair damaged oil plants lengthened progressively as the campaign developed because the intricate piping systems were weakened by the early attacks to such an extent that the shocks from later bombs exploding anywhere in the target area caused leaks to occur throughout the plants. Also, the necessity of returning more vital sections to working order sometimes led to severely damaged sections being abandoned.

The construction and dispersal programmes included plans to build seven large Bergius hydrogenation plants underground, and a number of smaller plants in the hills, in woods, and in the ruins of bombed factories which the Germans hoped would escape the attention of Medmenham's Photographic Interpreters. In spite of the large sums of money spent, and diverting a large amount of skilled labour from armaments factories, none of the large underground plants were ever completed. If they had been completed, it was doubtful if they would have been able to add significantly to the amount of supplies because, by 1945, the transport system in Germany had become incapable of dealing with the supply and distribution of raw materials. The view that bombing oil storage tanks was of little value did not hold when the transport system began to show signs of collapsing. Several cases were recorded where oil production stopped because either there were not enough storage tanks available to hold raw materials or there was nowhere to put the end product.

The difficulties experienced by PRUs in obtaining good and regular photographic coverage of the oil installations led to a greater reliance on Ultra. In the early part of the campaign deciphered messages provided detailed information concerning the effects of attacks on individual plants, but that type of report became less frequent after July. Fortunately, they were replaced by better reports which dealt with the existence and effects of fuel shortages.

The first indication that operational flights were being curtailed, came in a deciphered message on 10 August: the OKL had ordered that operational flights by four-engined aircraft were to be made only after reference to a higher command. The same signal stated that reconnaissance flights could be made only if absolutely essential, and that all aircraft were to fly operational sorties only if there was a good chance of success.[20]

In a similar message from Berlin on 13 August, German supply units were ordered to convert as many vehicles as was possible to producer gas by the end of October. Further decoded messages were all found to contain references to the effects of bombing the oil installations and the consequent fuel shortages. During that period, von Kluge, who had taken over from Rommel as C-in-C West, cited the fuel shortage as the main reason for his request to pull out of the Fallaise Pocket.

As unwilling as Harris was to become involved in the attacks on oil targets, RAF Bomber Command, aided by improved G-H equipment, had better results from its night bombing than the USAAF had when bombing during the day. However, if the target could be seen clearly, the American bomb aimers recorded more hits in the target areas. As with the attacks on the ball-bearing plants, it was dicovered, after the war, that the heavier bombs dropped by the RAF did more lasting damage than an equivalent weight of smaller American bombs. Another interesting result was found in the differing methods of attack. Attacks by close formations of American bombers lasted a few minutes only, and the Germans were sometimes able to extinguish fires quickly before they took hold; the RAF's method of using bomber streams, often in two phases, delayed fire fighting and caused the fear of yet another wave catching the defenders out in the open.[21]

Because the aim of the oil plan was never really defined, it was difficult to draw any conclusions as to whether or not the aim had been achieved. Spaatz got the plan accepted by saying that it would put the finishing touches to a Luftwaffe already weakened by 'Point

Blank'. The fact remained that there were more German fighters in existence in September than there were in June 1944. That there was no fuel for the engines or pilots to fly them was not the result of achieving the 'Point Blank' aims, but of the destruction of the means of producing and distributing aircraft fuel.

Notes

1 The Hartley Committee in conjunction with the American Enemy Objectives Unit and MEW. *British Intelligence in the Second World War* Vol III Pt.
2 The USAAF Fifteenth Air Force had attacked Ploiesti in August 1943 but without fighter cover. The attack was not successful and was very costly in terms of aircraft missing.
3 *British Intelligence in the Second World War* Vol III, Pt 2 p505 fn.
4 Craven and Cate, *Army Air Forces in World War II* Part 3.
5 PRO Air 41/56.
6 PRO DEFE 3/156 KV 4021.
7 Speer, *Inside the Third Reich*.
8 Ibid.
9 50–55% of all fighters were committed already to the defence of the Reich.
10 The defence of the oil plants in central Germany was entrusted to the 14th Flak Division.
11 The movement of road convoys at night also created problems in that the accident rate increased sharply. Bennett, *Ultra in the West* p89.
12 Ibid p90.
13 PRO DEFE 3/169. KV 9468.
14 PRO WO 219/1873.
15 A table in the Air Historical Branch Narrative. PRO Air 41/56.
16 For an example see notes 17 and 18.
17 PRO Air 41/56 Appx 17.
18 The same percentages as those given in Air 41/56 are 54.5, 25.2 and 20.3.
19 Speer, *Inside the Third Reich* p350.
20 PRO DEFE 3/117 XL 5773.
21 Cooke and Nesbit, *Target Hitler's Oil*.

CHAPTER TWENTY-THREE

Delays Imposed upon the German Army

We must blast our way on shore and gain a good lodgement before the enemy can bring up sufficient reserves to turn us out.

That was Montgomery's solution to the problem of getting the Allied armies into Normandy and making sure that they stayed there. To what extent did the Overlord Transportation Plan help in achieving that aim?

The Transportation Plan began to affect rail movements into and throughout France quite soon after the initial attack on Trappes in March 1944. By then, some German Army units were being redeployed in order to meet the threatened Allied attack. Although some of the moves were accompanied by slight delays, the time factor was not critical, and the set-backs were no more than minor irritations to be overcome by the Transportation Officers of OB West. However, as those early delays grew, they led to the realisation amongst German commanders that, if the destruction of the railways continued, there would come the time when normal reinforcement and resupply by rail might become impracticable, and that as many moves as possible should be made before that time arrived.

Severely hampered by the lack of any firm intelligence on the area chosen by the Allies for their assault, and misled by Operation Fortitude, the Germans were forced to deploy troops over a wide front, and only three of those pre-invasion moves actually provided any additional strength in the Normandy area. The problems of moving troops after D-Day would, they hoped, be overcome by local commanders and German ingenuity.

The three moves into the Normandy area were those of the Panzer Lehr Division from Budapest to the Chartres/Châteaudun area in early May, the 21st Panzer Division from Rennes to the Argentan area in late April, and, the most worrying for the Allied Intelligence Officers, the move of the 91st Air Landing Division from Germany to the Cherbourg Peninsula and into the very area chosen for the landing of the American airborne forces! Having trained itself in airborne operations it was well suited to dealing with enemy operations of that nature. The possibility of 'Overlord' being compromised caused great concern among Allied Counter Intelligence Staffs, but it was concluded finally that the Germans had just been extremely lucky in their choice of location. Nevertheless the plans were changed in favour of a new dropping zone behind the 'Omaha' and 'Utah' beaches.[1]

Although the records of the Transportation Officer of the German 7th Army contained certain details of trains used in the pre-invasion moves,[2] only a few of the trains were subject to the same extensive analysis as that of later train movements. Therefore, there is not much detail of the delays resulting from the early attacks on the French railway system. Nevertheless, correlating that information which is available with the narratives in Part 2 and Appendix 9 of this book provides an interesting link between the attacks on railways, German unit movements at that time, and the association between the number of bombs dropped and the fall in rail traffic described in Chapter 21.

Concerning the German troop movements, I examined ten of these. With one exception all were divisional moves and included the three moves into the Normandy area, previously mentioned. The moves have been arranged in date order, more or less.

21st Panzer Division
The Division made two moves prior to D-Day. Between 20 and 24 March it moved from its area around Vernon, northwest of Paris, to new locations near Rennes approximately 150 miles southwest of Vernon. I found no mention of any specific delays, but it is almost certain that the Division would have travelled via Trappes, and that some trains were routed through Le Mans. Trappes was still recovering from the Allied attack of 6/7 March, and Le Mans had been heavily attacked twice in the two weeks prior to the move; the second attack, by more than 200 Halifaxes of Nos 4 and 6 Groups, RAF Bomber Command, took place on the night of 13/14 March.

The second move occurred after a visit by the Inspector General of Panzer Troops, General Guderian.[3] Between 26 and 30 April the Division moved northeast to take up new positions between Argentan and Caen, from where it became the first tank division to move against the Normandy beaches. The name given to the Division's second move was 'Mandelbute'; because the move took place entirely within a part of the SNCF's Western Region which had escaped the attention of the RAF, there were few, if any, delays.

116th Panzer Division (formerly the 179th Reserve Panzer Division)
The Division effectively swapped areas with the 21st Panzer Division when the latter moved from its positions around Vernon. The transfer from Rennes took place between 22 and 27 March and some units seemed to have moved as far north as Beauvais, which, being in the SNCF's Northern Region was already feeling the effects of the attacks on Amiens (15 and 16 March). During the move, reports were received of the attack on Aulnoye during the night of 25/26 March,

and the Division considered itself lucky to have completed its move before the onset of the serious trouble which was to engulf the SNCF's Northern Region.

9th Panzer Division (formerly the 155th Reserve Panzer Division)

According to the log of the 7th Army Transportation Officer,[4] elements of the 155th Reserve Panzer Division moved from Laval/ Fourges to Vernon/Beauvais between 21 March and 4 April. Those units then joined others from the 155th Reserve Panzer Division and the old 9th Panzer Division at Nîmes in the South of France, and came under the control of the German 19th Army. There was no record of any serious delays during all these moves, but the Paris marshalling yards had been attacked already, and the first attack on Trappes and one on Vaires by Nos 4 and 6 Groups during the night of 29/30 March caused routing problems. A more serious situation developed when the units moved into the SNCF's Southeast and Southwest Regions where sabotage by French Resistance groups was becoming a major hazard to rail and road movements.

77th Infantry Division

A twenty-nine train convoy named 'Kornblume' carried elements of the Division from an area south of Caen to new posiitons near St Malo during the week 29 April–4 May. The ninety-mile journey took place entirely within the SNCF's Western Region which, largely because of Operation Fortitude, had not been subjected to too much attention by the RAF, and there did not appear to have been any problems with the move.

91st Air Landing Division

A large part of the Division moved in a thirty-five train convoy named 'Lenore'. Starting at Barnsholder-Bitsch on 2 May, most of the convoy had arrived in the Carentan area of the Cherbourg Peninsula by approximately 11 May. The route was via Petit Croix (Dijon) and Saincaize (Nevers), but at least five of the trains bound for Saincaize went to Montargis sixty or more miles to the north. The move took place over the area most affected by the first USAAF Eighth Air Force attacks on Blainville (27 April) and on Troyes, Metz and Saareguemines on 1 May. The American attacks had extended rail disruption into the SNCF's East and Southeast Regions, but the heavy USAAF attacks on Belfort, Mulhausen and Epinal on 11 May were apparently too late to catch the tail end of the convoy. Short delays only were experienced, resulting in an overall decrease of three per cent in the planned speeds.

101st Werfer Regiment (Mortars)

The movements of heavy mortar units were always of interest to Allied Intelligence Staffs. The fire power of those units was considerable, and they had come to be feared by all who had been subjected to the effects of the multi-barrelled 'Nebelwerfer'. Under the code name 'Korinthe', five trains moved the regiment 250 miles, from Bethune to the Cherbourg Peninsula just before the attacks began on the Seine bridges. Even so, heavy attacks by RAF Bomber Command both on Mantes (6/7 May) and Rouen (late April) added to the chaos that was building up in the SNCF's Northern Region and the trains barely averaged six miles an hour in the two-days period 10/11 May.

Panzer Lehr Division

As well as being the largest, and perhaps the most important pre-invasion move, the Division's transfer from Budapest was interesting because, although the final destination was the Orléans, Le Mans and Chartres triangle, the eighty-one train convoy, named Rosa, was planned to take a southerly route through France. In the event, twenty-one trains, routed initially via Moulins and Saincaize, eventually passed through Laroche and Malesherbes well north and east of Orléans. Increased incidents of sabotage in the SNCF's Southeast Region could have led to that change of route, or possibly the conditions around the Paris area were not as bad as had been expected at the time of the move, which took place between 2 and 9 May.

There had been no further attacks on Le Mans since 14 March, but a heavy raid by No 5 Group, RAF Bomber Command, on Tours in April, and a lighter one by the same Group on 1/2 May could both have ruled out the possibility of trying to reach Le Mans via the southern route which would have taken the convoy through Saincaize and Tours. The change of route was puzzling when the effects of the recent USAAF atacks in the area southeast of Paris and the heavy RAF attack on Villeneuve St George were both taken into consideration. Twenty-nine trains on the Avricourt-Malesherbes rail section were nine hours late arriving. On average, the trains in convoy 'Rosa' arrived at their destinations between six and nine hours late, and provided the Germans with their first hint of the problems which were beginning to build up.

A small convoy of twenty trains, carrying tanks and guns, was named 'König' and moved from Belgium to Beauvais between 5 and 6 May. Cuts in the main lines around Douai and Valenciennes forced the trains onto secondary lines and the average delay for each train, over the planned journey of 140 miles, was four hours. Both the 2nd

Panzer and 12th SS Panzer Divisions were thought to be moving at that time, but it seems more likely that only the 2nd SS Panzer Division was moving because it was known to be receiving new equipment and establishing itself in the Amiens/Beauvais area. By the time of that move there had been thirteen heavy attacks on the SNCF's Northern Region, including those on Lille, Aulnoye and Tergnier, and reports of ammunition trains having been hit during the attack on Lille in April could possibly have been connected with the move of the 12th SS Panzer Division from Antwerp to Evreux, which was taking place at that time.

As part of the German naval plans to counter the invasion, Admiral Krancke, Commander Naval Group West, had planned to add to the already extensive minefield between Le Havre and Calais by laying an additional barrage between Le Havre and Cherbourg during April and May. However, Transportation Plan attacks delayed the arrival of the mines, which had been routed through the SNCF's Northern Region, to such an extent that by that time they arrived in Le Havre the special mine-laying force, which had been gathered together for the task, had been decimated almost completely by the Royal Navy and RAF Coastal Command which had both intercepted the vessels on their way from Brest.

Prior to examining the 'battle of the build-up', Allied plans for landing troops and equipment in Normandy must be taken into consideration, together with a review of the various intelligence estimates of the rates at which the Germans were expected to move their Divisions towards the battle. Allied commanders knew, only too well, that any miscalculation concerning the opposing forces could lead to disaster. Calculations concerning the rates at which Allied troops and equipment could be got ashore were checked and re-checked, and there were probably more Intelligence appreciations concerning possible German reactions than in any other subject connected with 'Overlord'.[5]

COSSAC's original plan for 'Overlord', outlined at the Quebec Conference in 1943, was that nine Divisions would be used for the assault phase, and that the breakout would occur when a further twenty Divisions had been landed. The initial plan pre-supposed that the Germans would have only twelve full-strength Divisions, interspersed with 'static' divisions situated in the West. A further fifteen Divisions could be moved in from Russia, or elsewhere, during the first two months after the landings.

By May 1944 the JIC estimated the number of German Divisions located in the West to be: ten Panzer, fourteen Infantry, and thirty-four or thirty-five 'limited employment' Divisions, and that the total number of Divisions could reach sixty-two by D-Day. At the same time the JIC estimated the possible build-up rates of German and Allied Divisions as*:

	German	Allied
D-Day AM	3	8+
D-Day PM	5	?
D-Day + 2 days	6–7	10½
D-Day + 8 days	11–14	15+

* The number of divisions in contact or close enough to be used in battle.

In his final presentation of 'Overlord' at St Paul's School on 15 May 1944, Montgomery presented his idea of how the build-up could proceed. He thought that six enemy Divisions would initially oppose the landing of seven and a half Allied ones. The following day there would be ten and a half Allied Divisions ashore facing nine enemy Divisions, of which five would be armoured. On 8 June both sides would have twelve Divisions in contact; according to Montgomery, that would be the crucial time. Thereafter, by 11 June the Allies should have fifteen Divisions ashore which could oppose the twelve enemy Divisions that would be present on 8 June plus elements of a further thirteen Divisions which would be moving towards the Front. By 14 June Montgomery hoped to have eighteen Divisions ashore, but warned that the enemy could have twenty-four, of which ten could be armoured.[6]

Average figures based on some of the many intelligence estimates, produced at that time, showed that the Allies expected German Divisions to build up during June as follows:

6 June (D-Day) AM One Panzer and five Infantry Divisions

PM Two Panzer and seven Infantry Divisions

15 June Five Panzer and fourteen Infantry Divisions

30 June Nine Panzer and twenty-one Infantry Divisions

In the event the German build up amounted to:

6 June 1.3 Panzer and five Infantry Divisions

15 June Six Panzer and twelve Infantry Divisions

30 June Eight Panzer and eighteen Infantry Divisions

The plot illustrated on page 193 summarises both the expected and the actual build-up rates. However, it should be noted that some of the German Divisions were subjected to intense air attack during their approach, and that they were already at reduced strength by the time they reached the Front.

The first few weeks were critical times for both sides, and during that time they both suffered serious delays in the race to build up their forces. Two problems affected the Allies. The first was the great storm of 19 to 22 June, which wrecked the American and severely damaged the British 'Mulberry' harbours, thereby reducing the discharge of troops and equipment to such an extent that a British attack across the River Odon, set for 22 June, had to be postponed. The second problem was the general lack of storage space in the beachhead area, caused by slow progress in the British sector.

The initial problem for the Germans was indecision on the part of the High Command, who still believed that the Normandy landings were a feint and that a second landing would take place in the Pas de Calais area. When reserves were finally released, they were subjected to long delays when they tried to move on practically non-existent railways, or they were continually shot up as they moved along roads

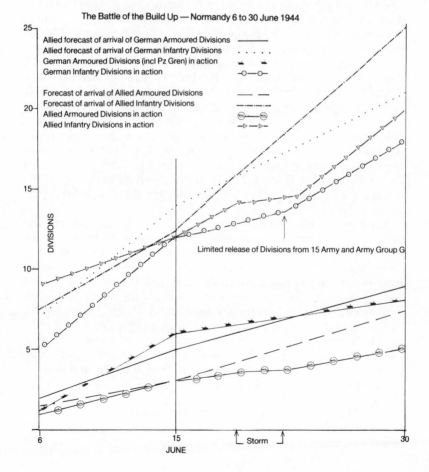

The Battle of the Build Up — Normandy 6 to 30 June 1944

Allied forecast of arrival of German Armoured Divisions
Allied forecast of arrival of German Infantry Divisions
German Armoured Divisions (incl Pz Gren) in action
German Infantry Divisions in action

Forecast of arrival of Allied Armoured Divisions
Forecast of arrival of Allied Infantry Divisions
Allied Armoured Divisions in action
Allied Infantry Divisions in action

Limited release of Divisions from 15 Army and Army Group G

DIVISIONS

Storm

JUNE

patrolled constantly by Allied bombers and fighters. In retrospect, it seemed that neither side took full advantage of the other's difficulties. The British failure to do so became the subject of much adverse comment by Air Force commanders. The Germans were unable perhaps to exploit the effects of the storm because of the restrictions imposed on the movements of their troops by fuel shortages, Allied air attacks and sabotage.

The delays imposed on some of the more important moves of German reinforcements after D-Day, and the extent to which those delays affected the outcome of the battle, will now be examined.

It was quite late on D-Day before German commanders appreciated the full extent of the attack, and Runstedt's immediate request for the release both of the 12th SS Panzer and the Panzer Lehr Divisions from the OKW reserve was not granted for several hours. It was not until the evening of 6 June that the two Divisions were given formal permission to head for the battle to join the five infantry divisions and the 21st Panzer Division which had all met the initial onslaught. Also released during that first evening were the 17th SS Panzer Grenadier, the 3rd Paratroop and the 77th Infantry Divisions from northern Brittany. Orders to move were also sent to the 1st SS Panzer Division in Antwerp, the 2nd SS Panzer Division near Toulouse, and the 2nd Panzer Division at Amiens. In fact, the 12th SS Panzer Division had jumped the gun a little and started to move from its concentration near Dreux during D-Day. Although it was held back by the order to stand fast, and by the air attacks which had reduced their progress to four miles per hour, the first elements approached Caen at approximately 1900 hr. The units were short of fuel; a dump, near Evreux, had been destroyed during the day, and both slow and static running had seriously upset the mpg figures for all the vehicles.

The Panzer Lehr Division also moved before formal consent had been given. Air attacks soon drove it off the main roads; even when dispersed on minor roads it was forced to increase the gaps in its convoys from the normal 25 yd to 100 yd. The division was harassed from the air all the way through Alencon and Domfront, and some reports suggest that, as the forward elements approached the battlefront, they came under fire from naval 15- and 16-inch guns, which were pumping shells into the Caen area at the rate of two every minute. Devoid of any rail transport and therefore running on their own tracks, the bulk of the Division's tanks did not reach Thury Harcourt, south of Caen, until approximately midday on 8 June — thirty-six hours after it had left its bases near Châteaudun only 135 miles away.

Allied Intelligence forecast that the Division could be in action on 7 June. The Divisional Commander, General Bayerlein, was a veteran of North Africa and appreciated the need for camouflage, but the slightest movement attracted swarms of AEAF fighter bombers, and by the end of 7 June, the Division had lost forty petrol wagons, eighty-four half track, personnel and gun towing vehicles, and ninety trucks. Almost twenty per cent of the tanks were not fit for battle because of mechanical problems caused by slow running and moving on their own tracks over metalled roads. Bayerlein's troops had christened the road running north from Vire as the 'Jabo rennstrecke' — the fighter-bomber racecourse.[7]

The 17th Panzer Grenadier Division's move from south of the River Loire started on 7 June. Initially, Rommel directed it to the west coast of the Cotentin, but later changed that, first to Balleroy, then to Carentan. The Division's troubles began soon after it left the Poitiers area. French Resistance attacks started before they reached the Loire bridges, some of which had already been destroyed by the USAAF Eighth Air Force during its attacks of 7 and 8 June. Heavy attacks by RAF Bomber Command during the ensuing three nights on all the rail centres in both eastern Brittany and the Cotentin caused general chaos on those railways which were being used by the division. The now-famous blocking of the Saumur tunnel by No 617 Squadron on the night of 8/9 June came just at the wrong time for five of the trains which, unable to get any further, disgorged their troops with orders to land march.

By 9 June, SHAEF Intelligence estimated that there was one serviceable double-tracked line only, connecting Tours and Le Mans with Argentan. The bridge over the canal at Tours had two of its six lines working, and convoy 'Mimose' was in serious trouble. Decoded signals from the local German Army Commander at Châteauroux, dated 9 June, provided details of many railway lines in his area which had been cut by the French Resistance. The main Paris–Toulouse line was cut in several places, forty miles of track near Issoudun had been cut several times, and terrorists had been caught trying to blow a bridge near Buzancais, where they had also stolen urgently needed trucks. The signal added that French railway workers were on strike, demanding protection against air and terrorist attacks in the area.[8]

Bad weather on 9 June gave the Division some breathing space from the air attacks. At midday on 10 June, leading elements of the lighter units joined up with units of the 3rd Paratroop Division near St Lô. However, they had run out of fuel, and were unable to help in closing the gap made in the German line by the sudden advance of the American 1st Division. The first major engagement of the Division's troops did not take place until early on 13 June, more than six days after they had received orders to move from their pre-invasion locations 175 miles to the south. The Division's failure to arrive earlier probably led to both the German predicament and the desperate situation in the Caumont area. There, General Marcks, a one-legged veteran of the Russian Front and the Commander of the

German LXXXIV Corps, met his death. Caught on the road by Allied fighters, his artificial leg prevented him from taking cover before cannon shells ripped into his car.

The 3rd Paratroop Division was also involved in trying to save the situation in west Normandy. Orders to move from its bases around Brest were received on the evening of D-Day. Twelve trains reached Rennes before the crippling attack by No 5 Group, RAF Bomber Command, on 8/9 June closed that station. From Rennes, the Division was supposed to travel by motorised transport but, with only enough army transport for one regiment, requests were made to the German Navy, which managed to provide a few vehicles.

The bulk of the Division appeared to have made its dangerous journey east in old buses, commandeered from the French. The first units reached Caumont without too much trouble, but Allied air attacks on the so-called choke points at Fourges and St Lô on 7 and 8 June, and RAF Bomber Command attacks on Fourges and Rennes on the night of 8/9 June, created such a mess in the area that the remainder of the Division soon ran into difficulties. It was reported that the approach road to St Lo, the final destination, was cratered heavily over its last twenty miles. By the evening of 9 June, most of the Division had got only as far as Brecey, east of Avranches. By 10 June, a lack of fuel was becoming the primary reason for slow progress.[9]

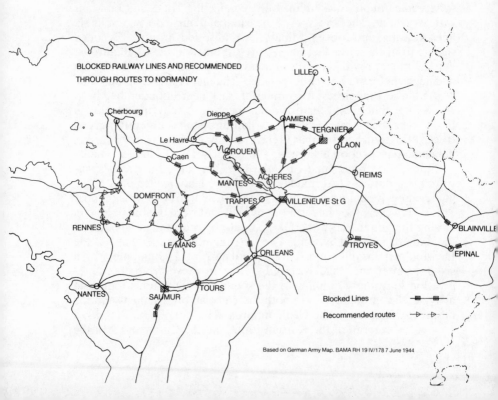

BLOCKED RAILWAY LINES AND RECOMMENDED THROUGH ROUTES TO NORMANDY

Blocked Lines

Recommended routes

Based on German Army Map. BAMA RH 19 IV/178 7 June 1944

The division was first in action at 1300 hr on 12 June, and then only in a defensive role 'until full fighting efficiency could be achieved'.[10] It had taken some units five and a half days to travel approximately 160 miles. A SHAEF appreciation dated 3 June warned that the Division would probably arrive at the battlefield on 9 June.

Another Division expected to arrive by 9 June was the 77th Infantry Division from the St Malo/St-Brieuc area. Ordered to the west coast of the Cotentin on the evening of D-Day, the Division began moving on 7 June. Having a limited amount of commandeered transport only, it was not long before fuel shortages and air attacks both slowed its progress to the point where some units were ordered onto bicycles while their heavy equipment followed in horse-drawn wagons. There was no suggestion that the Division ever tried to use trains for its short journey to the Front (50–80 miles).

The 265th Infantry Division made a bold start from its positions at Vannes and Quimper on the Brest Peninsula. After some delay, caused by the cutting of telephone lines,[11] a few trains were assembled and, moving by night only, the Division got as far as Fourges. There, the leading train was bombed and cut in two; the rear half, which contained the Division's horses, rolled back down the line for four miles. When the wagons came to rest finally, the French released the horses, and a 'Wild West'-type of round-up followed, in which German soldiers wasted a lot of time acting as cowboys! As with the other Divisions which had tried to travel through the area, it seemed that the Bomber Command attacks on Rennes and Fourges during the night of 8/9 June had caused the Division to abandon its attempts at rail movement. Most of the troops, including Headquarters staff, detrained at Rennes and proceeded in commandeered transport, on bicycles or on foot. The first battle groups of the Division were not identified by Allied Intelligence Officers until 17 June, in the area southwest of Carentan, ten days after they had started to move from their bases 200 miles away.

On 15 June, the French Resistance reported that all rail traffic in south Brittany had come to a halt, except for one single-tracked line running from Nantes to Rennes. The line Dinan–Dol–Avranches was cut at Pontaubault where the viaduct was badly damaged, and all the rail bridges over the Loire had been cut. In an Intelligence Summary, dated 15 June, the British 21st Army Group reviewed the state of the build-up of enemy forces. Revised estimates had predicted that nine Panzer and sixteen Infantry divisions would have been assembled against the invading armies by that time.[12] In fact, there were elements of six Panzer and twelve Infantry Divisions only, which included the 3rd Paratroop Division.

The Allies' primary concern was the movements of the Panzer Divisions, which were known to be moving towards the battlefront.

However, only a few Divisions had arrived, and some had not been seen at all. The Divisions concerned were the 1st and 2nd SS Panzer, 2nd Panzer, 11th Panzer, 116th Panzer, together with the 9th and 10th SS Panzer Divisions which were known to be on their way from Warsaw.

The attacks made by the French Resistance on the 2nd SS Panzer Division (Das Reich) provided the basis for several books on the subject of the massacre at Oradour,[13] therefore those accounts will not be repeated in this book. The account of the Division's move to Normandy will be confined to the known facts about the delays imposed upon it, both by air and partisan actions.

The Division was ordered to move from its bases around Toulouse on 8 June. Signals Intelligence confirmed, on 11 June, that the Divisions was on the move, that the main entraining points were in the Perigueux area, and that the move would be via Poitiers,[14] In that knowledge, Allied Staffs estimated that the Division would be in action by 14 June. Its request that fuel be available at Châtellerault by 13 June confirmed that the Division, less its heavy tanks, was land-marching via Tours.[15] Elements of the Division passed through Champsecret on 15 June. On 18 June, elements were reported to be assembling near St Lô where, deprived of its Panther tanks which were held up south of Angers, it was to wait in reserve. Lighter elements were engaged in the 'Epsom' battle between 23 and 27 June.

In spite of the much-publicised and acknowledged value of the attacks by the Maquis on the motorised columns, it was the attacks on the railways made by both the French Resistance and the Allied Air Forces that delayed the arrival at the battlefield of the essential elements of the Division, namely its heavy tanks and self-propelled guns. The incident concerning the substitution of carburundum paste for axle grease (mentioned in Chapter 20); the bombing of Montauban on 11 June by the USAAF Eighth Air Force just as some tanks were loading; and the bridge episode at Tours in which the train had to be pushed across because the bridge was too weak to take the weight of a locomotive, all of these incidents were but a small part of the troubles experienced on the railways at the time of the Division's move. An attempt to continue the move by rail via Le Mans, as late as 24 June, ended when two trains were caught in the open and attacked, blocking the lines to such an extent that any further organised railway movements in the area were virtually abandoned.[16] The heavy tanks did not arrive until the end of the month.

The 1st SS Panzer Division was ordered to move on 8 June and agents in Belgium reported the loading of tank units that evening. Air reconnaissance detected the movement of armour on the Paris–Dreux line at approximately that time, and Allied Intelligence Staffs predicted that the Division would arrive just after the Panzer Lehr,

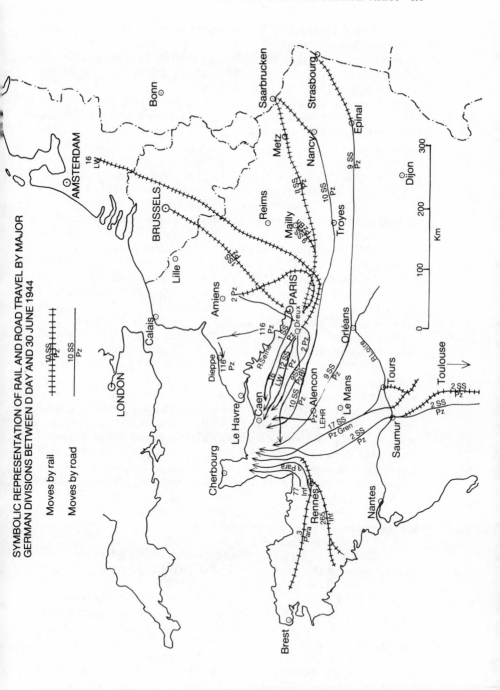

SYMBOLIC REPRESENTATION OF RAIL AND ROAD TRAVEL BY MAJOR
GERMAN DIVISIONS BETWEEN D DAY AND 30 JUNE 1944

Moves by rail

Moves by road

12th SS Panzer and 17th SS Panzer Grenadiers.[17] Further movement of the Division was stopped on 10 June because a German double agent had reported that the Allies planned to land in the Pas de Calais. On 17 June, British Sigint established that the bulk of the Division was still in Belgium on 16 June.

The Division did not start its move to Normandy until 19 June when, under the name of 'Teerose', forty-six trains set out for Normandy. On the ninety-mile run from Guignicourt to the Paris area, thirty-four of the trains clocked up delays averaging sixty hours. When unable to make any further progress by rail, the troops were given the order to land-march to the Front. Of the forty-six trains, fourteen were diverted, and thirty-five ended up at places other than those planned. The average speed of the trains was 7 mph.

Although the major part of the Division had reached the Front by 23 June, its Panther tanks were still at Rouen, unable to cross the Seine and waiting for traction around the south of Paris.

The Division became a fighting entity on 29 June when it was in action against the British Odon Salient. In addition to the ten days lost through indecision on the part of the German High Command, it took a further ten days to cover the 275-mile journey from Belgium to Normandy. It had been expected in Normandy by 13 June.

The loss of the Seine bridges and the general state of the railways in the Northern Region and around Paris, meant that German units trying to reach Normandy by rail from areas north of the Seine had to make long detours via the south of Paris and the Paris/Orléans gap. Sometimes the detours extended as far south and east as Troyes. Although much of the damage in the Paris area was caused by RAF Bomber Command pre-invasion attacks on the Parisian rail centres, many of the delays imposed after D-Day were the direct results of Bomber Command attacks on these centres on the nights of 6/7, 7/8 and 10/11 June, together with these on Dreux, Amiens, Cambrai and Aulnoye on 10/11, 12/13, 14/15 and 17/18 June respectively. Attacks by AEAF medium bombers cut the lines at Reims on 23 June and those at Nanteuil on 25 June, and were probably directly responsible for the wide diversions of nineteen trains, which had entered France via Givet and Hirson between 24 and 25 June.

The 2nd Panzer Division was released from its positions in the Amiens area on the morning of 8 June. On the morning of 10 June, eleven trains (code-name 'Konstantine') left Amiens bound for the German LXXXIV Corps area in west Normandy. Ultra warned Montgomery that the Division was marching to an assembly area thirty-five miles south of Caen on 12 June.[18] However, it was without its tanks, which could only travel by rail flats which themselves were confined to main lines because of their heavy axle loading. There was also the nagging question in German minds that the Allies might yet invade the Pas de Calais area, and that probably accounted for the general lack of urgency to move the Division from that area.

The first reports that the Division had reached the battle area came when infantry units from the Division attacked the British 7th Armoured Division (during its drive towards Caumont) on 12 June. However, such reports had emanated from intelligence confused by the German decision to alter all the cover names of their armoured divisions. On 12 June, 21st Army Group Intelligence Staff warned of the probable arrival of the Division by 14 June. In fact, its reconnaissance battalion had reached the Balleroy/Caumont area by the night of 12 June, when it then became evident that the Division had been directed to that area, not Caen as had been expected. The attack on the British 7th Armoured Division had been carried out by units of the 101st Heavy Panzer Battalion.

Although there was some confusion concerning the movements of the 2nd Panzer Division, the familiar note 'land-march' appeared against the move of one of the 'Konstantine' trains, which confirmed that the bulk of the Division moved through the Paris area by road, and that, as a result of the bombing of the Seine bridges and the Paris rail centres, its tanks had to make a very wide sweep to the south of the city. The formation first appeared on British situation maps, as a fully constituted armoured division, on 17 June, three days after the latest date forecast by Allied Intelligence Staffs.

The armoured division which seems to have suffered most from German indecision connected with Operation Fortitude was the 116th Panzer Division. From its D-Day positions astride the Seine, northwest of Paris, it was moved, first towards the Somme, then to an area between Dieppe and Le Treport. It was in much the same area when it was visited by Rommel on 19 June. On 23 June, Ultra revealed that its commander, General Schwerin, had complained that no one was bothering to keep him informed about the battle![19] It seemed that the Division remained in the Amiens–Rouen–Dieppe triangle for the ensuing two weeks, and that, apart from being bombed on 1 July, it was not involved in any proceedings until 9 July when the imposition of a wireless silence suggested that it was about to move. In fact, it was a further nine days before Hitler released the Division in response to OKW's requests, and it began to move towards Falaise.

By 23 July, the Germans were rearranging their forces in anticipation of another British attack, east of the river Orne. The 116th Panzer Division was assembling in the area of St Sylvain, six miles south of Caen; later, it was moved west to counter the American breakout during Operation Cobra. There was little information available concerning the Division's move from the 15th Army area. When it was moved, it took four days to get to its destination 100 miles away, which indicated that it suffered much the same difficulties as had other divisions. The Division was one of those listed by Montgomery, in his May briefing, as being likely to arrive at Normandy by 7 June. Had it been released on D-Day, it would probably not have arrived until 10 June.

Hitler's decision to recall the 2nd SS Panzer Corps from Russia was taken on 11 June,[20] and the two divisions, the 9th and 10th SS Panzer, began to move towards Normandy the next day. Elements of the 10th SS Panzer Division started to load their tanks at Sokol and Krystynopol on the morning of 12 June, and left there at 1730 hr.[21] Their first destination was Saarbrücken; they were warned to expect trouble from partisans as they travelled through Poland, and when they reached France. Their route was via Jarroslau, Breslau and Cottbus; having arrived in Germany, they approached Saarbrücken via Cologne and Frankfurt. The first twenty-one trains (code-named 'Viktoria') from Saarbrücken met up with the Division's Panther tank Regiment (9th SS), which had been training at Mailly le Camp. Together, they got as far as Dreux, apparently, where they unloaded on 18 June, six days after setting out from Poland, and two days after leaving Saarbrücken. Some units of the Division were routed via Nancy from whence they proceeded by road, via Troyes, Sens and Chartres.

The 9th SS Panzer Division left Poland after the 10th SS Panzer Division. Taking a more southerly route, it entered France via Strasbourg. The sixty-five trains of convoy 'Tekla' reached Epinal where most of the troops were forced to detrain because the lines from there would not take the heavy loads. They travelled by road, with great difficulty, via Orléans and Alencon, and rendezvoused with the 10th SS Panzer Division, at an assembly area southwest of Caen, on 28 June. Elements of both Divisions were involved in an attack on the Odon Salient on 29 June.[22]

An analysis showed that of the 141 trains used in France by the 'Viktoria' convoy (76 trains) and the 'Tekla' convoy (65 trains), twenty-one travelled more than 300 miles in France, fifty-one travelled 2–300 miles, the remainder travelled short distances only, to Epinal or Nancy. Seven of the eight trains destined for Malesherbes were halted between Troyes and Monterau. The average late-arrival time for the longer journeys was eight hours, and four hours for the shorter ones.

The worst delay, sixteen hours, was incurred by three trains which attempted to pass too close to the south of Paris. RAF Bomber Command had bombed the Paris rail centres on the night 7/8 June, but many of the delays incurred were the results of daily attacks by the USAAF Eighth Air Force on bridges and other rail facilities in north France between 8 and 15 June. Consequently, the entire rail system had been disrupted by that time. The American attacks on Saarbrücken of 28 June and 13 July came too late to interfere with the movements of the 9th and 10th SS Panzer Divisions.

Two further moves took place at approximately the same time as that of the 2nd SS Panzer Corps. The first was code-named 'Erbdeeren', in which fifty-seven trains transported the 16th Luftwaffe Field Division from Holland. Twenty-one of the trains were diverted, and three went to destinations other than those planned. Five trains were cancelled on 20/21 June (probably because the tracks had been cut at Château-Thiery), and cuts in the line at Saulces on 19 June caused five trains to be diverted via Liert. Long delays of up to ninety hours were recorded. Reims was bombed heavily by the AEAF on 23 June, and Melun was bombed by the USAAF Eighth Air Force on 22 June. The tail end of the Division cleared the Dutch border on 25 June; and was asembling near Mézidon, southeast of Caen, on 30 June. It was just north of that position when it was mauled badly by RAF Bomber Command on 18 July.[23]

The long journey made by the 271st Infantry Division, from Montpellier in the South of France to the Seine/Somme area, took place between 1 and 10 July. The fifty-one train convoy ('Chrysantheme') was subjected to many attacks by both the Maquis and Allied fighter bombers. One train was machine-gunned and set on fire between Cosne and Gien; thirteen trains were diverted via Moulins and Nevers, instead of passing through Dijon; seven trains were diverted (the records are incomplete as to their final detraining points); fourteen trains went to known points other than those planned; and thirteen trains ended up at unknown destinations. Three of the trains were recorded to have reached their correct destinations within a reasonable time. Delays of up to eight days were recorded for some of the trains.

Another cause of delay affected particularly those armoured units which were under the command of Panzer Group West. On 10 June the Group's Battle Headquarters was located in an orchard near the village of La Caine, twelve miles south of Caen. The Group's commander, General von Schweppenburg, was planning the first serious, armoured counterattack against the Allied beachhead. Given the amount of signals traffic, Ultra was able to guide air reconnaissance aircraft to the spot.[24] The Headquarters was bombed by the RAF; the Chief of Staff and seventeen staff officers were killed, all its radio trucks were destroyed, and the Headquarters ceased to exist as such. Command of the Panzer forces was taken over by the 1st SS Panzer Corps, but there was no hope of implementing the plan to 'drive the invaders back into the sea'.

I believe that incident, which came at such a critical time in the race to build up forces, added substantially to the general disruption of German tactical movements, and helped to weight the scales in Montgomery's favour.

Notes

1 *British Intelligence in the Second World War* Vol III, Pt 2, Appx 9.
2 BAMA RH 20–7/377 7th Army Transport Officer's log.
3 Bennett, *Ultra in the West* p58.
4 See Note 2.
5 For an example see *British Intelligence in the Second World War* Vol III, Pt 2, Chaps 43 and 44.
6 Nigel Hamilton, *Master of the Battlefield* Chap 9.
7 Wilmot, *Struggle for Europe* p329.
8 PRO DEFE 3/168 KV 71859.
9 Wilmot, *Struggle for Europe* p335.
10 PRO DEFE 3/170 KV 7591. The tail end of that division was welcomed by Rommel at St Lô on 16 June.
11 *Army Air Forces in World War II* Vol III, p220.
12 *British Intelligence in the Second World War* Vol III, Pt 2, p187. Based on PRO W 171/129.
13 See Bibliography.
14 PRO DEFE 3/169–170.
15 The expression 'Land march' was used frequently in the log of the Transport Officer of the 7th German Army to indicate that the trains could make no further progress.
16 *Army Air Forces in World War II* Vol III, p221.
17 2nd Panzer and 116 Panzer Divisions were on the move also, and there was some doubt as to which formation was seen.
18 Bennett, *Ultra in the West* p80. Other reports suggest that some infantry units from that Division were in action already, near Caumont, on 13 June.
19 Ibid p83.
20 See Chapter 5.
21 William Tierke, *Im Feuersturm Letzer Kriegtahre* (History of the 2nd SS Panzer Korps).
22 *British Intelligence in the Second World War* Vol III, Pt 2, p195.
23 See Chapter 19.
24 PRO DEFE 3/168.

CHAPTER TWENTY-FOUR

Conclusions

During the course of collecting material for and writing this book, I sometimes experienced those feelings that are well-known to those people who have had occasion to sit on a civilian jury, or have been members of a military court martial. On some days, I was convinced that Air Marshal Harris and General Spaatz were both right to resist the placing of their commands under General Eisenhower, and that the war in Europe might have ended sooner (possibly with less casualties, and certainly with less destruction in the countries of Occupied Europe), if they had been allowed, or encouraged, to use their immensely powerful forces solely against Nazi Germany. On other occasions, I discovered facts which made it appear that the Allied armies would have been unable to remain in Normandy if they had not had the support of heavy bombers, both before and after the actual landings.

I have always thought that it is wrong to criticise from a distance, or in retrospect, those decisions that have been taken by responsible and local commanders, and I have a natural tendency to avoid doing so by presenting facts and allowing others to make up their own minds about this or that. Some comment is however admissable, provided that is based on facts and is clearly separated from them. Readers of those facts have some right to expect such comments and conclusions, and I have therefore acceded to those expectations.

Several questions arising from this book should be answered. Did the Transportation Plan work? To what extent did its implementation affect the outcome of the battle in Normandy? Would an alternative plan have had the same results? Could the results of the Transportation Plan have been achieved more economically? Finally, to what extent did the tactical employment of heavy bombers contribute to the defeat of the German Army? When discussing the Transportation Plan, it should be noted that this book is concerned only with that part of the Plan that affected the railways of France and Belgium.

I will start by reviewing the forces involved. RAF Bomber Command was so strong in 1944 that it was able to take on the targets allotted to it, under the Transportation Plan, and maintain a sizeable effort against purely strategic targets in Germany. Most of the Transportation Plan targets were within 'Oboe' range, consequently, the accuracy of the Command's attacks against the rail centres confounded both its critics and its champions. The accuracy was relevant, however, both in terms of the period in which the attacks occurred (at a time when target-marking techniques were at last proving effective), and in the size of the targets which were much smaller than 'area bombing' targets. If ten per cent of those bombs dropped fell within the prescribed target area, that was considered to be acceptable. A great number of the bombs fell on urban areas mainly occupied by 'friendly' civilians. Casualty figures amongst the French and Belgian communities, although not as high as it was once feared they would be, were high enough to do more than raise the odd eyebrow.

The casualty figures for those civilians living close to the rail centres would have been far greater had it not been for the warnings given by the BBC and the good briefings given to the bomber crews. To that extent, Churchill's pledge to President Roosevelt that *all possible care will be taken to minimise this slaughter of friendly civilian life*[1] was honoured by some crews, at least, who brought their bombs home if they could not identify the target.

The losses amongst RAF Bomber Command crews were light to begin with but, when the Germans began to appreciate the significance of the attacks, German fighter strength was increased and more control centres were set up close to the routes taken by the bomber streams. The bad night at Mailly le Camp put an end to an order which decreed that a sortie over France would count as one-third of an operation for the purpose of calculating the thirty trips required to complete an operational tour. In spite of the growing casualty rate, the Transportation Plan did provide crews with some welcome relief from the depressing prospect of long trips to Berlin, which they had to endure during the winter of 1943/44. I am sure that most of the crews appreciated the opportunity of being in on 'the big shows' at the time of the Allied invasion of Normandy.

Because of their commitments to General Spaatz's Oil Plan and to 'Crossbow' targets, the USAAF Eighth Air Force Bomber Command joined the Transportation Plan at a late stage, but had equally good results. In daylight, under heavy fighter escort, it completed its programme of destroying railways in Belgium and in the East and Southeast Regions of the SNCF. Like their RAF counterparts, the crews welcomed the break from the long hauls to central Germany, and their casualty rate, when attacking Transportation Plan targets in France, was very light generally.

Given good weather conditions, Eighth Air Force bombing was more accurate than that carried out by the RAF, but its use of blind bombing aids did not reach the high standards achieved by the RAF, which bombed its Transportation Plan targets at night. Bombing in large formations produced results less accurate than those which could have been achieved by aircraft bombing singly. However, by using the large formation technique, rather than the RAF 'bomber stream', the raids were completed more quickly. They were also less terrifying to the civilian population who, often forewarned, were sometimes able to observe the attacks in comparative safety, from some vantage point well outside the target area. However, as with the RAF attacks, accuracy was relevant, and as the bombing of Troyes described in Chapter 13 shows, even those attacks which were considered to have been very accurate did bring about considerable destruction amongst nearby civilian housing estates.

The strength of the USAAF Eighth Air Force in early 1944 was such that it was also able to cope with a wide variety of targets. The build-up rate of their force of bombers and fighters in East Anglia, and the extent to which their logistical back-up increased, could only be described as phenomenal, and, combined with the prospects of an early end to the war, almost led to a 'throw away' situation in which damaged bombers, that could have been repaired, were scrapped and replaced by new ones.

The earlier attention to German synthetic oil production was a brave move by Spaatz, who was able to co-ordinate the efforts of both the USAAF Eighth and Fifteenth Air Forces. The build-up of a long-range fighter escort was the key factor in the success of those attacks. Earlier attacks on 'Pointblank' targets, deep in the heart of Germany, had emphasised that, in spite of the heavy defensive armament carried by the Fortresses and Liberators, bomber formations were not able to defend themselves adequately in daylight. No matter what form of fighting 'box' was devised, some of the determined enemy fighters would always get through to reduce such formations to groups of stragglers, which then became 'easy meat'. American aircraft were not suited to night operations and the escort fighters were soon regarded as essential. RAF disasters at the beginning of the war, together with the Battle of Britain, should have warned the American Air Generals. (I have found no record of 'Bomber' Harris having said to Eaker 'I told you so', but I bet he thought it.)

The demise of the Luftwaffe, which was the purpose of 'Point Blank', was, very much, a cumulative and progressive business. Some authors have suggested that the Luftwaffe fighter arm was broken during 'Big Week' in February 1944, but there were plenty of examples of a very strong come-back after that time — Nuremberg and Mailly being two of them. German fighter production kept going well into the last quarter of 1944, and more fighters were produced between March and September 1944 than in any other six-month period. It was the 'knock on' effects of shortages of aviation fuel which led to curtailment of pilot training, which in turn led to such a devastating loss of pilots and aircraft that, in the end, there were no pilots to fly newly built machines, which were grounded through lack of fuel anyway.

It is my belief that the most important achievement made by 'Point Blank' and the entire Combined Bomber Offensive, was not so much the knocking out, by one means or another, of the Luftwaffe fighter arm, but rather the fact that the Germans were forced onto the defensive and consequently had little or no offensive capability. Some bombers will always get through a defensive screen and, had the Germans had half or even a quarter of the number of bombers that were available to the Allied Air Force Commanders, things could have been very different during 'Neptune' and on the overcrowded Allied beach-head. The same argument applied to the Luftwaffe Flak Arm, where many of the excellent dual-purpose 88 mm guns were kept back for the defence of the Reich, instead of being sent to the Front where they would have been better employed knocking out Allied tanks.

The main problem the German Army had was a lack of intelligence concerning Allied intentions and preparations for 'Overlord'. Not only was the Luftwaffe unable to mount any worthwhile offensive operations, it also failed to provide regular and penetrating photo-graphic reconnaissance. Such photography would have revealed the extent and progress of the build-up of the Allied armies in south Britain, and would have cast serious doubts about the existence of the dreaded 'FUSAG'. Troops and supplies could have been better positioned prior to the Allied attack, and reserve forces might have been released to take part in the battle at a time when the Allies were least able to deal with them.

The Germans did not have the advantage of extensive agent networks such as the British had in Occupied Europe, or the priceless 'Ultra'; and there remained the possibility that the head of 'Foreign Armies West' was acting under the misguided belief that he might save lives by providing false intelligence, consequently misleading the German Army to such an extent that it would loose the battle more quickly.

I have investigated the delays imposed upon the tactical moves of the German Army by the destruction of the French railway systems, and have narrated the other difficulties they experienced, consequent upon being forced onto the roads. That the German Army, notwith-standing its difficulties and shortages, was able to prevent the Allied armies from attaining many of their initial objectives within the times specified in Montgomery's original plan, remained a tribute to the efficiency of its organisation and the fighting qualities of its soldiers. By contrast, many of the advantages enjoyed by the British and American armies appeared not to have been exploited fully in the early stages of the campaign, and some of the criticism levelled at them by Air Force commanders at the time, seems to have been justified.

The great contribution made to the Transportation Plan by the AEAF should be noted also. Both the RAF 2nd Tactical Air Force and the American USAAF Ninth Air Force were quick to respond, were more accurate in their attacks than the heavy bombers, and were often able to operate below cloud which prevented operations by the four-engined aircraft of both RAF Bomber Command and the USAAF Eighth Air Force. The part played by the medium bombers in closing, and keeping closed, the Seine and Loire bridges, became almost legendary, and the fighter bombers (known to the Germans as the 'jabos') which pounced on any German movement by rail or road, ensured the fulfilment of the secondary aim of the Transportation Plan, which was to drive the Germans onto the roads where they would use up petrol before being destroyed.

In Chapter 6, I gave a detailed account of the arguments that raged prior to the acceptance of Zuckerman's Transportation Plan. Both commanders of the strategic air forces, Harris and Spaatz, believed that the war could be won without a land battle. That view was, to some extent, supported by Albert Speer, the formidable German Minister for Armament Production, but was not echoed by other military leaders on both sides of the English Channel.[2] The subject remained a point of speculation for many established and would-be military historians. The insoluble question was, what would have happened if Harris and Spaatz had had their way and Germany *had* collapsed under the weight of strategic bombing alone; would the Russians have taken advantage of the situation and built the East/West wall along, say, the Dutch border, or even created a new Atlantic Wall?

More easily answered was the question of whether or not Eisenhower's decision to back the strategic phase of the Transportation Plan was justified. Should he have supported his countryman's counter-suggestion to go for Hitler's oil? In the event, the weather was so unpredictable at the time of 'Neptune' that it would not have been possible to carry out the alternative interdiction programme put forward by those opposed to Zuckerman's plan, and the latter's insistence that the problem was strategic, rather than tactical, must have been later recognised by all those concerned as having been the correct approach. Spaatz's oil plan must also be acknowledged as having played a major part in the lack of mobility of both the Luftwaffe and the German Army in Normandy. The pre-invasion bombing of the rail centres, particular by RAF Bomber Command, the subsequent attacks on bridges by the AEAF medium bombers, and the fuel shortages imposed on the German Army by a combination of these attacks and the bombing of the refineries, must be seen as having been entirely complementary. The pity was that no one could take the credit for having planned it that way, and a lot of time and effort was wasted in trying to prove that one approach to the problem stood a better chance of success than others.

Turning to the results of the attacks in support of 'Overlord', I believe that it is important to distinguish between the results and the effects which these had on the actual battle in Normandy. In Part 2 of this book I examined the results of the attacks on Transportation Plan and oil targets, and statistical and scientific analysis leaves no doubt that both the Transportation and Oil Plans achieved their aims, namely a marked reduction in the rail traffic of Belgium and France, and a substantial fall in the stocks of fuel available to the German armed forces.

The part played by the French Resistance in the disruption of the SNCF was important, but not vital. I think it true to say that the strength of the Resistance Movement lay more in its ability to cut communications and power lines more precisely than could be achieved by bombing. The cutting of wires controlling signalling systems and telephone links between rail centres, and the denial of power to electric locomotives in the SNCF's Southeast Region, was both economical in effort and highly effective. Cutting railway lines using explosives, although a nuisance, did not result in serious delays. The statement made in Foot's official history of the Resistance in France, that the Saumur rail tunnel could have been blocked just as well by a young WAAF officer with a few pounds of explosive, is misleading.

Such acts of sabotage against the railways, coupled with armed attacks by the Maquis on road convoys, created a problem for the German Army which is now fully appreciated by British and American armies. Tying down large numbers of regular troops using small bands of terrorists is a feature of guerrilla warfare. The Germans were not only delayed by such tactics but were also forced to divert a considerable number of troops to protect their lines of communications. Another important side-effect of cutting communications was the fact that the German Army and the Luftwaffe both had to resort to using radios. The airwaves were filled with many useful bits of information which 'Ultra' nets scooped up eagerly. So quickly were these messages deciphered that some became of tactical rather than strategic importance, and led to the bombing of convoys or temporary fuel dumps.

The arguments put forward by some of the anti-Transportation Plan lobby, that the French rail network was so extensive that alternative routes would always be found, did not appear to be so convincing when the axle loading factor was introduced. Tanks and guns are heavy things, and those people who are familiar with those little yellow discs on British service vehicles will know that some vehicles can not travel on all types of roads or over all bridges. The same applies to the loading of railway 'flats' which are normally used to transport tanks and guns to a point near enough to the battlefield for them to make their own way by road or across country. Many of the minor rail lines and roads in France were simply not capable of accepting heavily loaded wagons.

Another major point of contention was the availability of locomotives and rolling stock. In spite of the bombing, there was no real
shortage of wagons, but their destruction in marshalling yards did
become an important factor, because heavy cranes were needed to
clear away the debris before lines could be repaired. Even when the
cranes were available, the clearing up process added to the time
taken to restore the place to working order. The unavailability of
locomotives was, perhaps, the most important factor in the breakdown of the railway systems. Those people who had argued that there
were so many locomotives available that there would not be enough
time to reduce the number to a level which would create a problem,
were wrong. The reduction in the number of locomotives available in
Belgium and northern France began with the first attack on Trappes
in March, and the steady and progressive destruction of locomotive
servicing and repair facilities further reduced their number. In that
respect, RAF Bomber Command must take the lion's share of the
credit. The AEAF and USAAF Eighth Air Force Fighter Commands
made a significant contribution towards the number of locomotives
damaged whilst they were in motion, but damage by machine-gun or
rocket fire was often repairable, or would have been if the repair
sheds had been working at anything like their normal capacities.
Attacks by medium bombers on locomotive sheds and workshops,
although perhaps more accurate, did not bring the same lasting
damage as attacks made by the heavy bombers; the former could only
carry light bombs, which damaged the buildings, but did not always
destroy the machine tools contained in them.

In spite of all that was written and said at that time, I believe that
the American attacks on the synthetic oil plants, which began early in
May, did have an almost immediate effect on the ability of the
German Army to react, as it would have wished, to the Allied
landings in Normandy in June. In concluding its report on the effects
of the strategic air war against Germany,[3] the British Bombing
Survey Unit claimed that 'oil stocks in France were sufficient, by
German standards, to counter the invasion', but there was plenty of
evidence to prove that that was not the case. It is true that many of
the cries for help by German commanders about shortages of fuel
were in fact the result of transportation difficulties, but there were
other occasions when 'Ultra' provided evidence, quite early in the
campaign, that stocks had run out, or had been destroyed by
bombing. Authors are united in their descriptions of the problems
caused by the shortage of aviation fuels, but I prefer to emphasise the
fact that the *indirect* effects of the attacks on oil mattered most in the
early stages of the land battle. Diverting from Normandy much-
needed fighter cover, guns and ammunition for the defence of the oil
plants increased the suffering of the German Army, which was
undergoing constant and devastating attacks by Allied aircraft of all
types.

Conclusions concerning the use of heavy bombers against the V-weapon sites in north France are varied. It is difficult to determine the extent to which the pre-D-Day attacks on the original V-1 sites delayed the start of the V-1's operations. The fact that the modified 'Ski' sites were almost certainly introduced as a result of the earlier bombing, suggested that the programme was delayed by several months. However, many of the new sites were in existence in April, nearly two months before the first launchings in June; therefore the delay could have been caused by production or other technical problems, and not by Allied bombing. It seems likely that the early bombing attacks delayed the start by two or three months, which meant that the ships gathering for 'Neptune' were spared from what could have been disruptive, and even dangerous, attacks by V-1s during the latter part of May.

When V-1 operations began, on 13 June 1944, the so-called 'Buzz Bombs' were directed mostly against London, and although casualties were not excessive, they did result in urgent calls to use heavy bombers against the launch sites in the Pas de Calais. That diversion from tactical targets in direct support of the Allied armies came at a most inconvenient time, and it was fortunate that the RAF and the USAAF both had the capacity to deal with the ever increasing and wide variety of calls for their assistance.

The use of heavy bombers during 'Neptune' proved to be somewhat disappointing, and emphasised the difficulties created by the weather, which was far from ideal for precision bombing and the accurate release of airborne troops. Electronic countermeasures and the main 'spoof' raids were all carried out with precision and great skill, and the fact that those operations provoked only a limited reaction from the Germans, at that time, was more a result of their intransigent belief that the weather and tides were unsuitable for the landings. The fact that 7th Army Generals were attending 'war games' in Rennes, and that Rommel was absent from the scene during the night of the invasion, both support that conclusion.

The bombing of coastal defence batteries, although accurate enough in most cases, did not silence all the guns for any length of time. This was not entirely the fault of the bombers. In some cases, the fault lay with a lack of up-to-date intelligence (for example, some of the guns had been moved just prior to D-Day and replaced with dummies). In other cases, it was simply a matter of being unable to destroy those guns which were heavily encased in concrete; gun crews were deafened and reduced to mindless zombies, but the guns still worked and, when the crews recovered, they were directed onto the beaches.

Confirmation of the wisdom of the plan to bomb the railways well before D-Day was never more evident than during the first few days after the landings. The attacks on so-called 'choke points' by the heavy bombers of the USAAF Eighth Air Force had to be cancelled because of cloud cover. Some of those proposed attacks were carried out by RAF Bomber Command, using 'Oboe'; others were replaced with attacks by medium bombers operating below the persistent cloud. That was precisely the situation envisaged by Zuckerman and his followers, and it was just as well that their arguments won the day.

The tactical use of heavy bombers during Operation Goodwood was remarkably successful, and left the Germans dazed and disorganised. Nevertheless, the Operation came to an early and abortive halt, and became the subject of much acrimonious discussion between Allied air and army commanders.

The American heavy bombers, which were called upon to support Operation Cobra, were unfortunate in not having had the experience of 'Master Bomber' techniques, which the RAF had perfected during its night raids and had used during the 'Goodwood' bombing. The serious misplacement of bombs by the USAAF Eighth Air Force caused quite severe casualties among American troops, and made American Army commanders cautious about asking for support from high-flying aircraft. The obvious defects of the 'Cobra' bombing were made the subject of a special study, and efforts were intensified to find ways of overcoming problems, such as the enemy moving into exclusion zones as soon as the American Army pulled back in preparation for an air strike ahead of their positions. Eisenhower had some difficulty in convincing his divisional commanders that 'Cobra' had been won because of the support given by the heavy bombers! However, there were plenty of statements made by German generals which supported that conclusion.

'Ultra' decrypts in the early part of 1944 and the post-war interrogations of German generals and the Armaments Minister, Albert Speer, all provided ample evidence of the success of both the Transportation and Oil Plans, and of the value of the heavy bombers in the close support role.

In a message of May 1944, Hitler's Chief of the OKW, Keitel, complained that the OKW's requirements for the repair of damaged railways was not being met, and instructed military commanders in Belgium and France to ensure that all the necessary work was carried out. In an appreciation, dated 8 May, Von Runstedt reported that while air attacks on bridges were having no lasting effects, the systematic destruction of the railways had disrupted the supply system and troop movements. However, at his post-war interrogation he changed his mind and said that the strategic bombing of the French railways had had little or no effect until July. At the same time, the Transportation Officer of OB West was reported to have agreed with his former chief and said that the interdiction programme (on bridges) had had more effect on movement than the strategic bombing. Other senior German officers, however, claimed that strategic bombing of rail centres had been decisive in stopping rail traffic.[4]

Questioned about the effects on the battle of Normandy of bombing the French railways, Albert Speer replied:

As far as I know they were decisive, tanks for example had to be off-loaded at Reims and moved by road to Normandy. This resulted in a considerable loss of MT and substantial wastage before ever the tanks got into action, quite apart from the great expenditure of fuel.[5]

Air Marshal Sir John Slessor, in his book *The Central Blue*, having had some doubts about Zuckerman's plan, altered his opinion, and concluded:

The enormous importance of the intensive air bombardment of the enemy's rail communications in Northern France before the invasion is now a matter of history.

Churchill summed up the effects of the Transportation Plan:

With the approach of D-Day a rapidly spreading paralysis was creeping over the railway network of the Region Nord . . . the movement of German troops and material had thus become a matter of great difficulty and hazard well before any landings had been made.

Albert Speer's interrogation provided, perhaps, the most balanced views on the effects of the attacks on German oil production. Five important points emerged:

1 The shortage of aviation fuel became unsupportable from September 1944.
2 Stocks of Romanian natural oil in Germany enabled the manufacture of petrol and diesel fuel to be continued into the early part of 1945.
3 Some reduction in production was brought about by a shortage of tank wagons because there was inadequate storage capacity at the refineries (caused by bombing).
4 RAF night attacks were of longer duration and were more effective.
5 Repair times increased progressively as the attacks continued.

As with the effects of the Transportation Plan there were many 'Ultra'-deciphered messages and plenty of reports from German generals which spoke of aircraft grounded and of tanks being used as immobile pill boxes or being abandoned completely because of fuel shortages.

The effects of attacks by heavy bombers on troop concentrations were the subject of many reports and complaints by German generals. Field Marshal Gunther von Kluge, who had just replaced Runstedt, wrote to Hitler on 21 July, three days after the 'Goodwood' bombing:

> *Whole armoured formations, allotted to the counter attack, were caught in a bomb carpet of the greatest intensity so that they could be extricated from the torn up ground only by prolonged effort and in some cases only by dragging them out. The result was that they arrived too late . . . The psychological effect of such a mass of bombs coming down, with all the power of elemental nature on fighting forces, especially the infantry, is a factor which has to be taken into very serious consideration. It is immaterial whether such a carpet catches good troops or bad, they are more or less annihilated and, above all, their equipment is shattered.*

Harris estimated, on one occasion, that, at any given moment, 1000 of his heavy bombers could put down a barrage which was equivalent in weight to the shells from 4000 guns. Seen in that light, and looking at aerial photographs of the areas subjected to that type of bombing, it was not difficult to understand Kluge's remarks, or doubt that his account of events at Caen was anything but entirely accurate.

Montgomery, in a message of congratulation to Harris after Bomber Command had broken up a concentration of German armour near Caen on 7 July, wrote:

> *Again the Allied armies in France would like to thank you for your magnificent cooperation last night. We know that your main work lies further afield, and we applaud your continuous and sustained bombing of German war industries, and the effects that this has had on the German war effort, but we also know that you are always ready to bring your mighty effort closer and cooperate in our tactical battle.*

From all those accolades three main conclusions can be drawn:

1 The Transportation Plan was successful in that it did produce the required "railway desert" in north France, drove the Germans onto the roads, and delayed supplies. The major factor in its success was the pre-invasion bombing of the rail centres.

2 Contrary to some expert opinion, there was not enough fuel in German dumps in Normandy, and fuel shortages did affect the German Army almost from the start of the campaign. Those shortages were aggravated by three things: the extra use of motor transport, the loss of fuel in dumps attacked by Allied aircraft, and the difficulty in transferring stocks from one part of the battlefield to another. Thus the Transportation and Oil Plans complemented each other.

3 The use of heavy bombers in the tactical role was not easy, and could be contemplated only if target-marking methods were foolproof and there was some form of direct control of the attack, such as that used by the RAF in their ground-marking and Master Bomber techniques.

In spite of all this, and not withstanding the fact that some units were delayed by indecision on the part of the German High Command, it has to be acknowledged that some German troop trains did get through, and reserve units did arrive, sometimes battered and weakened by Allied air attacks, but in time to contain the Allied bridgehead for an uncomfortably long period. That awkward fact suggested that there may have been other and deeper reasons why the German Army was pushed back finally from its positions surrounding the British and American Armies.

Nearly all of the accounts of that period have cited Allied air superiority as the main reason for the defeat of the German Army, in Normandy and elsewhere in northwest Europe, in 1944/45. I agree with that conclusion; however, I believe that there is a subtle difference between Allied air supremacy and the German lack of any offensive capability in the air. The former explains the difficulties of movement and shortages of fuel experienced by the German Army in Normandy, the latter explains why the Germans were unable to prevent the arrival of a succession of Allied troops and equipment, which in the end, just had to burst out of the limited and overcrowded area. In the first few weeks the only disruption of the flow of men and supplies to the Allied beaches was caused by the obstruction and demolitions in Cherbourg Harbour and a few mines laid in the English Channel. The storm of 19-22 June was the only really serious setback in the Allied programme.[6]

In a final analysis of the subject, it is my belief that the Allied bombers *did* play a major role in imposing the required delays upon German reinforcements and supplies approaching Normandy. They provided a significant level of direct tactical support for the Allied armies also. I hope that those facts will be appreciated more readily by all those people who study that phase of the war.

It is my belief also that the root cause of the German defeat in Normandy lay, not so much on the ability of the Allied Air Forces to roam, almost unmolested, over the battlefield, but on the inability of the Luftwaffe to mount any, other than a token number of, offensive sorties against the Allied beaches and lines of supply.

The collapse of the Luftwaffe began with the Combined Bomber Offensive and 'Point Blank' in 1943. It was then that the Germans decided to concentrate on the production of fighters for the defence of the Reich, and stopped producing the bombers and ground attack aircraft which might have reduced the value of the superior resources available to the Allies. Therefore, there was a direct link between 'Point Blank' and the Transportation and Oil Plans. That link was the mutual aim of defeating the German Army. All the arguments concerning the best use of the heavy bombers were unnecessary; they were required for all three plans; their versatility enabled them to cope with those plans and a lot more.

The question of whether or not earlier attacks on the German oil industry and on the transport systems, by both the British and American heavy bombers, would have brought an earlier end to the War has to remain unanswered for the time being, but I personally doubt that strategic bombing alone would have won the War.

The cost in airmen's lives during the period we have been discussing was heavy enough; between 1 April and 5 June the Allied Air Forces lost over 12,000 men and 2000 aircraft, of which approximately 4000 men and 700 aircraft belonged to the RAF. About 83 per cent of the RAF Bomber Command effort had been in support of 'Overlord' in one way or another, nearly 40 per cent being spent on the Transportation Plan. From D-Day to 28 June the Allied armies lost approximately 8000 killed. How many more would have died? As a one-time Lance Corporal who completed his infantry training on the day the war ended in Europe, I have every reason to reflect on the possible outcome if the heavy bombers had not helped to end the war in Europe at that time.

Notes

1 Churchill, *The Second World War* Vol V, p410.
2 *Army Air Forces in World War II* Vol III, p786.
3 Zuckerman, *From Apes to Warlords* Appx 6.
4 *Army Air Forces in World War II* Vol III, p160.
5 Webster and Frankland, *Strategic Air Offensive against Germany* Appx 37. Interrogation of Albert Speer.
6 The SHAEF records show that more than 1,500,000 men, 332,000 vehicles and 1,500,000 tons of stores were landed between D-Day and 29 July.

CHAPTER TWENTY-FIVE

Epilogue

I began by telling my readers how I became involved in the subject of this book. I was not a member of the Royal Air Force; instead, I chose to serve in the infantry. I was then transferred to an armoured regiment and, finally, to the Intelligence Corps. Two of my elder brothers had been aircrew members of RAF Bomber Command (a third brother was fighting his way to France via Italy).

A major part of my post-war service was spent as a photographic interpreter, living sometimes in a joint service environment, but mostly in RAF establishments, where I shared offices or 'syndicate' rooms with RAF officers, many of whom had been aircrew in Bomber Command at the time of the Allied invasion of Normandy. The wild parties, in which I often became involved, reflected the relief that my friends in blue felt at having survived the war. I was young then and, unashamedly, joined in as if I too had survived those 'chop nights' which they were trying to forget. The truth was that I had survived because of their help in breaking up one of the most evil regimes of modern times.

I have made some play in this book about the number of casualties amongst French and Belgian civilians. That was done deliberately because, in the same way that I have tried to redress the balance of credit owed to bomber crews for their part in 'Overlord', it became apparent during my research that there was an equal need to draw attention to the suffering which those civilians endured in the name of Liberation.

When I first visited Voué, in search of my brother's grave, in 1986, I received nothing but praise and admiration for the RAF. Voué was close to Troyes and Mailly le Camp, and it was Louis Clement, an ex-Mayor of Voué, who actually witnessed the last moments of my brother's aircraft. The reception I received in 1986 was extraordinary; it was almost as if the villagers had been waiting for years for someone to whom they could pour our their praise for the RAF, and in particular for those crews that had 'smashed the Bosch at Mailly'.

The subsequent memorial service in 1987, which I mentioned in my prologue, was no small affair. Louis Clement and his council voted to invite representatives from the French Air Force and Army, the Commandant of the French barracks at Mailly, past members of the local French Resistance (some of whom had helped aircrew evade capture), and many other local dignitaries.

I became an Associate Member of both the Bomber Command and

No 101 Squadron Associations, and through their help I was able to bring together a sizeable party of ex-aircrew who had been on the Mailly raid. By kind permission of the AOC of No 1 Group RAF, and Wing Commanders Jim Uprichard and Peter Day (the commanders of No 101 and No 617 Squadrons at that time) and the British Air Attaché in Paris, aircraft from Nos 101 and 617 Squadrons flew over the church at Voué during the ceremony and continued north towards Mailly.

In all approximately 300 people sat down to 'lunch', which ended around midnight, but it was some time after that when No 101 Squadron members finally retrieved their hats — from the local fire brigade! The warmth of the hospitality and display of friendship towards the group of ex-aircrew, which included Group Captain Cheshire (who was the chief marker at Mailly), was something which none of those present will ever forget.

Was such a feeling of friendliness towards the RAF general throughout all those areas of France attacked by the British and American bombers? To find the answer I set out in June 1989 to visit some of the rail centres which had been hit so badly in the early part of 1944.

I entered France via Boulogne, and it was there that I discovered that the attacks on the railways and the E-boat pens had caused so much destruction that the French have taken advantage of the demolition of the wartime facilities by relocating the main passenger and goods stations and even realigning the river.

From Boulogne I went towards Lille, staying overnight at La Motte au Bois, where the remains of a V-1 launching site are situated. Lille was a little disappointing and, although I found the marshalling yards at La Delivrance, the weather was misty, and the whole complex was so vast that I was unable to get any useful photographs or find any survivors of the wartime attack within the limited time available to me.

Tergnier and Aulnoye were both rewarding in that I was able to identify the Aim Points marked on wartime target prints, and there were several buildings which still bore the scars of the bombing. At Tergnier, I walked around the housing estate which has replaced that which had been badly damaged during the attacks in April 1944. There, I met Monsieur Moeglin and Madame Dehegne who, as teenagers, had been evacuated from the area following warnings broadcast over the BBC. Both recounted how they had survived but had returned to find their homes destroyed. They bore no ill feeling, and in answer to my standard question about the attitude of the French people to the bombing they gave what was to become an equally standard reply: 'It was necessary for our liberation'. The locomotive workshops at Tergnier appeared to have been repaired and the arched roof looked just the same as it did in wartime photographs. A concrete air-raid shelter, used by the German controllers during the attacks still exists.

At Troyes, where I stayed again with my friend Louis Clement, I met Jacques Collard. He had been a railway controller at Troyes during the American attacks in May 1944. He and Madame Collard described how they had watched the first attack from high ground, north of the city. Monsieur Collard had not been as lucky during the second attack. Caught in the yards, he had been forced to take cover under the abutments of a concrete bridge; fortunately, it was not hit. He showed me a handsome scrapbook containing many photographs and cuttings taken at the time of the bombings. In answer to my usual question he replied, somewhat phlegmatically, 'The dead are not able to give their views'.

During my visit to Troyes, I met Jim Carpenter (in 1989, he was the Chairman of the RAF Air Gunners' Association) and his friend John Ackroyd, whose exploits I have described in this book. Both were in the company of Monsieur Bernard, the local archivist, who had done much to foster good relations between ex-aircrew members and the local inhabitants. The two ex-aircrew were there to receive a parachute harness which had belonged to Sgt Burton, one of the air gunners in John Ackroyd's crew, who had been killed whilst baling out of his stricken Halifax. The harness was placed in the Elvington museum.

At Trappes, I met Madame Renée Guillerm, who had lived near the railway centre at the time of the first raid. She told me of the many casualties that had occurred when a church was hit. Apparently many people had taken cover in the building, believing that it was strong enough to withstand the bombing. Madame Guillerm told me also of attempts by the Germans to capitalise on the fact that the Allies had caused so much suffering amongst the civilian population, and that the ordinary German soldiers had been particularly nice to them at that time, handing out sweets and the like. Some of those 'hearts and minds' campaigns could have been successful in the Paris area, where I found the least sympathy with and understanding of the air attacks.

At both Le Mans and Tours, the rail centres were recognized to be much the same as at the time of the bombing, but both were very quiet. I suspect that, as it is in many other parts of Europe, road transport is gaining the upper hand. (I wish that someone like Lord Zuckerman would come up with a Transportation Plan in reverse and drive everyone back onto the railways.)

On the way back to Britain, I visited some of the many churchyards that contain the graves of those airmen killed during the pre-invasion bombing in north France. At Poix, south of Amiens, I counted 149 graves of airmen from Britain, Canada, New Zealand and Australia; many of the men had been killed during the raids on Tergnier. All the graves in all the churchyards I visited were tended by French civilians working for the Commonwealth War Graves Commission; all the graves were immaculate.

Was it worth it? As well as those graves that I visited, there are so many more in larger cemeteries, and there are long lists of men who have no known grave. What of the French and Belgian civilians? How many of them died? Where are they buried? What was the cost of rebuilding 9000 homes in Caen? The first question is surely answered by the final outcome of the war. Hitler and his gang were eliminated; considering the atrocities and killings that occurred during their period of fanatical power, that was just as well. The sacrifices made by the Allies in the Second World War were far more justified than any sacrifice made before or since.

Appendix One
RAF Bomber Command Orders of Battle
March and June 1944
9 March 1944
(Based on PRO 41/56)

Squadron	Location	No aircraft established	Aircraft type	On unit charge	Remarks
No 1 Group	**HQ Bawtry**				
12	Wickenby	20	Lancaster I & III	21	
100	Grimsby	20	Lancaster I & III	21	
101	Ludford Magna	30	Lancaster I & III	32	ABC-equipped
103	Elsham Wolds	20	Lancaster I & III	21	
166	Kirmington	30	Lancaster I & III	31	
460 RAAF	Binbrook	30	Lancaster I & III	27	
550	N. Killingholme	20	Lancaster I & III	20	
576	Elsham Wolds	20	Lancaster I & III	21	
625	Kelstern	20	Lancaster I & III	20	
626	Wickenby	20	Lancaster I & III	22	
Not operational					
300 Polish	Faldingworth	9	Lancaster I & III	11	To re-equip 16 Wellingtons
		9	Wellington X	10	& 4 Lancasters
No 3 Group	**HQ Exning**				
15	Mildenhall	20	Lancaster I & III	21	
75 (NZ)	Mepal	30	Stirling	29	

Squadron	Location	No aircraft established	Aircraft type	On unit charge	Remarks
No 3 Group	**HQ Exning**				
90	Tuddenham	30	Stirling	28	
115	Witchford	30	Lancaster II	27	
138 (spec)	Tempsford	18	Halifax V	13	
149	Lakenheath	20	Stirling	19	
161 (spec)	Tempsford	13	Lysander	6	
		6	Halifax V	7	
		6	Hudson III/IIIA	5	Two Mk Is
199	Lakenheath	20	Stirling	19	
514	Waterbeach	30	Lancaster II	28	
622	Mildenhall	20	Lancaster I & III	21	
Not operational					
218	Woolfox Lodge	20	Stirling	18	
No 4 Group	**HQ York**				
10	Melbourne	30	Halifax II	25	
51	Snaith	30	Halifax III	31	
			Halifax II	1	2 flights operational
76	Holme on Spalding	30	Halifax III	30	
			Halifax V	1	
77	Elvington	30	Halifax V	20	2 flights operational
			Halifax II	6	
78	Breighton	30	Halifax III	30	
158	Lissett	20	Halifax III	25	
			Halifax II	1	
466 (RAAF)	Leconfield	20	Halifax III	19	
			Halifax II	3	
578	Burn	20	Halifax III	20	
640	Leconfield	20	Halifax III	20	

Squadron	Location	No aircraft established	Aircraft type	On unit charge	Remarks
No 5 Group	**HQ Swinderby**				
9	Bardney	20	Lancaster I & III	21	
44	Dunholme Lodge	20	Lancaster I & III	20	
49	Fiskerton	20	Lancaster I & III	22	
50	Skellingthorpe	20	Lancaster I & III	20	
57	East Kirkby	20	Lancaster I & III	21	
61	Coningsby	20	Lancaster I & III	22	
106	Metheringham	20	Lancaster I & III	21	
207	Spilsby	20	Lancaster I & II	21	
463 (RAAF)	Waddington	20	Lancaster I & III	21	
467 (RAAF)	Waddington	20	Lancaster I & III	18	
617	Woodhall Spa	20	Lancaster I & III	32	
619	Coningsby	20	Lancaster I & III	22	
630	East Kirkby	20	Lancaster I & III	21	
No 6 (Cdn) Group	**HQ Allerton**				
408	Linton on Ouse	20	Lancaster II	20	
419	Middleton St George	20	Lancaster X	1	Operational on Halifax II
			Halifax II	13	
420	Tholthorpe	20	Halifax III	20	
424	Skipton on Swale	20	Halifax III	20	
425	Tholthorpe	20	Halifax III	22	
426	Linton on Ouse	20	Lancaster II	20	
427	Leeming	20	Halifax III	20	
428	Middleton St George	20	Halifax II	17	
429	Leeming	20	Halifax III	32	
431	Croft	20	Halifax V	1	
			Halifax V	20	
432	East Moor	20	Halifax III	19	
433	Skipton on Swale	20	Lancaster II	1	
			Halifax III	20	
434	Croft	20	Halifax V	21	

Squadron	Location	No aircraft established	Aircraft type	On unit charge	Remarks
No 8 (PFF) Group	**HQ Huntingdon**				
7	Oakington	30	Lancaster I & II	28	
			Lancaster VI	1	
35	Graveley	30	Lancaster I & III	20	
			Halifax III	24	
			Halifax II	7	
83	Wyton	20	Lancaster I & III	22	
97	Bourne	30	Lancaster I & III	30	
105	Marham	18	Mosquito IX/XVI	22	'Oboe'-equipped
			Mosquito IV	1	
109	Marham	30	Mosquito IX/XVI	24	'Oboe'-equipped
			Mosquito IV	8	
139	Upwood	18	Mosquito IV/XX	12	
			Mosquito IX/XVI	6	
156	Upwood	30	Lancaster I & III	29	
405 (Cdn)	Gransden Lodge	20	Lancaster I & III	20	
627	Oakington	18	Mosquito IV	10	
692	Graveley	18	Mosquito IV/XX	9	Forming, half operational
No 100 (SP) Group	**HQ West Raynham**				
192	Foulsham	7	Wellington X	7	
		3	Mosquito IV	3	
		10	Halifax III & V	10	ECM
		1	Anson	1	
515	Little Snoring	18	Beaufighter I/II	10	
Not operational					
141	West Raynham	18	Mosquito II	13	
169	Little Snoring	18	Mosquito II	17	
			Beaufighter	4	
214	Sculthorpe	14	Fortress	21	ABC-equipped
239	West Raynham	18	Mosquito II & V	18	

1 June 1944

Squadron	Location	No aircraft established	Aircraft type	On unit charge	Remarks
No 1 Group	**HQ Bawtry**				
12	Wickenby	20	Lancaster I & III	21	
100	Grimsby	20	Lancaster I & III	20	
101	Ludford Magna	30	Lancaster I & III	27	ABC-equipped
103	Elsham Wolds	20	Lancaster I & III	20	
166	Kirmington	30	Lancaster I & III	29	
300 (Polish)	Faldingworth	20	Lancaster I & III	19	One flight operational
460 RAAF	Binbrook	30	Lancaster I & III	32	
550	N. Killingholme	20	Lancaster I & III	20	
576	Elsham Wolds	20	Lancaster I & III	20	
625	Kelstern	20	Lancaster I & III	18	
626	Wickenby	20	Lancaster I & III	22	
No 3 Group	**HQ Exning**				
15	Mildenhall	20	Lancaster I & III	16	
75	Mepal	30	Lancaster I & III	26	
90	Tuddenham	30	Lancaster I & III	11	Operational two flights
			Stirling	22	Stirling
115	Witchford	30	Lancaster I & III	28	
138 (SD)	Tempsford	18	Stirling IV (SD)	17	
			Halifax V	21	Operational on Halifax
149	Methwold	20	Stirling	11	
161 (SD)	Tempsford	13	Lysander	7	
		6	Halifax V	7	
		6	Hudson III/IIIA		
514	Waterbeach	30	Lancaster II	24	Inc. two Mk Is
622	Mildenhall	20	Lancaster I & III	20	

Squadron	Location	No aircraft established	Aircraft type	On unit charge	Remarks
Not operational					
218	Woolfox Lodge	20	Stirling	19	
No 4 Group	**HQ York**				
10	Melbourne	30	Halifax III	31	
51	Snaith	30	Halifax III	29	
76	Holme on Spalding Moor	30	Halifax III	31	
77	Full Sutton	30	Halifax III	21	Operational 1 flight
			Halifax II/V	3	1 flight Elvington non-operational
78	Breighton	30	Halifax III	29	
102	Pocklington	30	Halifax III	32	
158	Lissett	30	Halifax III	31	
346 (FF)	Elvington	20	Halifax V	23	To re-equip Halifax III 10/6
			Halifax II	1	
466 (RAAF)	Leconfield	20	Halifax III	19	
578	Bourn	30	Halifax III	31	To Driffield 4/6
640	Leconfield	20	Halifax III	20	
No 5 Group	**HQ Swinderby**				
9	Bardney	20	Lancaster I & III	19	
44 (Rhod)	Dunholme Lodge	20	Lancaster I & III	20	
49	Fiskerton	20	Lancaster I & III	22	
50	Skellingthorpe	20	Lancaster I & III	19	
57	East Kirkby	20	Lancaster I & III	20	
61	Skellingthorpe	20	Lancaster I & III	18	
83 (PFF)	Coningsby	20	Lancaster I & III	20	On loan form 8 Grp

Squadron	Base		Aircraft		Notes
No 5 Group	**HQ Swinderby**				
97 (PFF)	Coningsby	20	Lancaster I & III	20	On loan from 8 Grp
106	Metheringham	20	Lancaster I & III	18	
207	Spilsby	20	Lancaster I & III	20	
463 (RAAF)	Waddington	20	Lancaster I & III	21	
467 (RAAF)	Waddington	20	Lancaster I & III	20	
617	Woodhall Spa	20	Lancaster I & III	34	Special tasks
			Mosquito VI	1	
619	Dunholme Lodge	20	Lancaster I & III	20	
627 (PFF)	Woodhall Spa	18	Mosquito IV	22	On loan from 8 Grp
630	East Kirkby	20	Lancaster I & III	20	
No 6 (Cdn) Group	**HQ Allerton**				
408	Linton on Ouse	20	Lancaster II	29	
419	Middleton St George	20	Lancaster X	20	
420	Tholthorpe	20	Halifax III	20	
424	Skipton on Swale	20	Halifax III	20	
425	Tholthorpe	20	Halifax III	19	
426	Linton on Ouse	20	Halifax III	19	
427	Leeming	20	Halifax III	18	
428	Middleton St George	20	Lancaster X	4	Operational on Halifax
			Halifax II	19	
429	Leeming	20	Halifax III	19	
431	Croft	20	Halifax III	21	
432	East Moor	20	Halifax III	27	
433	Skipton on Swale	20	Halifax III	21	
434	Croft	20	Halifax III	20	
No 8 (PFF) Group	**HQ Huntingdon**				
7	Oakington	20	Lancaster I & III	20	
35	Graveley	20	Lancaster I & III	20	Inc. one Mk VI

No 8 (PFF) Group   HQ Huntingdon

Squadron	Location	No.	Aircraft	No.	Remarks
83			Lancaster I & III		
97	Bourn	30	Lancaster I & III	30	
105	Little Staughton	30	Mosquito IX/XVI	30	Detached 5 Grp (qv)
109			Mosquito IX/XVI	31	'Oboe'-equipped
			Mosquito IV	1	'Oboe'-equipped
139	Upwood	18	Mosquito IV/XX	10	
			Mosquito IX	4	
156	Upwood	20	Lancaster I & III	19	
405 (Cdn)	Gransden Lodge	20	Lancaster I & III	20	
571	Oakington	20	Mosquito IX/XVI	20	Inc. two Mk VIs
			Mosquito IV	19	Det to 5 Group
582	Little Staughton	20	Lancaster I & III	20	
635	Downham Market	20	Lancaster I & III	20	
692	Graveley	18	Mosquito IV/XX	11	
			Mosquito XVI	4	

No 100 Group   HQ Bylaugh Hall

Squadron	Location	No.	Aircraft	No.	Remarks
141 (BS)	West Raynham	18	Mosquito VI	16	Mk II held
169 (BS)	Little Snoring	18	Mosquito VI	15	Mk II held
192 (BS)	Foulsham	10	Halifax III	9	ECM
		7	Wellington X	8	
		7	Mosquito IV	5	
		1	Anson	1	
214 (BS)	Oulton	18	Fortress	10	Operational one flight only. ABC
239 (BS)	West Raynham	18	Mosquito II	17	One Mk VI
515 (BS)	Little Snoring	18	Mosquito VI	17	Intruder

Not operational

23	Little Snoring	18	Mosquito VI	16	Intruder
85 (BS)	Swannington	18	Mosquito XIX	18	
			Mosquito XVII	8	
157 (BS)	Swannington	18	Mosquito XIX	16	
			Mosquito II	3	
199	North Creake	20	Stirling	20	

Appendix Two
USAAF Eighth Air Force Bomber Command
Order of Battle 5 June 1944

1st Bombardment Division

1st Combat Bombardment Wing:

91st	Group	Bassingbourn	B-17 Fortress
381st	Group	Ridgewell	B-17 Fortress
398th	Group	Nuthamstead	B-17 Fortress

40th Combat Bombardment Wing:

92nd	Group	Podington	B-17 Fortress
305th	Group	Chelveston	B-17 Fortress
306th	Group	Thurleigh	B-17 Fortress

41st Combat Bombardment Wing:

303rd	Group	Molesworth	B-17 Fortress
379th	Group	Kimbolton	B-17 Fortress
384th	Group	Grafton Underwood	B-17 Fortress

94th Combat Bombardment Wing:

351st	Group	Polebrook	B-17 Fortress
401st	Group	Deenethorpe	B-17 Fortress
457th	Group	Glatton	B-17 Fortress

2nd Bombardment Division

2nd Combat Bombardment Wing:

389th	Group	Hethel	B-24 Liberator
445th	Group	Tibenham	B-24 Liberator
453rd	Group	Old Buckenham	B-24 Liberator

14th Combat Bombardment Wing:

44th	Group	Shipdham	B-24 Liberator
392nd	Group	Wedling	B-24 Liberator
492nd	Group	North Pickenham	B-24 Liberator

20th Combat Bombardment Wing:

93rd	Group	Hardwick	B-24 Liberator
446th	Group	Flixton	B-24 Liberator
448th	Group	Seething	B-24 Liberator

95th Combat Bombardment Wing:

489th	Group	Halesworth	B-24 Liberator
491th	Group	Metfield	B-24 Liberator

96th Combat Bombardment Wing:

458th	Group	Horsham St Faith	B-24 Liberator
466th	Group	Attlebridge	B-24 Liberator
467th	Group	Rackheath	B-24 Liberator

3rd Bombardment Division

4th Combat Bombardment Wing:
94th Group	Bury St Edmunds	B-17 Fortress
385th Group	Great Ashfield	B-17 Fortress
447th Group	Rattlesden	B-17 Fortress

13th Combat Bombardment Wing:
95th Group	Horham	B-17 Fortress
100th Group	Thorpe Abbots	B-17 Fortress
390th Group	Framlingham	B-17 Fortress

45th Combat Bombardment Wing:
96th Group	Snetterton Heath	B-17 Fortress
388th Group	Knettishal	B-17 Fortress
452nd Group	Deopham Green	B-17 Fortress

92nd Combat Bombardment Wing:
486th Group	Sudbury	B-24 Liberator
487th Group	Lavenham	B-24 Liberator

93rd Combat Bombardment Wing:
34th Group	Mendlesham	B-24 Liberator
490th Group	Eye	B-24 Liberator
493rd Group	Debach	B-24 Liberator

7th Photographic Reconnaissance Group
Mount Farm	Lightning, Spitfire

25th Bombardment Group (R) (Weather)
Watlon	B-24D, B-24H, Mosquito

Appendix Three
Marking and Master Bomber Techniques Used by the RAF
During Transportation Plan Offensives
Types of Marking Technique

Note

Minor variations in and development of marking techniques occurred almost daily and the following summary is intended as a guide only to the main methods used.

Sky Marking Using 'Oboe' (Musical Wanganui)

This method was normally used in any weather conditions when ground markers could not be seen by the Main Force. Sky marking flares (usually either red flares with green stars, or vice versa) were released by 'Oboe'-equipped aircraft. Each aircraft was controlled by two ground radio stations, located some distance apart, known as 'Cat' and 'Mouse', which controlled one 'Oboe'-equipped aircraft every ten minutes. The 'Cat' guided the aircraft in a controlled curve by transmitting radio signals which were picked up by the aircraft and reflected back to the station. By timing the interval between the signal and its reflection, the ground station was able to determine how far the aircraft was off course and, by emitting a certain distinctive signal, could guide it back onto the curve again. The mouse was similarly measuring the distance between itself and the aircraft, and when the aircraft reached a given point on the curve, the station instructed it to release its flares.

Main Force aircraft were routed to join the curve at a given point, usually approximately thirty miles from the target. They flew along the curve and approached the target on a given heading at 165 mph, with their bomb sights set at zero wind.

Ground Marking Using 'Oboe' (Musical Parramatta)

In this method, 'Oboe'-equipped aircraft dropped ground target indicators instead of release point flares. To guard against failure, additional, or back-up, aircraft flew in at intervals of one or two minutes to drop TIs of a different colour on the 'Oboe'-dropped TIs, if possible. If the 'Oboe'-dropped TIs had gone out by the time the back-up aircraft arrived, TIs were dropped onto those dropped by previous back-up aircraft.

Note

As further 'Oboe' channels were opened up and because of the short duration of the raids on Transportation Plan targets, 'Musical Parramatta' usually entailed blind 'Oboe' ground marking and did not use back-up aircraft.

Controlled 'Oboe'

In this method TIs were dropped by 'Oboe'-equipped aircraft, and the Master Bomber, flying ahead of the Main Force, estimated visually the most accurate TI and directed the Main Force by R/T to bomb on that TI. Frequently, he dropped additional marks of a distinctive colour onto the TIs and directed the Main Force aircraft to bomb on those. This method was used frequently in the attacks on the marshalling yards.

No 8 (PFF) Group Visual Technique

In this technique, developed by No 8 Group, the Master Bomber flew with the 'Oboe'-equipped aircraft. At zero hour minus eight minutes, he selected the best marker and dropped one of his own on that. 'Oboe'-dropped markers were of a short duration and had usually gone out by the time the first Main Force aircraft arrived to bomb the target. Consequently, they bombed on the marker dropped by the Master Bomber.

Note

'Oboe' was limited in range to 250 miles. Outside that range, marking had to be done either visually or by using H2S.

Ground Marking Using H2S (H2S Parramatta)

The main difference between H2S marking and that done using 'Oboe' was the degree of marking error. The average 'Oboe' error was approximately 300 yd whereas an H2S error was equal roughly to the mean radius of the target under attack. Because H2S marking was less accurate than that done using 'Oboe', the fundamental timing used in 'Musical' marking could not be employed. Therefore, as many H2S-equipped aircraft as possible (usually twelve) were sent to reach the target at approximately zero hour minus two or three minutes. The H2S aircraft dropped a scattered mass of TIs and back-up aircraft then estimated the mean point of impact and dropped additional markers on that. A succession of aircraft followed, usually at one- or two-minute intervals, to maintain the continuity of those markers on the mean point of impact.

Sky Marking Using H2S (Wanganui)

H2S-equipped aircraft dropped flares on the release point and, as for 'Musical Wanganui', those flares were bombed on by the Main Force on a given heading.

H2S Newhaven

This was a modification of and was similar to H2S Parramatta. A large number of H2S-equipped aircraft dropped TIs 'blind', to be used as proximity markers, prior to zero hour. In addition, they dropped reconnaissance flares and were followed immediately by aircraft who marked visually (usually expert PFF crews who dropped distinctively coloured TIs visually by the light of flares, at zero hour. The continuity of the marking was kept up by back-up aircraft who flew in at one- or two-minute intervals. This had to be done because once the bombing got underway, clouds of smoke and the glare from the incendiaries both prevented visual identification of the Aim Point.

Attacks using the H2S Newhaven technique were as short as possible because the flares dropped by back-up aircraft had a tendency to be inaccurate when the attack progressed. If the aircraft using visual marking techniques were unable to identify the Aim Point (because of bad weather conditions), they would use the blind H2S Parramatta technique. If the weather precluded any attempts to mark the Aim Point, Wanganui flares were then dropped.

Musical Newhaven

This development of the Newhaven technique was introduced during the attacks on the marshalling yards. Four sets of aircraft were used. Initially, TIs were dropped by 'Oboe'-equipped aircraft. Using the TIs as a guide, further aircraft dropped flares to illuminate the target, followed by aircraft who marked the target visually, and back-up aircraft. The method was considered generally to lead to inaccurate marking.

Visual Marking (No 5 Group Method)
This technique, developed by No 5 Group, proved itself to be very successful. Outside 'Oboe' range, trail-blazer aircraft used H2S to find the target where they dropped flares. In the light of these flares expert marking crews dropped Red Spot Fires visually, dive bombing from low-level. Within 'Oboe' range, No 8 Group 'Oboe'-equipped aircraft marked the target initially. They were followed by aircraft from No 5 Group who illuminated the target, then visual marking was done using Red Spot Fires.

Marking Point Technique
There was a danger that Red Spot Fires could be either obscured by smoke, or blown up by the bombs dropped during attacks. Consequently, No 5 Group developed the marking point technique. Visually marking aircraft aimed their Red Spot Fires at pre-arranged marking points, a short distance from the Aim Point. The positions of the RSFs in relation to the Aim Point were then estimated and broadcast to the Controller. Basing his calculations on that information, the Controller then broadcast a false wind setting for the Main Force to set their aircrafts' bomb sights. As a result, bombs aimed on the RSFs could be calculated to fall on the Aim Point.

Notes on the Master Bomber Technique
The use of the Master Bomber to assist accurate night bombing became a recognised necessity in RAF Bomber Command and was a result of the success achieved by Nos 5 and 8 Groups using that method.

It was considered, however, that the efficiency of the Master Bomber had, on occasion, been impaired by too much talking and interruptions by Main Force crews on the R/T. Also, there had been occasions when, instead of limiting himself to definite and clear-cut instructions, the Master Bomber had used the R/T to encourage crews by general remarks, which were of no assistance.

A letter sent to Groups on 3 May 1944, stated that orders were to be issued to ensure that Master Bombers limited themselves to giving clear-cut and definite instructions to crews and that Main Force crews were to maintain rigid R/T silence, except in exceptional circumstances.

Further instructions were issued on 4 May 1944, to the effect that all crews arriving at the target at or after zero hour should commence bombing on the markers without further orders, unless instructions to the contrary were issued by the Master Bomber or his Deputy. The Master Bomber was empowered to stop or reposition the bombing, but was not to initiate it. The instructions were issued to cover the possibility of a failure in an aircraft, or the R/T or W/T in the aircraft of a Master Bomber or his Deputy, and to eliminate the possibility of aircraft of the Main Force having to circle the target for an unnecessarily long period while awaiting the order to start.

Following a suggestion from No 5 Group, the D/C-in-C wrote to ACAS (Ops) on 14 May 1944, stating that experience with the new marking technique carried out by No 5 Group had shown that the success of the operation depended very largely on the efficiency of the Master Bomber in preparing and executing his duties. It was essential for him to study most carefully the tactical plan for each operation and to practise and be thoroughly conversant in the detailed technique of directing the markers and the Main Force over the target area.

While hitherto the Master and Deputy Master Bombers had both been drawn from the most experienced Squadron or Flight Commanders, in practice it had been found that the duties of the Master Bomber constituted a full-time job which could not be combined effectively with Squadron and Flight Commander duties.

It was therefore considered to be essential for the Master Bomber to be free from other administrative and operational duties and the D/C-in-C stated that an application would be made to establish four Wing Commander posts as Master Bombers at No 54 Squadron's base, Coningsby (No 5 Group). He added that further posts might be required in other operational Groups, according to the success and adoption of No 5 Group's technique. Establishing the four posts within No 5 Group was agreed subsequently by the Air Ministry.

Appendix Four
German Army Command in the West, June 1944

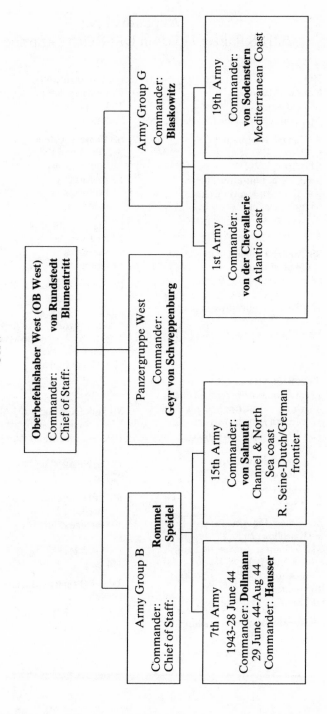

OKW

Oberbefehlshaber West (OB West)
Commander: **von Rundstedt**
Chief of Staff: **Blumentritt**

Army Group B
Commander: **Rommel**
Chief of Staff: **Speidel**

Panzergruppe West
Commander: **Geyr von Schweppenburg**

Army Group G
Commander: **Blaskowitz**

7th Army
1943-28 June 44
Commander: **Dollmann**
29 June 44-Aug 44
Commander: **Hausser**

15th Army
Commander: **von Salmuth**
Channel & North
Sea coast
R. Seine-Dutch/German
frontier

1st Army
Commander: **von der Chevallerie**
Atlantic Coast

19th Army
Commander: **von Sodenstern**
Mediterranean Coast

Appendix Five
2nd SS Panzer Division Das Reich — Spring 1944

HQ
8 motorcycles
32 vehicles
141 men

SS Panzer Regiment 2
62 Panzer KW V
64 Panzer KW IV
8 x 3.7 cm anti-aircraft guns
6 x 20 mm anti-aircraft guns
53 motorcycles
313 vehicles
2401 men

SS Panzer-Grenadier Regiment 3
(Deutschland)
88 motorcycles
6 x 15 cm guns/howitzers
12 x 10.5 cm guns/howitzers
24 flame throwers
12 x 12 cm mortars
527 vehicles
3242 men

SS Panzer Artillery Regiment 2
12 x 17 cm guns/howitzers
6 x 15 cm self-propelled guns
12 x 15 cm guns/howitzers
12 x 10.5 cm self-propelled
  guns
12 x 10.5 cm guns/howitzers
40 motorcycles
534 vehicles
2167 men

SS Panzer Jag Abteilung
(Battalion) 2
31 x 7.5 cm self-propelled guns
12 x 40 mm Pak
17 motorcycles
135 vehicles
513 men

SS Reconnaissance Abteilung 2
13 x 7.5 cm self-propelled guns
35 x 20 mm Pak

6 flame throwers
22 motorcycles
193 vehicles
942 men

SS Pioneer Abteilung 2
3 x 20/28 mm Pak
20 flame throwers
52 motorcycles
212 vehicles
984 men

SS Signals Abteilung 2
14 motorcycles
114 vehicles
515 men

SS Panzer-Grenadier Regiment 4
(Der Führer)
88 motorcycles
6 x 15 cm guns/howitzers
12 x 10.5 cm guns/howitzers
24 flame throwers
12 x 12 cm mortars
527 vehicles
3242 men

SS Flak (Anti-aircraft) Abteilung 2
12 x 8.8 cm anti-aircraft guns
18 x 20 mm anti-aircraft guns
16 motorcycles
181 vehicles
824 men

SS Sturmgeschutz (Assault gun)
Abteilung 2
30 sturmgeschuts III/IV
11 motorcycles
100 vehicles
344 men

SS Nebelwerfer (Mortar) Abteilung 2
18 Nebelwerfer
8 motorcycles
107 vehicles
473 men

Appendix Six

Summary of the Arguments Concerning the
Role of RAF Bomber Command in the First Half of 1944

NOTE: Comments on Bomber Command Memorandum for the Employment of Night Bombers in Connection with 'Overlord' are contained in D.C.A.S. 27 January 1944. PRO AIR./41/56.

Further Comments by Air Staff in the Light of Experience of Bomber Command's Operations in Support of 'Overlord' are contained in D.B. Ops 26715A 28 June 1944. PRO AIR. 20/5817.

Statements of C-in-C's Memorandum	Comments by AEAF	Comments by the Air Staff (27 January 1944)	Comments by the Air Staff (28 June 1944)
Role of Bomber Command The Memorandum states without qualification that Bomber Command's task is the destruction of the enemy's industrial centres.	It is presumed that Bomber Command will have its role extended to include as and when required, the maximum assistance to 'Overlord'.	From a date in the preparatory phase of 'Overlord' yet to be selected, the primary object of Bomber Command will become the support of that operation and all or part of the forces of Bomber Command will be at the disposal of the Supreme Commander. That support will be, in the words of the directive, 'in the manner most effective'. Once the type of support required from Bomber Command has been decided — and this will be done in conjunction with advisers from Bomber Command — it will be the duty of the C-in-C to do his best to fulfil these tasks.	Under the direction of the Deputy Supreme Allied Commander and in accordance with the Combined Chiefs of Staff's ruling, the whole of the forces of Bomber Command have been available for the support of 'Overlord' 'in the manner most effective'. This has been fully justified by events. The C-in-C Bomber Command has cooperated wholeheartedly in fulfilling the tasks allotted to him and the results achieved have far exceeded expectations.
Limitation of Bomber Command's Operations The nature of Bomber Command's operations is limited by the highly specialised aircraft and the complex operational technique employed.	It is not clear why targets in FRANCE should be any less suitable than industrial centres in GERMANY, provided they are carefully selected ones, e.g. railway centres or towns where the enemy's reserves are concentrated.	Although the heavy bomber force has been developed as an independent strategic force its task is not necessarily the destruction of enemy industrial centres. The highly specialised equipment and operational technique has been evolved to enable the force to place its bombs accurately on the desired target. Although bombing accuracy so far achieved has only enabled the force to carry area bombing by night, the aim is still to achieve the most accurate bombing possible; all technical development is to this end. The unavoidable limitations of Bomber Command in support of 'Overlord' are due to inability to achieve a high accuracy of bombing and not to the nature and extent of any specialisation which is taking place.	Events have shown that capabilities of the night bomber force in the support of 'Overlord' have not been limited to any appreciable extent; on the contrary, Bomber Command have demonstrated their ability to achieve an accuracy and concentration on small targets far exceeding that which can be achieved by the American heavies by day; furthermore, they have achieved such concentrations by night below a 10/10ths cloud base, while the American day heavies in similar conditions have been forced to abandon their task. The following wide diversity of targets has been successfully attacked: transportation targets; coastal batteries; dumps; camps; airfields; radar stations; tactical targets. The earlier Air Staff comment 'that the aim is still to achieve the most accurate bombing' has been justified beyond expectation. The density of attack achieved by Bomber Command throughout its operations in support of 'Overlord' has been most creditable and in many attacks such as Juvissy, Mailly le Camp, Aulnay, etc. an amazing density has been achieved.

Paras of Memo	Statements of C-in-C's Memorandum	Comments by AEAF	Comments by the Air Staff (27 January 1944)	Comments by the Air Sta (28 June 1944)
3.	**Day Operations** Because of training, armament and ceilings when flying in formations, day operations are absolutely out of the question and could in no circumstances be undertaken.	It is not anticipated that our night bombers will normally be called upon for day operations.	Bomber Command have within the last two years carried out daylight raids on Augsburg, Danzig, Creusot and Milan. These were done with little previous daylight training, and if necessary squadrons could again be trained to operate in daylight probably with less than six weeks being set aside for the purpose, especially in view of the shorter ranges involved and the degree of fighter cover which would be afforded in this theatre of operations. Their armament is no less efficient than some squadrons in the Tactical Air Forces; the height at which it would be necessary to fly would be dependent on the flak opposition in the 'Overlord' area. Tactical Air Forces are already operating at heights and below those heights at which our heavy bombers could operate. It is considered, however, that there would be little if any call for the R.A.F. Bomber Command to operate by day since they can be effectively employed at night in support of landing operations. Moreover, American heavy bomber forces in numbers equal to those of R.A.F. Bomber Command will be available for precision daylight attack.	The C-in-C's statement t daylight operations were absolutely out of the que and could in no circumst be undertaken, has been directly contradicted by Bomber Command have carried out a large numb heavy scale daylight atta smaller losses than they against the same targets night. The previous Air S view as to the feasibility daylight operations has b proved correct.

Statements of C-in-C's Memorandum	Comments by AEAF	Comments by the Air Staff (27 January 1944)	Comments by the Air Staff (28 June 1944)
Night Operations — Pathfinder Technique			
It is necessary always to use some form of Pathfinder technique.	Whatever the result obtained through the use of PFF for targets in GERMANY, they should be improved for targets in FRANCE. The Memorandum admits that individual bombing can be successful in suitable conditions such as excellent visibility, bright moonlight and meagre opposition. The conditions might well exist for 'Overlord'. In any event, Bomber Command's statement seems to have been written with special reference to targets deep in GERMANY. The limitations of the aids are well realised and there is no suggestion that they should be used in attacks against unsuitable targets. With the exception of H2S, greater accuracy with these aids can be obtained against short range targets in FRANCE than against those at longer ranges in GERMANY.	Paras 4 and 5 give an incorrect impression of the potential uses of existing navigational aids and marking technique in support of military operations and belittle the accuracy which is to be expected from 'Oboe', H2S or H2X for bombing strips of coastline in preparation for a landing. Results to be achieved by H2S alone are shown by the attached chart . . . giving the appearance of Baltic coast near Peenemünde on an H2S screen. The bomb plot and photographs of results achieved in this attack are shown at Appendix B. H2S or H2X are more effective in picking out coastline than in other circumstances. It is therefore incorrect to state that H2S gives its best results when used against 'isolated and densely built-up industrial areas surrounded by open country'. In fact water shows up much better than any other feature on H2S screen. The statement 'It is always necessary to use some form of Pathfinder Technique' is too sweeping. In an emergency and with clear moonlight the heavy bomber force might quite well use visual methods of bombing especially in the coastal areas. The extent of coverage of 'Oboe' as shown on the Bomber Command charts is misleading. There is considerable cover provided over the vital coastal area to the West of Paris.	The Air Staff comment that the C-in-C had given an incorrect impression as to the use of existing navigational aids has been confirmed by the 'Overlord' operations. Since the C-in-C's paper was written the technique of visual marking with the aid of flares has been developed and results achieved by the technique have been in many cases comparable to those achieved with the aid of 'Oboe'. It is true that some form of Pathfinder technique is always necessary, but this does not necessarily involve the use of 'Oboe', H2S or Gee-H.
The aids for the Pathfinder technique are 'Oboe', H2S, G-H. The limitations of these aids are emphasised.			
Weather Restrictions			
Choice of heavy bomber targets is chiefly governed by weather.	It is agreed that an adequate period must be allowed for the necessary bomber effort to be brought to bear on 'OVERLORD' targets. It should be remembered that the closer ranges of 'OVERLORD' targets permit of considerably greater accuracy of weather forecasts than for targets deep in GERMANY.	It is agreed that weather conditions will restrict the choice of targets but if defences are light and deep penetration is not required, restrictions on account of weather will not be so great as is general in Bomber Command operations. Night attacks need not necessarily be aided by blind bombing devices. The hooded flare has been developed with a degree of priority to enable targets to be found and visual bombing to be carried out. The comments of AEAF are agreed.	Weather has not been so great a limiting factor on operations over France as over Germany; owing to the light flak defences in France it has often been possible to make accurate and concentrated attacks from below the cloud base. Moreover in a period of extremely bad weather the effort has, in June, far exceeded that ever before put out by Bomber Command.

Paras of Memo	Statements of C-in-C's Memorandum	Comments by AEAF	Comments by the Air Staff (27 January 1944)	Comments by the Air St... (28 June 1944)
11	**Tactical Restrictions** Employment of the Pathfinder technique limits the number of targets which can be attacked on any night and also the number of consecutive nights over which attacks can be sustained (with present limitations Pathfinders can work 2 targets each night during two nights out of three for 12 days).	If the period during which targets are marked is reduced, and the targets are at shorter ranges from this country, it should be possible to raise the maximum number of targets that can be marked during a single night. In any case it is understood that P.F.F. capacity will have increased by time of 'OVERLORD'.	It is not agreed that it is impossible to mark more than two targets during the course of one night without crews and aircraft being used more than once. Targets can be marked by aircraft fitted with H2S, 'OBOE', G-H and in addition visual identification can be practised with the aid of flares.	The Air Staff view has be... fully substantiated. Duri... 'OVERLORD' operatio... to 10 targets have been a... in one night, a Pathfinde... technique being employe... against each target. The technique of visual mark... with the aid of flares has ... highly successful.
12–14	**Maximum Monthly Effort** The Maximum effort Bomber Command can sustain is approximately 5000 sorties per month assuming normal wastage. This allows for eight full-scale attacks per month.	Presumably this is based on deep penetration operations against targets in GERMANY. Short range operations against targets in FRANCE should allow a considerably greater numer of sorties to be carried out.	This paragraph is misleading. Last May, June and July Bomber Command averaged 5700 sorties a month. These were for the most part long range sorties accomplished with an average operational strength of 52 Squadron. If the same effort per squadron is expanded, the existing Bomber Command force should be able to put out 7300 sorties a month during 'OVERLORD'. This figure should be proportionately greater in view of the shorter sorties involved.	The Air Staff view that m... than 7300 sorties a month... should be possible during 'OVERLORD' is proved... correct by the fact that du... the 68 day period betwee... 14 and June 21, Bomber Command completed 24,... heavy bomber sorties. Th... average of approximately... 11,000 sorties per month,... is more than twice the fig... 5000 sorties per month wh... the C-in-C put forward as... effort that could be sustai... Bomber Command assum... normal wastage (total air... missing over this period amounted to 641 or 2.6 p... cent).
15.	**'Fleeting Targets'** The heavy bomber force is quite incapable of being brought into action quickly against 'fleeting targets'. The time required to refuel, service and bomb up the aircraft, brief the crews and marshal the force is such that with maximum efficiency some seven daylight hours are the minimum necessary between the decision to bomb a given target and take-off of aircraft. The target cannot be altered during that period without involving a new start. If the preparatory work has to be done in darkness the minimum period would be extended to nine or ten hours.	It is not proposed to whittle Bomber Command away by operations against 'fleeting targets'. In the main, tactical results will be achieved as a result against 'OVERLORD' strategical targets. The statement appears to refer to the 'turn-round' period. For operations against important transient targets connected with 'OVERLORD' during the criticial period, Bomber Command forces could be standing by and some simplified briefing procedure arranged. Under these circumstances it would seem that the period between the order to attack and the take-off could be reduced by day to something more in the order of 60 minutes.	This paragraph gives an exaggerated impression of the time necessary to bomb up for the attack of targets of the type likely to be attacked during the period of two weeks before and after D-Day. Standard bomb loads will be used and these can be prepared in advance at dispersal points. It is not correct to say that the target cannot be altered during the period of seven hours without involving a new start and consequent further delay. In bombing by marker technique the target can be changed at short notice.	No occasion has arisen for... testing the C-in-C's pessim... statement on the time tak... bomb up for the attack of targets in connection with 'OVERLORD'. The com... of the Air Staff are, howe... substantiated by the fact t... standardised bomb loads ... been employed against tac... targets and by the fact tha... force attacks have almost exclusively been on marke... therefore have called for l... no briefing.

Statements of C-in-C's Memorandum	Comments by AEAF	Comments by the Air Staff (27 January 1944)	Comments by the Air Staff (28 June 1944)
'Programme Bombing' 'Programme Bombing' except over a long period and in the most general terms is ruled out altogether as an operation of war. A planned schedule of heavy bomber operations to give immediate assistance to ground forces would be extremely unreliable and almost wholly futile. Beach drenching could be regarded only as a contingent possibility and could not form an integral part of any plan. In no circumstances would heavy bombers be relied on to destroy gun emplacements, nor are they suitable for cutting railway communications.	It is not accepted that 'programme bombing' cannot be undertaken in the 'OVERLORD' theatre of operations. This statement would appear to have been made without full knowledge of the tasks which the heavy bomber force would be called upon to perform in support of the Operation.	The drenching of beaches by heavy bomber attack will not necessarily involve the cratering of a large area of coast to an extent imposing limitations on our own troop movements. 500-lb bombs with instantaneous or air burst fuses should be used and little cratering will in fact result. The effect of bombing attacks on gun emplacements has been exhaustively examined by an Inter-Service Committee and they agreed that if guns are not provided with overhead cover a high degree of neutralisation can be effected. Similarly with air burst and instantaneous fused bombs appreciable casualties and lowering of morale can be caused to defenders in slit trenches. Professor Zuckerman's Report on bombing of communications in Sicily and Italy shows exclusively that great effect can be achieved by heavy bombers and that if it is to have immediate effect in the battle area the targets selected must be close to that area and not hundreds of miles away as is suggested in the C-in-C's memorandum.	Bomber Command were most successfully employed on 'programme bombing' in relation to 'OVERLORD' and their attacks on gun positions were highly effective. The C-in-C's statement that the heavy bomber force could in no circumstances be relied on to cut railway communications could not have been further from the truth. Whether the attacks have been on marshalling yards, junctions, tunnels or bridges in nearly every case most successful results have been achieved.
Cost of Changing Bomber Policy States the case for continuing the heavy bomber offensive on GERMANY and the consequences of a six-months break in this offensive.	The cost of diverting the whole or part of the heavy bomber effort to the direct support of 'OVERLORD' would certainly receive the fullest consideration and the decision to do so will be taken at the highest level.	The general contentions of these paragraphs that the effects of strategical bombing are cumulative and that there is recovery rate as well as destructive rate and that therefore any cessation of attacks on Germany is to be avoided is accepted. It is incorrect, however, to suggest that these arguments apply to an interruption of say two weeks or even to a temporary diminution of effort due to the needs of 'OVERLORD'. Weather conditions have many times imposed periods of interruption of the attack on Germany. It is incorrect to suggest that a relatively short interruption even of several weeks of the bombing of Germany would enable the enemy to redispose the major part of his air and ground defences and move them from central Germany to the Invasion Area.	It is true that 'OVERLORD' commitments have caused some diversion of effort from the bombing of German targets. This has not been considerable, however, since Bomber Command are in any case severely limited in their attacks on Germany by moonlight and by the short nights now being experienced. Bomber Command reverted at D + 6 to strategical bombing, when they attacked the synthetic oil plants in the Ruhr. 'OVERLORD' has provided an abundance of profitable targets for attack by Bomber Command during the recent moonlight periods. The Air Staff view that relatively short interruptions, even of several weeks, of the bombing of Germany would not enable the enemy to redispose the major part of his air and ground defences was correct. Any major movement by the enemy of ground defences or night fighters to the West has been influenced chiefly by the knowledge that Bomber Command were unlikely to operate further East than the Ruhr during the short periods of darkness.

Paras of Memo	Statements of C-in-C's Memorandum	Comments by AEAF	Comments by the Air Staff (27 January 1944)	Comments by the Air Sta (28 June 1944)
21.	**Morale** Germany would go wild with a sense of relief and reborn hope with a cessation or ponderable reduction of the bombing of GERMANY proper.	Failure of Operation 'OVERLORD' would result in far graver repercussions than a temporary cessation in the bombing of German centres.	Whilst it is entirely practicable for Bomber Command during certain phases of 'OVERLORD' materially to assist land operations, this can be done without allowing the German population to receive any appreciable respite from bombing attack. It should be possible even with the needs of 'OVERLORD' to maintain a sufficient degree of pressure on Germany so as to allow no recovery in morale. Indeed, some such constant pressure will be necessary in order to compel the enemy to maintain fighter forces in Germany and prevent complete concentration in the 'OVERLORD' area.	There is no indication 'th Germany has gone wild sense of relief and a sens relief and reborn hope w cessation or ponderable reduction of the bombing Germany proper'. The th the German population i great as ever and is main by such attacks as Bombe Command has made upo Ruhr and the Americans Berlin in recent weeks. On the contrary, the knowledge of the enorm effort which has been de to the support of 'OVERLORD' must hav viewed with considerable apprehension by the Ger population; an apprehens which will grow with succ the invasion. The Germa population fully realise th troops are being subjecte the very heavy bombing a normally directed at them that these attacks, by play their part in the successfu establishment of the bridgehead, may be even injurious in securing the c of Germany than if direct the population.
22.	**Conclusions** The Bomber Command Memorandum concludes by stating that it is clear that the best and indeed the only, effective support Bomber Command can give to Operation 'OVERLORD' is the intensification of the attacks against suitable industrial targets in GERMANY.	The desirability of maintaining the Bomber Command offensive against industrial centres in GERMANY is fully appreciated. Bomber Command must, however, be diverted in whole or part as required to the attack of suitable targets in support of Operation 'OVERLORD' in the preparatory phase, during the assault and subsequently.	The comments of AEAF are agreed. The extent to which the support of Bomber Command will be required in the various phases of 'OVERLORD' will be determined by the CCOS after they have had General Eisenhower's recommendations. The COS and CCOS are in a position to balance the respective needs of 'OVERLORD' and 'POINT BLANK' and can adjust the degree of support required from the strategical air forces, in accordance with the particular requirements at the time.	Generally, the conclusion the Bomber Command memorandum have prove entirely incorrect. The su which Bomber Command in fact, been capable of affording has played an outstanding part in the successful establishment c bridgehead. The statemer 'the only effective suppor Bomber Command could to operation 'OVERLOR was the intensification of against industrial targets i Germany' has proved to b far indeed from the truth.

Appendix Seven
Details of Aircraft Involved

Avro Lancaster I/III
Role: Heavy bomber
Crew: 7/8   Engines: 4   Maximum fuel load: 15,500 lb
Maximum speed: 280 mph   Operational ceiling: 24,500 ft
Maximum bomb capacity: 14,000 lb (some adapted to carry 'Grand Slam)
Armament: Eight .303 guns in three turrets
Remarks: ABC-equipped aircraft carried a crew of 8

Boeing B-17 Fortress
Role: Heavy bomber
Crew: 10/11   Engines: 4   Maximum range: 2700 miles
Maximum speed: 287 mph   Operational ceiling: 31,500 ft
Maximum bomb capacity: 12,800 lb
Armament: Ten .50 guns in five turrets and waist positions
Remarks: B-17 YB.40 carried fourteen .50 guns and 12,400 rounds of
         ammunition

Consolidated B-24 Liberator
Role: Heavy bomber
Crew: 8/10   Engines: 4   Maximum range: 2300 miles
Maximum speed: 270 mph   Operational ceiling: 28,000 ft
Maximum bomb capacity: 12,800 lb
Armament: Ten .50 guns

De Havilland Mosquito Mk VI
Role: Light bomber
Crew: 2   Engines: 2   Maximum range: 1795 miles with
                                     reduced bomb load
Maximum speed: 380 mph   Operational ceiling: 36,000 ft
Maximum bomb load: 2000 lb (4000 lb Mk XVI)
Armament: Four 20 mm cannon in fighter role
Remarks: No armament carried in PR or bomber versions. Later versions
         were faster and could operate at higher altitudes

Focke-Wulf Fw 190 A8
Role: Fighter
Crew: 1   Engines: 1   Maximum range: approximately 500 miles
                                     Operational ceiling: 35,000 ft
Armament: Two 13 mm and four 20 mm cannon

Handley Page Halifax II/III
Role: Heavy bomber
Crew: 7/8   Engines: 4   Maximum fuel load: 15,200 lb (19,350 lb)
Maximum speed: 265 mph   Operational ceiling: 24,000 ft
Maximum bomb load: 13,000 lb (13,750 lb)
Armament: Ten .303 guns in 3 or 4 turrets
Remarks: Mk III figures in brackets

Junkers Ju 88G
Role: Night fighter
Crew: 2   Engines: 2   Maximum range: 1200 miles
                                     Operational ceiling: 32,500 ft
Armament: Three 20 mm, one 13 mm, three 7.9 mm cannon

Martin B-26 Marauder III
Role: Medium bomber
Crew: 5   Engines: 2   Maximum range: 1200 miles
Maximum speed: 305 mph   Operational ceiling: 28,000 ft
Maximum bomb load: 4000 lb
Armament: Six to eight .50 guns

Messerschmitt Bf 109G
Role: Fighter
Crew: 1   Engines: 1   Maximum range: 620 miles
                                     Operational ceiling: 38,000 ft
Armament: One 30 mm or one 20 mm and two 13 mm cannon

Messerschmitt Me 110G
Role: Night fighter
Crew: 2   Engines: 2   Maximum range: 1300 miles
Maximum speed: 300 mph   Operational ceiling: 26,250 ft
Armament: Two 30 mm, two 20 mm and 7.9 mm cannon/guns
Remarks: Some aircraft equipped with Schräge Musik

Short Stirling
Role: Heavy bomber
Crew: 7   Engines: 4   Maximum fuel load: 16,250 lb
Maximum speed: 270 mph   Operational ceiling: 17,000 ft
Armament: Eight .303 guns in three turrets

Vickers-Supermarine Spitfire XI PR
Role: Photographic reconnaissance
Crew: 1   Engines: 1   Maximum range: up to 2000 miles with
                                     belly tanks
Maximum speed: 422 mph   Operational ceiling: 42,000 ft
Remarks: Carried no armament, carried two F52 and one K18 cameras

Appendix Eight
Bomb and Fuel Planning
Lancaster I/III (1), Halifax II (2), Halifax III (3), Sterling (4)

Overall Track Miles	Total Fuel Required (Galls)				Fuel Weight (lbs)				Weight Available For Bombs and 'Window'			
	(1)	(2)	(3)	(4)	(1)	(2)	(3)	(4)	(1)	(2)	(3)	(4)
600				1102				7950				12357
700		1075		1234		7750		8880			13750	11420
800	1040	1164	1200	1367	7500	8400	8140	9850	17200	11800	13360	10457
900	1150	1285	1325	1500	8300	9250	9540	10820	16400	10950	11960	9487
1000	1250	1400	1450	1645	9000	10080	10440	11845	15700	10120	11060	8462
1100	1358	1525	1575	1770	9775	10980	11340	12745	14925	9200	10160	7562
1200	1465	1650	1700	1900	10550	11880	12240	13680	14150	8320	9260	6625
1300	1570	1770	1825	2035	11300	12744	13140	14652	13400	7456	8360	5655
1400	1675	1882	1950	2168	12080	13600	14020	15610	12620	6600	7480	4695
1500	1780	2010	2075		12820	14480	14940		11880	5470	6560	
1600	1885		2200		13600		15840		11100		5600	
1700	1990		2335		14330		16812		10370		4688	
1800	2095		2452		15100		17654		9600		3846	

NOTES

1   Fuel required was based on the following formulae:

Lancaster I/III	$\dfrac{\text{Overall Track Miles}}{0.95}$	+ 200 Galls
Halifax II	$\dfrac{\text{Overall Track Miles}}{0.83}$	+ 200 Galls
Halifax III	$\dfrac{\text{Overall Track Miles}}{0.80}$	+ 200 Galls
Stirling	$\dfrac{\text{Overall Track Miles}}{0.75}$	+ 300 Galls

Overall track miles was base to base + reserve depending on winds.

2   The disposable loads were calculated by adding tare weights to service loads (i.e., crew, ammunition, oils, etc.) and taking this away from the maximum permissible take-off weight. Disposable loads for the four aircraft in the table were; Lancaster I/III – 24,700 lb, Halifax II – 20,200 lb, Halifax III – 21,500 lb and Stirling – 20,307 lb.

3   One gallon of petrol weighs 7.2 lb.

4   Bomb weights were calculated with any carriers and the following figures were used:

Bomb Type	Mean Weight for Calculation
12,000 lb HE	11,940 lb
8,000 lb HC	7,850 lb
4,000 lb HC	3,950 lb
2,000 lb HC	1,890 lb
1,000 lb GP	1,100 lb
500 lb MC	500 lb
60 x 4 lb incendiary	290 lb

Tables and figures based on information in PRO Air 24/269.

Appendix Nine

RAF Bomber Command Operations Against Transportation Targets

6 March–6 June 1944

Based on PRO Air 41/56 Appendix 10

Date	Target or Purpose	No. Aircraft Despatched	No. Aircraft Attacking	No. Aircraft Missing	Tonnage Bombs Dropped	RAF Groups Participating	Aircraft Types involved
March	**Railway Centres**						
6/7	Trappes	267	263	—	1260.7	4, 6, 8	Mosquito, Halifax
7/8	Le Mans	304	201	—	952.6	3, 4, 6	Halifax, Lancaster
13/14	Le Mans	222	208	1	965.0	4, 6	Halifax, Mosquito
15/16	Amiens	140	123	3	607.4	3, 4, 6, 8	Halifax, Stirling
16/17	Amiens	130	118	—	561.4	3, 4, 6	Mosquito, Stirling
23/24	Laon	143	72	2	292.7	3, 4, 6	Stirling, Halifax
25/26	Aulnoye	192	183	—	808.8	3, 4, 6, 8	Halifax, Lancaster
26/27	Courtrai	109	102	—	474.0	3, 4, 6	Halifax, Stirling
29/30	Paris (Vaires)	84	77	1	312.9	4, 6, 8	Halifax, Mosquito
April							
9/10	Villeneuve St George	225	213	—	993.8	1, 3, 4	Mosquito, Lancaster
						6, 8	Halifax
10/11	Lille	239	227	1	1054.7	3, 4, 6	Stirling, Halifax
	Tergnier	157	155	10	692.0	4	Halifax
	Ghent	122	118	—	615.3	6	Halifax
	Aulnoye	132	129	7	790.8	1	Lancaster
	Laon	148	147	1	766.6	3, 6, 8	Lancaster
	Tours	180	173	1	947.2	5	Lancaster
11/12	Aachen	350	342	9	1938.5	1, 3, 5, 8	Lancaster

Date	Target or Purpose	No. Aircraft Despatched	No. Aircraft Attacking	No. Aircraft Missing	Tonnage Bombs Dropped	RAF Groups Participating	Aircraft Types involved
18/19	Noisy le Sec	163	162	4	874.7	6, 8	Lancaster, Halifax
	Tergnier	163	159	6	719.6	4, 8	Lancaster, Halifax
	Tergnier — Noisy le Sec	8	5	—	—	8	Mosquito
20/21	Rouen	289	281	—	1538.1	1, 3, 8	Mosquito, Lancaster
	Juvisy	209	203	1	1105.7	5, 8	Mosquito, Lancaster
	Cologne	379	358	4	1767.0	1, 3, 6, 8	Lancaster, Mosquito
	Ottignies	196	190	1	916.2	4	Halifax, Lancaster Mosquito
	Paris (La Chappelle)	269	260	6	1265.4	5, 8	Lancaster, Mosquito
	Lens	175	170	1	849.4	6, 8	Lancaster, Mosquito Halifax
22/23	Chambly	14	4	1	16.1	3	Stirling
	Dusseldorf	596	567	29	2150.5	1, 3, 4, 6, 8	Halifax, Lancaster Mosquito
24/25	Laon	181	169	9	715.2	3, 4, 6	Stirling, Halifax
	Chambly	4	3	—	9.4	3	Stirling
26/27	Villeneuve St George	217	202	1	852.0	4, 6, 8	Halifax, Lancaster Mosquito
27/28	Chambly	10	—	—	—	3	Stirling
	Montzen	144	135	15	607.7	4, 6, 8	Halifax, Lancaster Mosquito
	Aulnoye	233	213	1	930.6	4, 6, 8	Halifax, Lancaster Mosquito
30/1	Acheres	128	122	—	529.5	4, 8	Halifax, Lancaster
	Somain	142	135	1	594.6	6, 8	Halifax, Mosquito
May 1/2	Chambly	120	113	5	530.5	3, 8	Stirling, Lancaster Mosquito
	Malines	132	120	2	535.6	4, 8	Halifax, Lancaster Mosquito

Date	Target or Purpose	No. Aircraft Despatched	No. Aircraft Attacking	No. Aircraft Missing	Tonnage Bombs Dropped	RAF Groups Participating	Aircraft Types involved
1/2	Tours	50	50	—	221.5	5	Lancaster, Mosquito
	Toulouse	139	136	—	289.8	5	Lancaster, Mosquito
	St Ghislaine	137	123	2	556.6	6, 8	Halifax, Lancaster
3/4	Montdidier	92	88	4	401.8	8	Lancaster, Mosquito
6/7	Mantes-Gassicourt	149	143	3	629.8	4, 8	Mosquito, Lancaster Halifax
8/9	Haine St Pierre	125	119	9	481.6	6, 8	Lancaster, Halifax Mosquito
10/11	Lens	125	121	—	534.5	4, 8	Halifax, Lancaster Mosquito
	Lille	89	85	12	418.9	5	Lancaster, Mosquito
	Ghent	126	118	—	425.6	6, 8	Lancaster, Halifax
	Courtrai	98	93	—	533.8	3, 8	Lancaster, Mosquito
11/12	Hasselt	128	39	5	231.2	1, 8	Lancaster, Mosquito
	Louvain	110	101	4	559.2	3, 8	Lancaster, Mosquito
12/13	Hasselt	111	105	7	437.2	4, 8	Lancaster, Halifax Mosquito
19/20	Louvain	120	103	5	356.7	6, 8	Lancaster, Halifax
	Orléans	122	112	1	617.7	1, 8	Lancaster, Mosquito
	Le Mans	116	110	3	555.5	3, 8	Lancaster, Mosquito
	Tours	117	107	—	477.4	5	Lancaster, Mosquito
	Boulogne	143	134	—	562.3	4, 8	Lancaster, Halifax
	Amiens	121	40	1	152.7	5, 8	Lancaster, Mosquito
22/23	Orléans	128	112	1	617.7	4, 8	Lancaster, Halifax Mosquito
	Le Mans	133	116	2	388.4	6, 8	Lancaster, Halifax Mosquito
24/25	Aachen	432	409	25	2036.5	1, 4, 3, 6, 8	Lancaster, Halifax
26/27	Aachen	11	11	—	19.6	8	Mosquito

Date	Target or Purpose	No. Aircraft Despatched	No. Aircraft Attacking	No. Aircraft Missing	Tonnage Bombs Dropped	RAF Groups Participating	Aircraft Types involved
27/28	Aachen	170	166	12	907.6	1, 3, 8	Lancaster, Mosquito
	Nantes	104	53	—	255.1	5	Lancaster, Mosquito
28/29	Angers	126	118	1	472.2	3, 8	Lancaster, Mosquito
	Laval	6	4	—	5.4	1	Lancaster
31/1	Trappes	219	202	4	872.0	1, 3, 4, 8	Lancaster, Halifax Mosquito
	Tergnier	115	101	2	538.7	1, 8	Lancaster, Mosquito
	Saumur	86	49	—	240.4	5	Lancaster, Mosquito
June							
1/2	Saumur	58	53	—	259.2	5	Lancaster, Mosquito
2/3	Trappes	128	124	16	480.8	1, 4, 8	Lancaster, Halifax Mosquito

Appendix Ten
Allocation of Transportation Plan Targets
19 April 1944

Part One — Occupied Territories

RAF Bomber Command

Location	Target No	Location	Target No
Amiens/Longeau	Z 446	Miramas	Z 631
Angers	?	Nantes	?
Aulnoye	Z 599	Orléans	?
Boulogne sur Mer	Z 805A	Ottignes	ZB 893
Courtrai	ZB 886	Paris/La Plaine	Z 799A
Ghent/Meirlebeke	ZB 884B	La Chappelle	
Hasselt	ZB 889	Paris/Noisy Le Sec/Juvissy	Z 800B
Juvisy	Z 605	Rouen/Sotteville	Z 435
Laon	Z 604	Saumur	?
Le Mans	Z 444A	Somain	Z 834
Lens	Z 798	St Ghislain	ZB 909
Lille/Delivrance	Z 571	Tergnier	Z 572
Lille/Fives	Z 183B	Trappes	Z 431
Louvain	ZB 917A/B	Tours/St Pierre des Corps/Town	Z 434A
Malines	?	Vaires	Z 606
Mantes/Gassincourt	Z 804	Villeneuve St Georges	Z 801
Montzen	ZB 907		

USAAF Eighth Force Bomber Command

Location	Target No	Location	Target No
Belfort	Z 822	Metz	Z 642
Blainville	Z 807	Mulhouse/Ile Napoleon	Z 813C
Brussels/Midi	ZB 928	Mulhouse/Main Station	Z 813A
Brussels/Schaerbeek	ZB 40B	Mulhouse/Nord	Z 813B
Châlons sur Marne	Z 809	Reims	Z 802
Chaumont	Z 826	Sarraguemines	Z 817
Epinal	Z 831	Strasbourg/Hausbergen	Z 298A
Liège/Guillemins	ZB 891B	Thionville	Z 615A/B/C/D/E
Liège/Kinkempois	ZB/891A		
Liège/Renory	ZB 891	Troyes	Z 803
Luxembourg	ZL 124		

USAAF Ninth Air Force

Location	Target No	Location	Target No
Aerschot	ZB 925	Haine St Pierre	ZB 876B
Arras	Z 436	Malines	ZB 918B
Antwerp/Dam	ZB 926	Mons	ZB 910
Bethune	Z 823	Mohon/Mezières	Z 643
Busigny	Z 824	Namur/Ronet	ZB 892
Calais	Z 825	Tourcoing	Z 835
Cambrai	Z 600	Tournai	ZB 908
Charleroi/Monceau	ZB 906	Valenciennes locomotive works	Z610
Charleroi/Montignies	ZB 115D		
Charleroi/St Martin	ZB 116B	Valenciennes marshalling yard	Z 819
Creil	Z 601		
Douai	Z 830		

USAAF Fifteenth Air Force Bomber Command

Location	Target No		
Amberieu	Z 238C	Lyon/Vaise	Z 812B
Avignon	Z 806	Lyon/Venissieux	Z 640E/D
Badan/Givors	Z 629	Marseilles/La Blancarde	Z 630C
Carnoules	Z 808	Marseilles/St Charles	Z 630D
Chambery	Z 810	Nice	Z 815
Grenoble	Z 811	Nîmes	Z 626
Lyon/Mouche	Z 812A	St Etienne	Z 816

Part Two — Germany

RAF Bomber Command

Location	Target No		
Aachen/Hauptbahnhof	GH 455	Aachen West	GH 627
Aachen/Rothe Erde	GS 5609B	Brunswick marshalling yard	GH 5515

USAAF Eighth Air Force Bomber Command

Location	Target No		
Enrang	GH 599	Konz	GH 5532A

USAAF Fifteenth Air Force Bomber Command

Location	Target No		
Munich/Laim	GH 606	Nurenburg/Rangierbahnhof	GH 632
Munich/Ost	GH 643	Regensburg	GH 638
Nurenburg/Betriebswerk West	GH 356	Stuttgart/Kornwestheim	GH 605
		Stuttgart/Unterturgheim	GH 575
Nurenburg/Rangerbahnhof	GH 574A	Villach	GH 5634

Appendix Eleven
Fate of Missing Crews

Note: This list is restricted to 43 crews reported missing at the time of the attacks mentioned in Chapters 7-11, 15 and 16. In order to avoid an overlengthy document the 42 crews missing from the attack on Mailly le Camp are not listed. I have tried to avoid errors in spelling names, but some records are not very clear. The following abbreviations are used throughout:

K – killed; b – buried; S – Safe; Ev – evaded capture; PW – Prisoner of War; B – Believed, used in conjunction with other abbreviations unless confirmation of death appears in the Commonwealth War Graves Registers; (A) – Australian; (C) – Canadian; (NZ) – New Zealand. All dates are 1944.

Lille 9/10 April

35 Sqn, Halifax 'F'

F/O R J Bordiss	Kb Abbeville
F/S L M Talbot	Kb Abbeville
F/S W Severs	BPW
Sgt P Obrien	Ev
F/O F B James	BPW
F/S T M Holder	BPW
Sgt J Robertson	BPW

Tergnier 10/11 April

10 Sqn, Halifax 'J'

F/L Barnes	BK
P/O Steel (C)	BS
F/O Pottier	BS
F/L Collier	BS
P/O Alliston	BS
Sgt Mathews	BS
Sgt G C Howell	Kb Longueval
Sgt Crossman	BK b ?

Tergnier 10/11 April

51 Sqn, Halifax 'C'

F/S H M Hall (A)	Kb Davenscourt
F/O Kirkwood	BS
F/O C T Hartley (C)	Kb Davenscourt
W O J B Osborn (A)	Kb Davenscourt
Sgt G J W Peck	Kb Davenscourt
Sgt Hagarthy	BS
F/S Fairclough	BS

78 Sqn, Halifax LV 877

P/O L Tait	Kb Poix
F/S V H Hawkins	Kb Poix
W/O C L Weatherby (C)	Kb Poix
Sgt Keenan	BS
Sgt W N Smith	Kb Poix
Sgt R R Rudd (A)	Kb Poix
Sgt R Graham	Kb Poix

158 Sqn, Halifax 'G'	F/S T E F Sims	Kb Meharicourt
	F/S P T Heard	"
	F/S R W Diss	"
	Sgt W Sommerville	"
	Sgt H Taylor	"
	Sgt L G Rowley	"
	Sgt P A Wenham	"
158 Sqn, Halifax 'X'	W/O A R A Gibson (C)	Kb Meharicourt
	W/O W Brayley	BS
	Sgt H J Jeffrey	BS
	Sgt P Dowdeswell	BS
	Sgt J C Williams	Kb Meharicourt
	Sgt D G Robbins	"
	Sgt J J Turner	"
158 Sqn, Halifax 'Y'	S/L W F Dredge	Kb Poix
	F/O A J Smith	"
	F/O J A Singleton	"
	Sgt J B Graham	"
	Sgt L Mills	"
	Sgt G Ingle	"
	Sgt J Sharp	"
158 Sqn, Halifax 'Z'	F/S L N Couchman (NZ)	Kb Poix
	F/O F S Langston	"
	F/O H M Elliot (C)	"
	Sgt W J Ansty	"
	Sgt K Lawry	"
	Sgt H E Lees	"
	Sgt G D Phoenix	"
466 Sqn, Halifax LV 875	F/S J C Bond (A)	Kb Meharicourt
	F/S J N Keys (A)	"
	W/O J H Maunder (A)	"
	F/S B L Sheean (A)	"
	F/S C Y Warren (A)	"
	Sgt D K Messenger	"
	Sgt J A White	"
466 Sqn, Halifax 'F'	F/O Lamb (A)	BK b ?
	F/S Jacob (A)	BK b ?
	F/O Slatter (A)	BS
	F/S Westerman (A)	BK b ?
	F/S Ince (A)	"
	F/S Burke (A)	"
	Sgt Harman	"
640 Sqn, Halifax 'T'	P/O R H Axton	Kb Roye
	Sgt A L Jackson	"
	F/O R Dunlop	"
	Sgt J McNaughton	"
	Sgt J Judd	"
	Sgt W M Phillips	"
	Sgt H W Whitfield	"

Tergnier 18/19 April

51 Sqn, Halifax 'J'	F/Sgt C Shackleton	Kb Grand-Seraucourt
	F/S E O Yorke	”
	Sgt D W Kennedy	”
	Sgt P Latchford	”
	Sgt C Christie	”
	Sgt W J Gilchrist	”
	F/S F Taylor	”
51 Sqn, Halifax 'Y'	F/S A Sarjantson	Kb Davenscourt
	F/O W G Meeson	”
	F/S St J Scheffler	”
	Sgt H D Nash	”
	Sgt M C McCarthy	”
	Sgt S G Myers	”
	Sgt J A Smith	”
466 Sqn, Halifax LV 956	F/S B W Casey (A)	Kb Poix
	Sgt Weisman	?
	F/S Wallace	?
	F/S Richards	?
	F/S J E Swann (A)	Kb Poix
	F/S W B Lyall (A)	Kb Poix
	Sgt Camp	?
158 Sqn, Halifax 'K'	F/O W A Hughes (C)	Kb Grand-Seraucourt
	F/S F R Salmond	”
	F/O B A Trewin (C)	”
	W/O J A Leaver (A)	”
	F/S J Heyes	”
	F/O R Stakes	”
	Sgt O Brown	”
158 Sqn, Halifax 'Q'	P/O P Kettles-Roy	Kb Meharicourt
	F/O P G Taylor	?
	F/S G McEwan	Kb Meharicourt
	? R V Wright	?
	Sgt M Madden	Kb Meharicourt
	Sgt A F Kneller	”
	? Sowden	?
640 Sqn, Halifax 'S'	F/L F N Boulton	Kb Grandcourt
	P/O L Meyer (C)	
	F/O J Ellis	?
	Sgt J Walton	Kb Grandcourt
	Sgt J Rayworth	?
	Sgt C Rose (C)	Kb Grandcourt
	Sgt J Varty	?

Chambly 1/2 May

218 Sqn, Stirling 'G'	P/O N Eliot	BS Ev
	Sgt N Wilson	"
	F/S G A Hassett	Kb Poix
	Sgt S Clayton	"
	Sgt K J Lynch	BS Ev
	Sgt C F Weir	BS Ev
	Sgt I R Grantham	Kb Poix
	F/O E G Hawkins	"
218 Sqn, Stirling 'P'	F/L I I Jones	Kb Poix
	F/O S D Taylor	BS Ev
	Sgt A Snook	Kb Poix
	F/S R H Osborne (A)	"
	F/O R E Twining	"
	W/O M R Bell (C)	"
	Sgt E W Wright	BS Ev
7 Sqn, Lancaster 'B'	P/O A R Speirs (NZ)	BS Ev
	F/O J H Wain (NZ)	Kb Nointel
	F/O J D Saidler	"
	F/S S Wallace	"
	Sgt G D Vine	"
	Sgt E Feather	"
	F/S J Clift (NZ)	"
75 Sqn, Lancaster ME 689	S/L E W Sachtler (NZ)	Kb Poix
	F/O A Heron	"
	P/O M F Lombard	"
	F/S D J MacKenzie (A)	"
	Sgt P Stevens	"
	F/S T A Peevers (NZ)	"
	Sgt J Pettifer	"
514 Sqn, Lancaster 'H2'	F/L R J Curtis	Kb St Sever
	F/O W L W Jones	"
	F/S B G Green	"
	F/S R S Cole	"
	F/O H C Bryant	"
	W/O R F Hall	"
	Sgt S F Martin	"

Orléans 19/20 May

166 Sqn, Lancaster ME 775	P/O J H Booth	Kb Dreux
	Sgt J Robinson	BPW
	Sgt J McGreggor	"
	F/O A L Hill (C)	"
	Sgt D G Blacknell	"
	Sgt J Terry	Kb Thoiry
	Sgt T Moffet	BEv

Le Mans 19/20 May

7 Sqn, Lancaster 'C'	W/Cdr J F Barron (NZ)	Kb Le Mans
	S/L J Baker	Kb Le Mans
		+ 4 Unknown
	S/L P R Coldwell	Kb Le Mans
	P/O A Price	?
	F/O J W Walters (NZ)	?
	F/S D W Wood	Kb Le Mans
	F/O R J Weatherall (C)	?
	W/O T Lamondsby	?
7 Sqn, Lancaster 'R'	S/L J M Dennis	Kb Le Mans
	F/O R J Hewett	Kb Le Mans
	F/L W F Porteous	Kb Le Mans
		+ 1 Unknown
	W/O R Hunt	?
	Sgt P J Kofoed	Kb Le Mans
	Sgt L Timmins	Kb Le Mans
	F/S A G Lawrence	Kb Le Mans
115 Sqn, Lancaster	P/O S S Atkin	Kb Le Mans
	F/O J V Hayward	"
	P/O K R Mather	"
	P/O R W Jones (A)	"
	F/S R Giles	"
	P/O L E Mehden (A)	"
	Sgt J Rafferty	"
	Sgt I C Plumb	"

Amiens 19/20 May

44 Sqn, Lancaster 'O'	P/O V F Hobbs	BPW
	Sgt A G Hall	BPW
	F/S T P Fenwick	Kb Abbeville
	W/O D G Scott	BK b ?
	Sgt J E Garnsey	Kb Abbeville
	Sgt C T Wright	BPW
	Sgt J B Ingram	BK b ?
	F/O R J Barber (C)	Kb Abbeville

Bourg Leopold 11/12 May

9 Sqn, Lancaster ND 951	P/O M Bunnagar	Kb Wilsele
	Sgt A Leggitt	"
	Sgt A Henderson	"
	F/O G Isfan	"
	Sgt G Chambers	"
	Sgt B Easterlow	"
	Sgt R Watson	"
61 Sqn, Lancaster	P/O J H Eastwood	Kb Schoonselhof
	F/O R P Kayser	
	Sgt E Kingman	?
	Sgt G Crump	?
	F/S A Ayre	?
	W/O E Middleton	?
	Sgt R O Ellis	BPW

630 Sqn, Lancaster 'S'	P/O W Watt (NZ)	Kb Heverlee
	Sgt R Witham	BPW
	Sgt L Thompson	Kb Schoonselhof
	F/S K Stuart ?	BPW
	Sgt P Amies	Kb Schoonselhof
	P/O A F Grant (C)	"
	Sgt P R Rowthorn	"

630 Sqn, Lancaster 'G'	P/O A Jackson	Not Known. Ditched?
	Sgt D Muddiman	"
	Sgt R M Cartlidge	"
	Sgt H E Owen	"
	F/O J Feldman	"
	Sgt A N Seago	"
	Sgt E Lewis	"

467 Sqn, Lancaster 'E'	G/Capt J R Balmer (A)	Kb Heverlee
	F/O P J Hammond (A)	"
	P/O L T Watson	Kb Leopoldsburg
	F/S A R Barber	"
	P/O J F Ward	Kb Heverlee
	F/L W R Hare	"
	F/S J Connelly	"
	Sgt T A Stevens	"

Bourg Leopold 27/28 May

101 Sqn, Lancaster 'K'	P/O T G Allen	Kb Sommelsdijk
	Sgt G E Benson	"
	F/S T Friedt	"
	Sgt R G Evans	"
	Sgt K Powers	"
	Sgt R G Nowens	"
	Sgt G Reid	"
	Sgt Harris	"

102 Sqn, Halifax 'Y'	F/O A H S Hughes	BPW
	F/O G H Godsell	"
	F/S L Collins	"
	Sgt G Welsh	"
	F/O G H Scott	"
	Sgt T Eburne	Kb Schoonselhof
	Sgt R Lethbridge	"

420 Sqn, Halifax 'U'	S/L G S Beall (C)	Kb Heverlee
	F/O E J Andrews (C)	"
	P/O W Woolley	"
	Sgt W Hickox (C)	"
	F/O J F Robinson (C)	"
	P/O W C Stainton (C)	"
	P/O A F Goodall (C)	"
	W/O O J Mohler (C)	"

424 Sqn, Halifax 'B'	F/L B L Mallett	BEv
	F/O R A Irwin (C)	Kb Heverlee
	W/O W Wakely (C)	"
	Sgt M Muir	Ev
	W/O K C Sweatman	Ev
	P/O G F Freeman (C)	Kb Heverlee
	F/S V Poppa	BPW
	F/O W A Elliot	Ev
427 Sqn, Halifax 'P'	P/O F G Devereaux (C)	Kb Baisy-Thy
(This aircraft collided	W/O N Stevenson (C)	Kb Heverlee
with 429 'Y'.)	P/O J F Brown (C)	"
	Sgt B J Roach	"
	F/O R D Ford (C)	"
	Sgt R Edwards	Kb Baisy-Thy
	P/O K L Patience (C)	Kb Heverlee
427 Sqn, Halifax LW 365	P/O B C Scobie (C)	Kb Heverlee
	F/O A G Smith (C)	"
	F/O N G Nahu (C)	"
	Sgt J H Rudge	"
	Sgt T J Whiteside	"
	P/O J Cardinall (C)	"
	P/O G F Vinett (C)	"
429 Sqn, Halifax 'Y'	P/O C V Ross (C)	Kb Heverlee
(This aircraft collided	P/O E L Bailey (C)	"
with 427 'P'.)	P/O B Dunlop (C)	"
	Sgt N Hornby	"
	F/O M Rabovsky (C)	"
	P/O P E Coltman (C)	"
	P/O L Kirton (C)	Kb Baisy-Thy
432 Sqn, Halifax 'N'	F/S H Menzies	Kb Nijmegen
	F/O G Grainlock	BEv
	F/S W S Rowan	BPW
	Sgt J Clarke	?
	F/O D Rutherford	BEv
	W/O H H Rodgers	BEv
	Sgt T McClay	BEv
	Sgt S Hall	BPW
466 Sqn, Halifax 'U'	P/O K C Page (A)	Kb Brussels
	W/O J E Browne (A)	"
	W/O W W Beavan (A)	Kb Brussels
	Sgt A G Cox (A)	BPW
	W/O L W Cain (A)	Kb Brussels
	Sgt W Impey	"
	F/S W J Moody (A)	"
640 Sqn, Halifax 'O'	F/O F Williams	Kb Schoonselhof
	F/S R P Olsen	BPW
	Sgt R P Crawford	BPW
	F/O K J Lambert	Kb Schoonselhof
	Sgt T H Riley	BPW
	Sgt H A Messenger	Kb Schoonselhof
	Sgt T S White	BPW

Appendix Twelve
Schräge Musik

The summer of 1917 marked the first offensive action by German fighters against night attacks by British bombers. The use of searchlights to illuminate targets caused difficulties for the German pilots, who had been trained to attack from above. One pilot, Lt Thiede, fitted two light machine guns into his aircraft in such a way that the barrels pointed upwards and slightly forwards, thus enabling him to attack his targets from below without being dazzled by the searchlights. Thiede was believed to have reminded the Luftwaffe of those tactics in 1938.[1]

In 1941, Hauptman Schoenert and many other German night fighter pilots complained of the difficulties of attacking British bombers from below — the obvious quarter because most aircraft were not fitted with ventral turrets. One of the problems was that German aircraft were being hit by pieces of wreckage falling off those of the enemy. Schoenert began to experiment with an arrangement of guns, similar to that used by Thiede, in a Dornier 217. In the summer of 1942 General Kammhuber authorised the fitting of three Dornier 217's with oblique armament for experimental purposes. Field tests began early in 1943, with Schoenert's old Staffel, 3/NJG/5, trying as many as six oblique-mounted MG 151 cannon.

The experiments were so successful that by June a standard set of equipment was being produced. Known as the R 22, it was fitted to Dornier 217s and Junkers 88 night fighters. Similar equipment was fitted later in 1943 to the Messerschmitt 110. The first officially recorded 'kill' using an oblique mounting was in May 1943, when Schoenert shot down a British bomber over Berlin. Experiments followed using the Luftwaffe's 'Spanner' infra red searchlight system in conjunction with airborne radar and the Schräge Musik cannon. The standard technique adopted was to detect the target using the 'Lichtenstein' radar, approach until approximatley 1000 ft below the target, then use the IR light to get closer to match the speed of the other aircraft. The pilot would then pull forward and downward, raking the target from tail to nose.

In Chapter 2 I mentioned that the first warning of that type of attack was apparently not issued by the Allies until July 1944. I looked for an official explanation for this, but did not find one amongst the Air 14 and Air 40 files contained in the Public Records Office. From other documents scattered between the Air 14 and 40 files and from those of the Bomber Command Air 24 series, I pieced together the following account.

Confirmation that the Germans had been aware of the vulnerability of British bombers to attacks from below came early in 1943, when an ADI(K) report discussed enemy interception methods. The report described a form of attack which had become popular with IV/NJG/1, but spoke only of the earlier type of attacks, made by pulling the aircraft's nose up — the form criticised by Schoenert and others as being both too difficult and too dangerous.[2]

In February 1943 at an Operational Research Committee meeting, the efficiency of the new AGLT (Automatic Gun Laying) in dealing with attacks from below was discussed. The question of whether or not the enemy had developed an upward-firing cannon was mentioned, but was 'to be kept under review' only.[3]

In March 1943, Dr Dickins stated in another ORC report that 'some of the damage which crews believed had been caused by light flak, had in fact come from aircraft cannon.[4] In June 1943 there was some correspondence between Mr Smeed of the ORS and Mr Capon of the Ministry of Aircraft Production. Smeed wrote, in reply to earlier letters from Capon, 'evidence has now come to light which seems to completely remove the possibility' (that the Germans were using upward-firing guns), and that the guns situated in the middle of Ju 88 aircraft were for defensive purposes only. Capon replied,

> *I do not suppose that the enemy has gone over entirely (if at all) to the use of upward firing, and the information about fixed guns does not throw any light on whether upward firing guns are used or not.*[5]

A report on the interrogation of a German PoW in June 1943 stated that, in reply to the question about upward facing guns, the subject had said that they were not using any upward facing system. However, Intelligence seemed to have been aware of the possibility, because they left the question in the Interrogator's brief.

SCHRÄGE MUSIK

The arrows show the gun mountings in the main types of night fighter; top Me 110, centre Ju 88, bottom Do 217

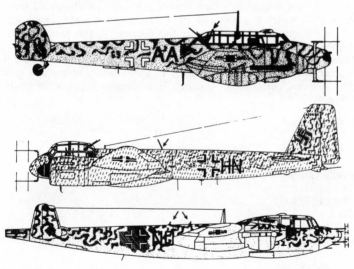

Original drawings by Martin Streetly

An analysis of aircraft losses incurred by Bomber Command in December 1943, showed that of the 4133 sorties flown, 170 aircraft had been lost, of which seventy-seven had been shot down by fighters, and sixty-one had been lost to unknown causes. The number of surprise attacks resulting in damage to aircraft was high (fifty-six out of 152), and in forty-seven cases of damage by enemy fighters which involved fires, twenty-nine had resulted in fires in the aircraft fuselage, as opposed to the engines or wings.[6] In a later and similar review of casualties, in 1944, it was estimated that the peak in losses to fighters occurred in March 1944, when, from 4500 sorties, 137 aircraft had been shot down and a further sixty-seven had been damaged by fighters. Twenty-nine aircraft had been shot down, and 105 had been damaged by flak, clearly indicating that attacks by fighters were twice as likely to prove fatal. In the period between October 1943 and September 1944, out of 16,315 sorties, 465 aircraft had been lost to fighters, and 111 to flak.

In its monthly report of May 1944, the ORS, having analyzed enemy methods of attack, concluded that thirty-six per cent of bombers (which got home to tell the tale) had been attacked from an unknown source. The value of the 'corkscrew' flying technique was emphasised by those cases in which the enemy had been seen before the attack. The report ended by recommending that the danger of unseen attacks be countered by better electronic warning devices. No mention was made in that report of the possibility of aircraft having encountered Schräge Musik.[7]

In June 1944 a secret, diplomatic source mentioned two 20 mm cannon fitted in a Messerschmitt 110, but a further month passed before official confirmation of the existence of Schräge Musik appeared in AI 2(g)'s Report No 1612, dated 21 July. The report also contained details of attack procedures which mostly agreed with those given above.

By September 1944 'the cat was' well and truly 'out of the bag'. The US Air Force Technical Intelligence Department published an illustrated report in January 1945, which was based on the examination of a Messerschmitt 110, which had been captured at Dreux the previous September. The report contained pictures of twin MG FF 20 mm cannon, mounted behind the pilot, and fixed to fire upward and forward by fifteen degrees.[8] It was easy to be wise after the event; I think that some of the criticism of the way that the Intelligence and Operational Research Departments handled the affair was justified.

Notes

1 Aders, *The History of the German Night Fighter Force*.

The following are all PRO references:
2 Air 14/3272.
3 Air 14/3274.
4 Ibid.
5 Air 14/3272.
6 Air 14/364.
7 Air 24/276.
8 Air 40/196.

Appendix Thirteen
Principal Staff and Command Appointments
June — July 1944

Note:
Throughout the text, and in order to conserve space, I have mostly referred to the main personalities by their surnames. I hope those concerned or their relatives will not interpret my action as any mark of disrespect. The following list shows those ranks or titles held at the time of 'Overlord'. I have omitted the great number of orders and decorations held by most of these great men.

British

Chief of the Air Staff
Marshal of the Royal Air Force Sir Charles Portal

Air Officer Commanding-in-Chief Bomber Command
ACM Sir Arthur Harris

Air Officer Commanding No 1 Group
AVM E A B Rice

Air Officer Commanding No 3 Group
AVM R Harrison

Air Officer Commanding No 4 Group
AVM C R Carr

Air Officer Commanding No 5 Group
AVM The Hon R A Cochrane

Air Officer Commanding No 6 Group (RCAF)
AVM C M McEwen

Air Officer Commanding No 8 (Pathfinder) Group
AVM D C T Bennett

Deputy Supreme Commander SHAEF
ACM Sir Arthur Tedder

Commander Allied Expeditionary Air Force (AEAF)
ACM Sir Trafford Leigh-Mallory

Commander 21st Army Group
Gen Sir Bernard Montgomery

Deputy Head of Operations AEAF
Air Cdre E J Kingston-McCloughry

Chief Scientific Advisor AEAF
Prof Solly Zuckerman

Director of Bomber Operations — Air Staff
Air Cdre S O Bufton

American

Supreme Commander Allied Expeditionary Forces
Gen Dwight D Eisenhower

Commanding General US Army Air Force
Gen H H Arnold

Commanding US Strategic Air Forces Europe
Gen Carl Spaatz

Commander US Army Air Forces United Kingdom
(Original USAAF Eighth Air Force)
Lt Gen Ira C Eaker

Commanding General USAAF Eighth Air Force
Maj Gen James Doolittle

German

Chief, High Command of the German Armed Forces (OKW)
FM Wilhelm Keitel

Chief of Operations Staff OKW
Col Gen Alfred Jodl

Commander in Chief German High Command in the West (OB West)
FM Gerd von Runstedt
July/August: FM Gunther von Kluge

Commander Army Group B
FM Erwin Rommel

Commander Panzer Group West
Gen Freiher Leo Gehr von Schweppenburg

Commander 1st SS Panzer Corps
Obergruppenführer de W SS Sepp Dietrich

Original Commander German Night Fighter Forces
Gen Joseph Kammhuber

Later Commander German Night Fighters
Gen Adolf Galland

Commander Luftflotte III
FM Hugo Sperrle

Reich Minister for Armaments Production
Albert Speer

Notes on Sources and Selected Bibliography

Most of the information contained in this book has been extracted from files held at the Public Record Office at Kew. The great number of files involved precludes noting all of them, but most were contained in the following classes.

Air series: 8, 14, 20, 22, 24, 25, 27, 34, 37, 40 and 41.

War Office series: 171, 208, 219 and 232.

Cabinet and Prime Minister's Papers: Cab 100 and Prem 3.

Defence and Home Office Papers: DEFE 3, HO 193.

I consulted also the following documents held at the Air Historical Branch: Translations in the VII series: 70, 75, 84, 89, 95, 133, 158 and 165.

Also, the Missing Aircraft card index.

The summaries of missions carried out by the USAAF Eighth Air Force were compiled both from the PRO Air 40 series and other reports photocopied for me by the Office of Air Force History, Washington D.C.

Information obtained via the Bundesarchiv/Militararchiv at Freiburg was found mainly in the RH-20-7 and RH-19 classes.

Information on the final burial places of those crews killed during the attacks, described in Part 2 of this book and listed in Appendix 11, was derived from the registers compiled by the Commonwealth War Graves Commission.

I had cause to refer to the following published material also:

Aders, G	*The History of the German Night Fighter Force* Janes 1979
Air Ministry	*The Rise and Fall of the German Air Force* HMSO
Babbington-Smith, C	*Evidence in Camera* 1958
Bower, C	*Bomber Barrons* Book Club Kimber 1983
Brickhill, P	*The Dam Busters* London 1978
Bryant, A	*Turn of the Tide* Collins 1977
Bennett, R	*Ultra in the West* Hutchinson 1979
Cheshire, L	*Bomber Pilot* Hutchinson 1943
Churchill, W L S	*The Second World War* Cassel
Collier, B	*Hidden Weapons* Hamilton
Cook/Conyers	*Target Hitler's Oil* Kimber 1985
Craven & Cate	*The Army Air Forces in World War II* Office of Air Force History, Washington D.C. 1983
Ellis, L F	*Victory in the West* HMSO 1962-68
Eisenhower, D	*Eisenhower at War 1943-1945*
Emerson, W	*Operation Point Blank* Harmon Memorial Lectures 1963
Freeman, R	*The Mighty Eighth* Macdonald and Jane's
Foot, M R D	*SOE in France* HMSO
Hansell, H S	*The Strategic Air War against Germany and Japan* Office of Air Force History, Washington D.C. 1986
Harris, Sir A	*Bomber Offensive* Collins
Hastings, M	*Bomber Command* Michael Joseph 1980
Hastings, M	*Overlord* Michael Joseph 1988
Hastings, M	*Das Reich* Pan Books 1983
Hamilton, N	*Master of the Battlefield* McGraw Hill 1983
Hinsley, F H	*British Intelligence in the Second World War* HMSO 1979-1989
Irving, D	*The Trail of the Fox* Weidenfeld & Nicolson
Irving, D	*The Rise and Fall of the Luftwaffe* Weidenfeld & Nicolson
Jones, R V	*Most Secret War* Hamish Hamilton 1978
Jones, W E	*Bomber Intelligence* Midland Counties
Keegan, J	*Six Armies in Normandy* Jonathan Cape

Liddel Hart, B H	*History of the Second World War* Cassel 1970	
Messenger, C	*Bomber Harris and the Strategic Bombing Offensive* Arms and Armour	
Middlebrook, M	*Bomber Command War Diaries* Allen Lane	
Middlebrook, M	*The Nuremberg Raid* Allen Lane	
Murray, W	*Luftwaffe* Allen and Unwin	
Musgrove, G	*Pathfinder Force* Macdonald and Jane's	
Overy, T	*The Air War 1935-45* Europa	
Price, A	*Instruments of Darkness* Macdonald and Jane's	
Revie, A	*The Lost Command* Bruce & Watson	
Rostow, W W	*Pre Invasion Bombing Strategy* Gower	
Saward, D	*Bomber Harris* Buchan and Enright	
Saward, D	*Victory Denied* Buchan and Enright 1984	
Slessor, Sir J	*The Central Blue* Cassel	
Speidel, H	*We Defended Normandy* Jenkins	
Speer, A	*Inside the Third Reich* Weidenfeld & Nicolson 1970	
Streetly, M	*Confound and Destroy* Macdonald & Jane's	
Terraine, J	*The Right of the Line* Hodder & Stoughton 1985	
Verity, H	*We Landed by Moonlight* Ian Allen 1978	
Webster, Sir C and Frankland, N	*The Strategic Air Offensive Against Germany* HMSO	
Wilmot, C	*The Struggle for Europe* Collins 1954	
Wynn & Young	*Overture to Overlord* Airlife 1983	
Zuckerman, Lord	*From Apes to Warlords* Hamish Hamilton	

USSBS Reports were seen mostly at the Imperial War Museum.

Glossary

ABC	Airborne Cigar. Airborne electronic countermeasure
ACIU	Allied Central Interpretation Unit
AEAF	Allied Expeditionary Air Force
AI	Air Intelligence, Airborne Intercept (radar)
AOC	Air Officer Commanding
AVM	Air Vice Marshal
Boozer	Radar warning device carried in bombers
Chop Night	A night on which many aircraft were lost
CAS	Chief of the Air Staff
CBO	Combined Bomber Offensive
CI	Counter Intelligence
CIU	Central Interpretation Unit (Air photographs)
Cookie	4000-lb bomb
COS	Chiefs of Staff (British)
COSSAC	Chief of Staff to the Supreme Allied Commander
Crossbow	Countermeasures against German V-weapons
DF	Radio direction finding
DR	Dead reckoning navigation
Enigma	German coding device
Flak	Fliegerabwehrkanonen. German anti-aircraft gun(fire)
Fortitude	Allied cover plan for Overlord
FUSAG	Notional 1st US Army Group
Gardening	Mine-laying sorties
Gee	RAF radio navigation aid
G-H	RAF blind bombing aid
H2S(H2X)	British (American) radar navigation aid
HCU	Heavy Conversion Unit
JAFU	German Fighter control HQ
JD	Jagdgeschwader. Fighter Wing
JIC	Joint Intelligence Sub Committee (of the COS)
Knickerbein	German beam navigation aid
Lichtenstein	German AI radar
Mandrel	British electronic jamming of German radar
MEW	Ministry of Economic Warfare
Newhaven	Target marking using H2S
NJG	Nachjagdeschwader. Night fighter wing
Oboe	British blind bombing aid
Nickel	Leaflet dropping operation
OKH	Oberkommando des Heeres. High Command of the German Army

OKL	Oberkommando der Luftwaffe. High Command of the German Air Force
ORG	Operational Research Group
ORS	Operational Research Section (Bomber Command)
OTU	Operational Training Unit
Overlord	The Allied Invasion of northwest Europe
Panzer	German tank (Unit)
PI	Photographic interpreter
PR	Photographic reconnaissance
PWE	Political Warfare Executive (American)
R/T	Radio transmission (Voice)
SAS	Special Air Service
SHAEF	Supreme Headquarters Allied Expeditionary Force
SIGINT	Signals Intelligence
SIS	Secret Intelligence Service
Spoof Raid	Diversionary attack
TAF	Tactical Air Force
Tallboy	12,000-lb bomb designed for maximum penetration
SOE	Special Operations Executive
Tame Boar	German controlled night fighter
TRE	Telecommunications Research Establishment
Ultra	Decoded messages based on Enigma signals
USAAF	United States Army Air Force
WAAF	Womans Auxiliary Air Force
Wild Boar	Freelance German night fighters
Window	Tinfoil strips dropped to confuse German ground radar
W/T	Wireless Transmission (Morse)
Wurzburg	German ground-to-air radar
X Gerat	German blind bombing aid
Y Gerat	German blind bombing aid
Y	The interception and analysis of enemy radio and signals

INDEX